NEVER CHARGED, NEVER CONVICTED

MY LIFE IN THE BOSTON DRUG TRADE

MARVIN CLARK
With CARL SENNA

Permissions
Strategic Media Inc.
782 Wofford St.
Rock Hill, SC 29730

ISBN-13: 978-1-939521-21-7
ISBN-10: 1-939521-21-1

Dedication

To my Father and Mother, sister Eva Clark, Esq. and brother Melvin—M.C.

ꟾ ꟾ

Acknowledgements

Special thanks to Eva Clark; former Massachusetts State Representative Melvin H. King; Strategic Media Books Publishing, Inc.; Barbara Casey of the Barbara Casey Agency; James Raynor; Clarence "Duval" Jenkins; and my wife Margaret A. Senna who provided invaluable assistance, evenings and weekends in the initial proofreading of the manuscript.—Carl Senna

ꕤ ꕤ

Table of Contents

ꟿ ꟿ

Foreword

In Boston I knew him as the friend of a boy living in the same six-story apartment building as my family. We were 1950s immigrants from Louisiana and Alabama, much as his parents were from 1940s South Carolina. The government subsidized housing project was in the city's Roxbury neighborhood. And it stood on a corner bounded by Whittier, Tremont, Ruggles and Cabot Streets. One block up Cabot Street, on the corner of Whittier where we lived, was Vernon Street. The Clark family lived in a three-decker building a few blocks up Vernon Street in the direction of the elevated commuter train—the Orange Line. On Vernon Street, a block away from the Clark address, I attended a Roman Catholic Church and its elementary school run by nuns. I was the only pupil of color in my class. My friends after school were my white classmates, at least for the first year. Clark attended public schools, so we did not travel in the same after-school circles. At some point, however, I must have met him when he visited another kid in our building. I recall him at the time because most of my white neighbors and the white families of my friends had begun moving to all-white parts of the city. I knew who he was and I am sure that we met for this reason: most of my friends were rivals of his friends in sports and in gangs disputing street turf. As I began to explore my neighborhood beyond the streets surrounding the projects, I am sure that we talked and played football or baseball in some of the lots. But except for those times in the late 1950s, I cannot recall seeing him after I began high school.

My connection to his book began in 2009 when I received a telephone call from a mutual friend still in touch with me from that time. I was teaching a writing course at a small community college in Calais, Maine along the Canadian border. The friend said that he had met Clark by chance and learned that he was writing a memoir. He asked me whether I could help him get Clark's book published. I wasn't sure, I replied, but he asked me if I would try to do so. And that was how this book came about.

Clark's memoir details an underworld life that I did not experience, although it was present all around me. The Boston that I knew then was still largely spared the illegal drug problems reported in New York City. Marvin was in high school when he began to surreptitiously distribute illegal drugs. His youthful curiosity seems to have drawn him to use them at first. But he quickly saw that he could profit from selling them. In the late 1960s, Boston had over a million temporary college students each September to June. Large universities like Northeastern and Boston University in the city expanded their campus sites, opening classrooms in and around the city. Summer school matriculation also was commencement for street marketing of marijuana and cocaine; recreational drugs and illegal prescription drugs became a boom business like prohibition era liquor. Marijuana, or pot, became the drug of choice for the city's youth culture. Until the 1960s, as Clark describes here, the kinds of misbehavior associated with our youth—underage smoking cigarettes and drinking beer at house parties, or "necking" with teenage girls—all seemed tame, or "lame," compared to what later generations were doing.

Drugs, tobacco and dating were mostly beyond my financial means. I became asthmatic, with severe allergies, in grade school. In high school I developed violent asthmatic attacks and hives brought on by peanuts, eggs, coconut, tobacco smoke, soaps, perfumes, and dust. As I grew older, my attacks worsened until I began to outgrow my allergies in my mid-twenties, just as I was about to get married. Perhaps I was sensitive to allergens because of the environmental toxins around me. I may even have had an unknown genetic predisposition. But I could not help noticing that many other kids like me developed asthma and some of the same allergies. Some also had severe cases of eczema or psoriasis. My asthma prevented me from smoking anything. My lungs simply closed when I inhaled smoke from someone's cigarette. Almost every evening I had to shut myself in a room away from my mother, a pack a day smoker of her "Coffin Nails," (unfiltered brand "Lucky Strikes") which she lit up after she returned home from work.

Clark also describes breathing problems that he later developed as an adult. There were large manufacturing plants on Vernon Street where he lived. Every morning the smoke stacks from the factories spewed acrid smoke into the city air. Hospitals and even the schools added to the pollutants in the air that we breathed. Worse, local residents used some toxic DDT aerosol bug sprays (since banned) to control roaches and other vermin. Not only rats and mice, but raccoons, foxes and possums from the nearby Fens Park, were attracted by uncollected garbage. Clark describes his susceptibility to colds. If he had allergies, he did not mention them. In any case, he was healthy enough to compete in track and field meets.

Until my senior year I did not know anyone actively involved in the drug trade in high school. I learned about the trade at English High. My source was a classmate who entered the school after being kicked out of Boston Latin School. The two high schools then faced one another across Louis Pasteur Avenue, up from the Harvard Medical and Dental Schools. Latin was the most selective city school, and he was in my advanced classes. As the months passed, he revealed his activities to me. My initial reaction to his story, like the one I had from my first reading of Clark's memoir, was disbelief. But his display of large sums of money persuaded me that he was telling the truth. At the time I did not know the details of his dealings or of Clark's. I had never known a kid to carry around so much cash. He was taller than most of my classmates, more mature, better read than many of our teachers. But he was our same age. He was also a drug dealer of sorts. And for obvious reasons, I shall call him "ABCD."

While I knew nothing of Clark's career as a drug dealer until I read his memoir, I learned of ABCD's role when I saw his affluent lifestyle. In retrospect, it doesn't seem odd that they both were involved in the drug trade. It was a quick way to make a buck even then. But the way that they were involved could not have been more different. ABCD's method seemed virtually arrest proof. First, as ABCD confided to me, he never consumed, possessed, or handled any illegal drugs. His role was restricted to the financing of transactions, a blind and invisible presence to street distribution of the drugs. He said that he was a hidden investor to dealers, loaning them money to make smaller loans to street distributors to purchase and distribute drugs. So he never had to deal with the drugs directly. His role was the same as the Yankee bankers of the slave trade who financed the trade without ever seeing the commodities, the African slaves sold in auctions in Cuba, New Orleans, Richmond, or Charleston. ABCD was a commodities banker to illegal traders, loaning money as an investment to drug dealers who then sold the drugs on the streets. Risks were minimal to ABCD from a defaulted loan. His security was to hold a borrower's expensive portable collateral—the latest electronics, new vehicles, rent-a-guns, jewelry, and gold—until the loan with interest was repaid. The collateral usually had a resale value worth far more on the streets than the money he loaned to buy drugs. ABCD seemed, therefore, not so much an investment banker to common drug dealers as an unlicensed pawnbroker to unlicensed loan sharks, the sharks in turn loaning even smaller loans with higher interest to unlicensed street pharmacists, or street dealers. ABCD controlled the disposition of very expensive property belonging to his debtors involved in trafficking. Meanwhile, he could easily sell the collateral for more money than the cash amount of his loan, in the event that his clients were ever busted, or there was a default for other reasons. As a naïve juvenile, I had the cynical attitudes of most youth from my neighborhood regarding the law; I was duly impressed by ABCD for out-slicking the authorities. Now, of course, many police forces have a law which enables them to seize suspicious assets without justification from suspected dealers (a federal "asset seizure" law). Today, an ABCD probably might still elude police suspicion, but his middlemen would be wise not to flash their ill-gotten loot or expensive life-styles.

I have no idea whether ABCD is alive today. Decades ago, a mutual friend informed me that the law finally caught up with ABCD, but, like Al Capone, he was allegedly jailed not for the crimes he committed, but for other offenses. The corollary of his career then may be that successful criminals in one area usually run afoul of the law for mistakes they make committing other crimes.

In contrast to ABCD, Clark states that he directly handled his sales. Either smuggling the drugs through customs or selling it on the streets, he was buying, packaging, delivering and consuming his stash of drugs. That meant he was constantly at risk of arrests and jail sentences his entire life. Yet he was never arrested, nor convicted. He trafficked in drugs almost casually while working legitimate jobs. Although his trafficking seems never to have been as lucrative for him as it was for ABCD, the money was enough for him to afford motorcycles, expensive automobiles, and a lifestyle that would have been difficult to obtain without his selling drugs. Perhaps, in spite of his boasts about evading the law, just before he passed away, he suffered a severe bout of pneumonia. For some reason, he reportedly had a bad reaction to his hospital treatment. Because he allegedly protested his treatment, while severely ill, the nursing staff confined him to a locked hospital ward for an unspecified time. I learned of his confinement from our mutual friend only weeks before he passed away.

Unlike the one out of four young working class black males in the courts today, Clark grew into adulthood unscathed by drug trafficking. Not only did he became a member of the black middle-class, but he would be a forerunner of pot dealers of the 1960s-1980s, lucky enough to survive until selling pot became legal. The parallels between the lucky pot dealers like Clark and Prohibitionist bootleggers like Joseph Kennedy, the patriarch of Boston's political dynasty, may be that neither type was arrested. But Clark never controlled an illegal network to profit anywhere nearly as much wealth as Kennedy did.

ABCD, of course, was in a different class of dealers. While Clark did not relate much of his dealings to anyone, ABCD seemed very candid about his ability to buy things no law-abiding kid could afford—a string of Vespa motor bikes, booze, new clothes and bling. In fact, he once gave me a motor bike he was going to sell as a gift. Over the years poverty and opportunity drew other youth to the drug trade, most of them not as lucky as Clark or as shrewd as ABCD.

While Clark emailed me parts of the draft of his memoir, I emailed back to him my editorial suggestions. But our collaborative efforts all ended just after we had completed his work-in-progress. In May 2011, while we were still looking for a publisher and finishing the final draft, I learned that he had passed away.

Clark grew up in a period that younger generations might benefit knowing from his perspective, even if they will not agree with many of his interpretations of events, or his arguments. Today, marijuana is legally sold in a growing numbers of state licensed clinics across the country; and many dealers like Clark have come out of the criminal underground. So what is missing in his account? As a witness, I believe that I can offer an overview of some details that Clark did not live long enough to include.

The most glaring omission for me is the absence of lethal violence in Clark's trafficking. Today, the news of violent crimes in the slums, barrios, or biker gangs rarely fails to mention related trafficking. When Clark got out of the trade, homicide had become an occupational hazard for traffickers. At first what seemed "new" about drug dealers was no longer new. Daily we began to read of drug rivalries and homicides connected to the trade in poor neighborhoods. At the 2012-13 trial of South Boston mobster James "Whitey" Bulger, reports showed just how lethal the trade had become even while Clark was blithely selling drugs to college kids. Not even he knew how much Bulger's mobs controlled his sources of drugs. According to court documents in the Bulger's trial, the mobs protected drug dealers. They enforced corruption and profiteering at all levels of the city's law enforcement. In the 1960s, the police were unable to solve over half of the city's homicides, many of them mob hits. So the chances of the police arresting dealers like Clark were remote.

Whitey Bulger's gang was the Winter Hill mob, an Irish South Boston-Somerville alliance with Sicilian mobsters based out of Providence, Rhode Island. Together the two mobs controlled most of the black drug trade in Boston, either as middle men or as major suppliers. And this was during the racial strife over court ordered integration of the public schools, when South Boston and Roxbury were not only racially segregated, but places where the opposite race visited only at their peril. The Bulger mob corrupted police administrators, city and state officials. Few levels of law enforcement were beyond their reach. They bribed officials at the local office of the Federal Bureau of Investigation when it was headed by future FBI director William Mueller. And the increased availability of cheap pot, cocaine and heroin seemed to be directly related to increased city homicides. In the 1960s-1980s, each year seemed to set a new city record for shooting deaths in Roxbury. Paradoxically, as Boston's City Hall mayors obtained more funding each year (ostensibly to fight illegal drug dealing), the unsolved murder rate kept rising in its poorer neighborhoods.

In the Bulger conviction trial, his fellow mobsters and hit men James Martorano and Stephen "the Rifleman" Flemmi testified against Bulger. They blamed him for several murders that the three had committed. In a sensational rebuttal, Bulger's defense lawyer revealed that all three had at one time or another received federal immunity from prosecution for helping the feds convict rival mob leaders. Martorano confessed to killing three black youths outside of Roxbury's popular Basin Street South Club at Northampton and Washington Streets, but he received federal immunity from prosecution for them. Flemmi assisted Bulger in the dismemberment of the teenage daughter of one of Bulger's girlfriends because the teenager was dating black men. The FBI gave both men federal immunity, although Flemmi was expelled from the federal witness protection program when he was arrested and convicted of new mob crimes. The FBI denied that Bulger was immune from prosecution for his murders while serving as one of their informants. Yet Bulger's secret ties to the FBI would never have been revealed had he not been apprehended for mob hits. Sometime in the 1970s or '80s, he lost his ability to corrupt several agents in Boston's FBI office.

While Bulger was getting away with murder, city-wide violence among teenage gangs dominated the news. Juveniles from single parent households almost had to seek protection in a street gang in order to protect themselves from daily bullying and harassment. Girl gangs affiliated with boy gangs. And the girl affiliate gangs engaged in the same kind of misbehavior as male juvenile gangs. Clark befriended one gang, the Emperors. And my friends and I organized one called the Marcel Dukes, another called the Barons, and we younger kids allied with the older gangs like the Park Boys and the Rays.

The highlight of street gangs in my experience was wearing colorful jackets and other insignia (inspired by films like "West Side Story"). 1958-1960 was a period of sharp racial change in our neighborhood. I described what I had witnessed during that period in an essay published in *Boston Magazine*:

> ....the racial conflict that pitted me and my largely black Protestant friends against a mostly white Catholic population during the busing-confrontation years. ..many of my white co-religionists were as much driven by false fears and political demagogues as we were....(Thankfully) The pitched battles my friends and I fought with the sons of Europe and the Emerald Isle in Cherry Valley, Uphams Corner, Eliot Square, Roxbury Crossing, Madison Park, Franklin Park, South Boston, Dorchester, and Mission Hill, and on Dudley Street, Huntington Avenue, Mass. Ave., and Boston Common are not the city's, or the church's, present. ("Reflections: A Catholic Boyhood," *Boston Magazine,* December 1989, pp 113-114)

Even as the city was embroiled in bitter racial battles over control and funding of the public schools, witnessing daily violent street confrontations, fighting over white police brutality and discrimination, challenging white injustice in the courts—here, after hours, when the bars and nightclubs like the High Hat, The Brown Derby, Basin Street South, and the Big M closed, whites and blacks of the night sat together joking and talking as though they were comrades in arms against the "straight" world.

Elsewhere, at night, when the strip clubs closed, one found patrons and club owners, strippers and their mobster boyfriends, journalists and wandering visitors, sitting comfortably next to vice squad detectives and uniformed cops, students from local universities looking for whores, nurses and emergency room doctors, pimps and prostitutes, street hoods and FBI agents in Chinatown after-hours restaurants for pre-dawn breakfast meals, or for illegal liquor. An underage college student looking for a beer could be served openly at a Chinese restaurant. Chances of the same student being served liquor after hours at the Businessman's Club or some of the other black after-hours clubs in and around the South End were nil. But for all the city's inter-racial tolerance after hours, daytime showed a community driven by racial division and discrimination.

Boston by day then was a city divided into ethnic and racial enclaves. In the race riots in Roxbury, while I was in college, a white reporter at the Bay State Banner described to me being on the 52nd floor of the Prudential Center Skyscraper which overlooks the city. During the riots over Martin Luther King Jr.'s assassination, he had a bird's eye view of the city. As he informed me, he noticed that from the border along the racially mixed South End and Back Bay neighborhoods, as he looked down on Lower Roxbury's black community, he saw no street lights. Rioters had either knocked out the lamps or the power companies had shut them off. From his vantage point in the "Pru," he saw Roxbury as a large dark hole inside the rest of the city. The "hood" was enveloped in darkness except for traffic headlamps, the flashing lights of fire trucks, riot police units, and other emergency vehicles, and buildings and cars burning. The police were trying, often brutally, to suppress mob stoning of whites trapped in vehicles along the major streets. Roaming black gangs preyed on white owned businesses, looting grocery, clothing and liquor stores, swarming unlucky non-black and black pedestrians.

Mayor Kevin White ordered school buses full of riot police to suppress the attacks, or to prevent looting and stoning traffic vehicles. In Roxbury the city restored city transit services with hours of shutting them down. Riot police wielding truncheons just as quickly surprised and beat marauders and innocent bystanders. The next day, the "hood" seemed like a war zone in a foreign country, its streets blocked by torched cars, store windows smashed and the stores looted, the smoldering remains of buildings everywhere.

This was not entirely a race riot. Many of the younger rioters were joined by white teenagers who had adopted the speech and behavior of their black friends in a kind of reverse racial assimilation. Years after abandoning that brief assimilated identity, some of them still could "translate" black street slang, or, for comic effect, adopt the behavior and manner of their former black selves in recalling jokes or playing the ritual verbal insult game, "The Dozens." It was amusing for many of us to see whites with fine straight hair following black males with kinky hair into local barber shops to have their hair also straightened and waved, into "du." Today when we see whites with Rastafarian hair braids, we know the person has not necessarily assumed a black hipster identity. He may be merely adopting a hair style. But a white boy in a black gang adopting a "marcel" during this period was considered a "white Negro." Poverty integrated some of them into black hipster culture in more ways than appearance.

In 1964 I became interim director of a social service agency, The Roxbury Community Council. It had offices on Warren Street next to Dudley Bus and El Train terminal in the heart of lower Roxbury. One of my jobs was to counsel ex-cons, dropouts, and vets to steer them into getting their general education degree, or high school diploma. I had access to their educational transcripts in order to assist them.

One striking pattern for many of the "White Negroes" who had adopted black culture was the change in their educational reports and test scores. On standardized measures of intelligence, the rank scores of those in the highest range dropped by as much as 2 percentiles in some cases. I was able to monitor the progress of some of them over a couple of years. I found that the shift in performance downwards on standardized tests in several cases was because of motivation, attention or lack of interest. I was astounded to see several of them as young adults recover early childhood rankings on standardized aptitude and intelligence tests. Gone was much of their former street gang swagger, their old street monikers (E.g., "Bang Bang," "Wop," "Grip," "Cap-Eye," "Crib") and gone, too, the behavioral display of "reverse assimilation" of the culture of black street gangs.

The social power vacuum from the larger white culture later reclaimed them, as adults. It restored their white cultural identity, a new mainstream persona and personality. The "white Negroes" became "white" in every respect of behavior and attitudes associated with members of the majority race. They abandoned the black street culture that had temporarily given them a black identity during the time their impoverished families had been unable to flee with other whites to new majority white neighborhoods. Personality changes in the "white Negro" lives paralleled historical descriptions of kidnapped white children raised for many years by Native American tribes.

Another consequence I observed of racial segregation was that it seemed to deprive both races of gender orientation tolerance. We males are never more than genetically half male: we are of female and male parentage. Until we understand how our rigid socially constructed gender divisions prevent us from seeing the female in males and vice versa, we blindly discriminate gays according to a gender fiction. If all people are half of each gender, it can only mean that some of us of either gender may behave more as the other than the one they appear to be. And they ought to be treated as equally today as we treated them and they treated minorities of all genders in the parties and cafes of the Civil Rights protest period.

Late in the second term of President Barack Obama, the Justice Department issued a directive that federal prosecutors no longer give priority to simple possession of marijuana by individuals. Clark today would still be arrested for distribution of it, but he could consume small amounts without fear of being targeted for arrest because of his consumption. The administration's action not to prosecute illegal drug consumers of small amounts of pot follows some state government decisions not to do so such as Colorado and the state of Washington. Clark would probably have been beheaded if he had been arrested and convicted for selling the plant cannabis or other banned drugs in countries like Saudi Arabia. Now that Colorado has legalized the sale of marijuana for personal use, as of January 1, 2014, for the first time in living memory Americans can buy cannabis seeds and plants from state licensed outlets for any reason. As more evidence of relaxed prosecution trends, President Obama in 2013 commuted the sentences of eight drug dealers of rock cocaine. His executive action followed Attorney General Eric Holder's decision earlier that the Justice Department give simple possession of pot low arrest priority, in effect leaving to states the discretion of how vigorously or not they wished to prosecute illegal drug use.

For reasons I was unable to determine, Clark suffered seasonal hospitalizations for pneumonia and bronchitis attacks. When he died in the locked ward of Massachusetts General Hospital, a family member reported to me that his death was related to pneumonia and an immune condition. I never learned whether his illness was related to his drug consumption, a hereditary condition, or some other health cause. I will not speculate further as to the reason for his death. I never saw the medical cause of his condition, but I well knew the risks of his life style when he was a young adult. I knew Boston's underside too. I knew of the places to avoid, even if not always the people to avoid. And like Clark, sometimes I fell in briefly with the wrong crowd while in elementary school, only to abandon them all by the time I found an ambition away from the "hood" in high school. By then my life choices, like Clark's, led me away from a time of life that has all but vanished.

--Carl Senna,

Saint John, New Brunswick and Portland, Maine, 2015

☙ ❧

Chapter 1:

Where the Seeds Were Planted

There was no way in heaven or hell that anyone other than the Lord himself could have predicted that, in the words of the great poet Robert Frost, "I would have taken the road less traveled." I came from a good family. By good family I mean that both of my loving and caring parents made a good home for me and my sister. My mother had a mission that we would experience some of the cultural activities of the affluent white homes where she worked as a maid shortly after my parents arrived in Boston from South Carolina in the 1940s.

I don't know what specific event motivated my parents to move as far North as Boston, but I am eternally grateful to them that they made the move so I'd grow up here. Had I grown up in Hampton, South Carolina, my mother's birthplace, under racial segregation, I doubt that I would still be alive to write about this experience. I doubt that I could have ever accepted the racist humiliations that my parents had experienced growing up in South Carolina. For a long time I thought of myself rather bravely, as the kind of black person who would have killed the first white person who said aloud in my presence that he wanted to "put a nigger in his place!" And sure as night follows day, I had no doubt in my imagination, given race relations at the time, that white retaliation would have quickly followed, and they would have killed me.

What I imagined was not at all imaginary. My parents recalled to us kids their memories of South Carolina, many times describing humiliations, injustices and violations of civil rights there. American history documented their experience of southern white racism that southern blacks were as oppressed as any of the peoples of Eastern Europe, supposedly part of the Soviet Empire. But in my innocence, I believed that I would never have submitted to segregation and white racism. I believed I was too proud and strong. I believed that I would have challenged and resisted living under the yoke of white racism that my parents and their parents experienced. But I was in for a rude awakening. I soon learned that I was not as brave or as tough as I supposed. To be sure, there would be times when the future when I could not be described as a coward. I would fight where I was clearly outmatched. On the other hand, I wasn't a fool, either. I understood the wisdom to live for another day. If I lost a fight in the schoolyard, for instance, I figured I would do better against my foe in a rematch. If I lost, I would train myself to fight with more skill than him, the next time. And usually that is what happened when I was in elementary school. And that was the way I thought it was to be. So at least I supposed.

After graduating from Roxbury Memorial High School in 1960, I was 17 going on 18. And I was like many young black men at the time with little opportunity other than the urgent need to find a way to make a living. My first summer after graduation, my parents helped me obtain a graduation gift in the form of a Harley Davidson motorcycle. It was an old stripped down model that once had a sidecar attached to it. Even though it was an old clunker, it was a prize for me. I became fascinated with motorcycles. I wanted to know everything about them. I had caught the cycle bug.

I soon got cocky. I took risks. And two summers later, almost predictably, perhaps inevitably, I got into an accident which destroyed the old bike. Did that kill my cycle bug? No! Without skipping a beat, I moved up to a 1961 Triumph Motorcycle. I bought it brand new for $1,169.00. Anything close to a Grand was a lot of money for me at the time. It was a helluva' beauty, as they say. And it performed. In a few weeks, I drove it all the way to Ohio.

When I decided to make the trip to Ohio, I was twenty years old. I had already survived gang fights in Roxbury. I had participated in race riots. I had been involved in melees on the streets, stoning of police cars, and fights in many school yards and housing projects. I had lost friends to gang violence. And though I had never been a gang banger, I had taken risks in street fighting. I had even survived a motorcycle accident. In hindsight, I had too much confidence for my age. What young man my age doesn't?

My first night layover was Elizabeth, New Jersey, where I stayed with relatives overnight. My second stop was in Philadelphia. There I was the guest in my aunt's home for a couple of days. Her nephew, who also happened to be named Marvin, was a year older than me. He had quite a dating list. I didn't have a steady girlfriend at the time, although I was sexually experienced. It didn't take long for me to ask him whether he could find a date for me. And at his suggestion, I contacted his best friend's sister, a 17-year-old girl. I found her very attractive. I forget her name, so here I shall call her Veronica, the V for vibrant and very friendly. She had delicate features, smooth café-au-lait color, short straightened black hair, and eyes as black as midnight. She wore firehouse red lipsticks, and that made her tempting to kiss on our first date.

That visit I recall us going to music concerts and afterward to a restaurant with Marvin and his girlfriend. Later, I returned with her to the apartment building where she lived with her family. Since they were sleeping inside the apartment, I made out passionately with her on the inside stairs of her hallway. I was surprised that making love on a hard floor could be as comfortable as it was. I confessed later to Marvin about my tryst. I confessed that I was deeply conflicted, about our initial sex. I didn't love Veronica. But I felt that I was taking advantage of her innocence. She was a virgin. And she was a young innocent girl. The next day, when I recalled our date and what happened in her hallway, I felt ashamed and guilty. I also felt that I had taken advantage of her friendship with Marvin.

Marvin turned out to be quite a bit more seasoned than me in the dating department. He dismissed my concerns, calling me naïve. In his view, Veronica's loss of innocence or virginity was simply a rite of passage, a natural thing, a matter of time. He said nearly every red blooded normal person loses their virginity, including men. For reasons that will become clear, his words stuck with me. His outlook and counsel helped me overcome my guilt. He laughed at me for not knowing what he did to virgins like Veronica. Marvin saw them as customers for male pleasure.

And he didn't have much difficulty in convincing them that they ought to want what he had, as opposed to that he should want what they had. Only someone as naïve as me, he said, would behave as though the girl held the advantage in a date. He ribbed me a lot for a day or so about my 'virginal' attitude, my dating guilt. By the way he spoke of sleeping with them I doubt that he felt either shame or guilt ever about women. Either that or he had long since forgotten those feelings. From that time onwards, whenever we got together alone, he chuckled, joshing me about Veronica. He never failed to ask me whether I remembered her or whether I wanted to check her out. By then I even had trouble trying to recall her first name. I only remembered what had transpired between us. In time she had become just one of my many sexual encounters with partners whose names are now lost to me. I probably would not even remember her first name except for his jogging my memory.

That next night of my layover in Elizabeth, I picked Veronica up on my motorcycle and we went to a large park on the Schuylkill River. There was a thick cover of weeping willow trees along the river bank that provided camouflage for us. It was a warm summer evening. The park was deserted. Across the river, there were railroad men coupling and uncoupling a line of freight cars to large electric locomotives. As dusk fell the mood overcame us. After an interlude in the dark, I returned to Marvin's house.

Early the next morning, I awoke from a sound sleep, feeling charged and eager to hit the road but a steady downpour had begun at dawn and continued all morning. I wasn't about to take to the road on my cycle in the storm. The rain meant I had to delay my departure until late afternoon rush hour. And wouldn't you just know it?—a little ways outside of town another shower stopped me under a highway bridge for three hours. I didn't hit open road until the skies cleared at dusk.

I spent the next day crossing Pennsylvania, with stops along the highway. My Massachusetts auto license plates attracted a lot of attention. Meeting a lot of people along the way, I found them curious, many fascinated to see a lone black youth from Boston on his new motorcycle. I felt like a celebrity of sorts. One elderly couple in a diner was especially generous to me. The husband slipped me a few dollars to help me pay for my gas. This was the first time I had experienced long distance travel. I would have welcomed the company of another rider. But I was comfortable going it alone. Truth to tell, I was, as Marvin said, very naïve. I didn't realize what a major undertaking the trip was for a 20-year old on the Pennsylvania Turnpike. The highway crossed through the mountains in the company of trailer trucks and traffic moving at speeds of 70 and 80 miles per hour.

Somewhere in western Pennsylvania, as the highway sloped sharply upwards the Allegheny Mountains, my ears popped inside my helmet. Beneath my leather jacket, I was wearing a large kidney belt that supported my back. By this time, my plastic windshield was covered with bugs and flies. The bugs were a nuisance, popping and splattering against the shield. I had to wipe them off the shield in order to see in front of me. I kept wiping them away with one hand while I held my bike handle bar with the other, something I do not recommend to anyone speeding along the highway. But it was better for the bugs to hit my windshield than that they hit my face at 70 miles an hour.

The highway was the first I ever saw with a tunnel carved through a mountain. There were times when I could see miles ahead on the horizon of the mountain peak as I climbed the steep highway. The road seemed to snake through endless corridors of rock. Day turned to night as I traveled on-and-on through the Pennsylvania mountains. Just before dawn, I exited the highway onto a street that had streetcar tracks. The street took me to the top of a hill. There I looked down on the city of Pittsburg. It was still early morning, hardly any vehicle traffic, and the sidewalks were empty.

One of my favorite singing groups, "The Skyliners," came from the city. And here I was in their very hometown while they were asleep! I was thrilled! My view of the city at that time of morning became in memory a surreal image. I recall a pink glow broken up by clouds of gray smog filling the city sky. Dark smokestacks as tall as skyscrapers blew columns of white steam above gray buildings. At the time, I didn't know that such pollution could be a major health problem. As I descended into the city, I began to gag from an irritating smell in the air. It irritated my nostrils and made me sneeze several times. And in the time I was there, I often broke into a cough or sneeze. I was happy to leave Pittsburgh. Just after dawn, I crossed a narrow bridge through Wheeling, West Virginia, into Ohio. I passed along one of the flattest landscapes I'd ever seen, a drab vista of farms, single homes, and fields. It soon became a boring landscape that repeated its patterns as I crossed miles of farmland. And I began to want my trip to end.

Cincinnati, Ohio, my next stop, was a letdown for me. I hadn't known what to expect, but I was disappointed with what I saw of that city. Accustomed to statues, historical landmarks, and streets full of people in "Bean Town," I expected the same of Cincinnati. I was deeply disappointed. I felt as though I must have taken a wrong turn to the Cincinnati I expected. Immediately, I was lost in the drab 'burbs, the city's uniform empty sidewalks, split-level homes and shopping malls. I didn't see thriving downtown theaters, arts centers, or museums; I didn't see a downtown store like Boston's Filenes, a Commons, or Public Gardens. The city felt so unwelcoming. I was relieved only by my visit to my kinfolk, my aunt, uncle, and their son Louis who was about ten years older than me.

Louis naturally wanted to ride on my motorcycle. After I rested for a few hours, I let him take me for a spin. He drove me to an apartment to meet one of his female friends, a heavyset, middle-aged, not very attractive woman. She became my date for the time I was there. That evening, Louis left us alone to run some errands, and we had just enough privacy and time "to get down." I seduced her on the spot. She was not a looker and her lovemaking wasn't great. I didn't do much else of note while I was visiting. My aunt and uncle, being retired, spent a lot of time at home. In a couple of days, I found myself bored to tears and ready to leave.

It seemed that most of the radio stations played nothing but hillbilly music, what we would call Country and Western music today. I was raised in a world of R&B. Country music just didn't do it for me at my age. Frankly, Country music singers had a southern white flavor, a stereotypical accent or redneck tone that turned me off. Part of the reason I felt that way had to do with my false notion that the South was a lot like Ohio, a place of racial bigotry against blacks. As I have more than hinted already, I didn't have warm feelings for the South and I had no desire to explore more of Ohio. Of course, those are no longer my views. We've all changed since the 1960s about race and gender and everything in between. I confess that I long ago freed myself of my former prejudice against the white South. Today, I enjoy listening to Country music.

I was now ready to return home. The next morning, I headed on the highway back east towards Philly. The hours seemed to pass more quickly for me on the road home than they had passed going the other way. Perhaps the return trip seemed to pass more quickly because of the few stops I made returning from Ohio. Although I wanted to reach Philadelphia by midnight, it was already early evening as I reached the halfway point on the highway somewhere in the mountains. In my eagerness to reach Philly, I didn't take note of the signs telling me where I was in the state and I began to wonder where I was. I found myself driving along the darkening road feeling lost and in the middle of nowhere. About then, I noticed in my rear view mirror a late model black station wagon which had been keeping up with me for almost the past fifty miles. At first it seemed nothing out of the ordinary.

Sometimes, on a long drive in the past, I have chosen to keep pace with another vehicle following me. I'd figure then that the driver behind me was doing what I often did to keep alert. I watched my speed, so as not to leave him too far behind me. For it seemed safe to help him stay with me. But I had been riding since I left Ohio. I hadn't taken a break and I was beginning to feel that I needed a good rest. When I spotted a sign to a rest area ahead, I followed the sign and pulled in for my break.

There were no other cars visible from the highway in the rest stop. When I pulled into the turn-off, the car behind me followed. There being no benches outside to sit, I parked my motorcycle next to a grassy spot where I could sit down. I was well visible under the rest lights. I had a good clear view around me. I noticed that the car following me was now parked next to a small cabin that served as a men's room. From a spot on the grass, I watched the driver go inside the rest room. He was a tall, heavy-set, middle-aged white guy with a moustache. When he came out, he walked over to me, making small talk. Abruptly, his friendly tone changed. And he said in a matter-of-fact manner, "I want to suck your dick and fuck you." Yes, you read that correctly! Even the crickets went quiet. And my mind went blank. I felt like the mythical Ulysses facing the cannibalistic, monstrous Cyclops. How could I talk my way out of this one? He didn't seem like he was joking. And he wasn't smiling. This was serious.

The creep towered over me. My first attempt to reason with him failed. I tried to talk him out of it by saying I wasn't like that. But he persisted with his proposal. Try as I might, my reasoning with him didn't matter. I pointed out to him that he didn't come across like a ------. I couldn't say the word to finish my sentence before he finished it for me: "Faggot," he said, smiling. In a level tone, he next said that he liked to fuck and fight "niggers," too.

Although I had a knife in my pocket for protection, I felt as unarmed as though I was carrying a toothpick. I didn't think that a stab-and-dash scenario would play out in my favor. I felt exhausted. I didn't have the energy to outfight or outrun him. And I didn't want to end up having to watch my back all the way to Philly. What if he ran me off the road? What if he attacked me now? The clock was ticking. It was getting very dark. There was no time for bravado. I was too far into redneck country to fight a white man trying to rape me.

Not one car had come into the rest area. "Fuck it!" I thought. Hoping he wouldn't kill me, I became resigned to letting him have his way with me.

We went over to some bushes as I slipped my knife into my back pocket. And he quickly got down to business. It was a "bite your sleeve, I'm coming in dry" moment that brought tears to my eyes. And between keeping an eye on him and keeping a lookout for anyone coming into the rest stop, I was a bundle of nerves. This incident scarred me enough to cause me later to suffer what is now known as erectile dysfunction. At the end, when he had finished with me, he drove off in a huff.

It was now getting dark. I waited a few minutes sore and nauseous, and left the rest area. I cleaned myself up at a gas station where I rested for a while. That was my first experience with a sexual predator or with a homosexual predator. What he did was not appealing to me. I promised myself it would never happen again. I felt dirty and unclean for many weeks and many months —a deep humiliation and shame. The rape stole part of my soul, an open, painful wound that never healed. Try as I might, I never have let my anger go over what happened, nor have I forgot the painful humiliation of my encounter. It comes back again and again to fill me with dread, shame, anger and terror.

I reached Philadelphia around midnight. I have never told anyone about what happened at the rest stop until this day. There would be days to come when I would be required to think quickly for my survival. And as the saying goes, reader, "You ain't seen nothing yet," of my life.

☙ ❧

Chapter 2:

My Better Angels

A group of friends and I started getting together about my senior year in high school to buy a quarter pound of reefer and divide it up. Sometimes the person who picked up the grass would add a few dollars to the price, or he'd receive a little extra grass for his trouble. I was no different than the others;: I smoked reefer before I dealt it. I soon changed, of course, as I quickly learned more about getting into the business.

I remember quite vividly some things about my early years in the trade. But I can't recall when exactly in time I began dealing in high school. In retrospect, having completed a long trip from 1960 to l990 wheeling and dealing dope, I can say that I was dealing to the day and to the hour I decided to give it up. Never arrested, never prosecuted, never convicted, never did time in jail - for either dealing dope or for consuming it. So I here offer my story of the trade—a story that I hesitate to call successful, because it's one that is mostly as shameful to recall as it is difficult to justify.

No; for all that, I kept my drug consumption well under wraps; but I can offer no excuses for living off the profits of a trade as addictive to some victims as liquor or tobacco cigarettes. My account is simply what I honestly still recall of that life. And I leave it to readers to judge it for what it's worth.

In time I came to renounce the trade. I don't know how I came to that point except as a moral reckoning with my better angels. In the end it was a moral decision based on lessons of right and wrong I got from my parents. I believe reasons like mine often get little credibility from people concerned about the spread of illegal drugs in our communities. The prosecution of illegal drugs in the United States fails to stop most of the street distributors and their suppliers like me. Professional health workers, lawmen, the courts, and the criminal justice system's Drug Enforcement Agencies discount a moral impulse as a tool against drug use. But often a moral appeal is the most effective argument to make with some of the most hardened drug dealers. And I write this from experience. Considering that thousands of dealers like me were never caught, what was it, I ask, that convinced me and the others to voluntarily give up the trade? Why, really, would we abandon easy money, lots of easy money, for risks that seemed easy enough for us to avoid? My answer is this: Moral appeals to give up the drug trade ought not altogether to be dismissed. It took a crisis of conscience, for instance, in another illicit trade, the slave trade, for slave traders like John Newton, the author of *Amazing Grace*, (1725-1807) to abandon his commitment to slavery. History books about the trade show that the most effective abolitionists, in writings and debates, were former slaves, former traders and former owners of slave plantations. Often a moral consideration by someone is the only thing standing between cruelty, participation, indifference to it, and the rejection of it. And such a moral or ethical discovery involves the wish to win back the respect of those we have always loved and respected. To recover that love means returning to standards of behavior according to principles we once held. One day my wish to reclaim such a past turned me away from the trade. It was a reverence for my parents that kept coming back to me all the while I was dealing; it was my memories of moral lessons that they had tried to instill in me. And now it has taken almost a life-time after they're gone for me to reclaim the lessons.

A lot of people I knew on the streets in Roxbury, where a large number of black Bostonians lived, and in Brookline, the affluent town that bordered Roxbury, didn't know when to stop before crossing the line between dealing and consuming the stuff. Most of them didn't survive for long on the streets. Very few of the dealers and consumers I knew, in fact, survived as long as me without doing time, or becoming a victim of the street violence never far from those in the trade. I came close to the end of my life at the very beginning of my career as a dealer. Why didn't I stop then, after a bad trip? So well you may ask. And all I can tell you is that I've since asked myself the same question a thousand times, without getting any convincing answer in terms of the risks. Perhaps I was blinded to the dangers by the goods and the good times that drug money easily enabled me to buy. Of course, nearly every druggie has a moment when you relax your guard, when danger rears its ugly head and before you know it all bets are off. It then doesn't matter how long you've survived. You're at the pearly gates. And yet, if you survive, most of you don't change. You keep on dealing, just like me.

And when you finally decide to stop as I did, when you're ready in your head and heart, it turns out that being terrified of how drugs almost killed you didn't matter. You turn away from the life not out of fear but out of love for people who love you, family, friends, lovers—the people you have always loved most. You realize that you're not worthy of their love unless you stop. And you want them to love you more than anything else in the world. But until then, you're in love with the life, the quick score, lots of easy money, and all that a lot of money can buy. And you're young enough to enjoy time, time that you control.

One of my worst drug collapses, however, was early on in the trade; and it ought to have given me second thoughts, but it didn't. But on a day I ought to have been up and about at work, one of my best friends in Roxbury, Norman, asked me to keep an eye on his house against break-ins. I agreed to watch the house. On the day he went out of town, I house-sat with his nephew, a young guy I shall call Wolfie. For reasons that were unclear to me, Norman did not trust Wolfie to watch his house while he was out of town. And I never enjoyed Wolfie's company. Unlike me, Wolfie was into crack and coke, but he had never offered to share his dope with me. I guess he knew that I was a street dealer, and as such, that I was in the business of making money. I wasn't the kind of dude who got high with something that I could sell. Clearly, I didn't have warm regards for Wolfie.

One reason I didn't like Wolfie was his stinginess: Always, since I first met him, I found that he was niggardly with everything, including with his "ciggies." He once made the statement that he didn't believe in buying cigarettes when he could bum them off people. I didn't deal him anything even if he could pay for it. When he sometimes asked for a hit, or freebie, I always told him I was "on empty."

As I recall, I came close to the end that day house-sitting. I was on the bed still half-asleep when Wolfie woke me in the bedroom. He was holding a nip bottle, its neck covered with a small piece of foil. There on a bed of ashes in the foil was a small white rock: I recognized it as crystal meth, something then still very new to me.

"Have a hit!" said Wolfie. And he handed me the bottle.

Still out of it, I took the bottle from him. As he lit a lighter to burn the rock, I inhaled the smoke. It was a hell of a hit! The room exploded in my head in a burst of colored lights. I couldn't see anything but the blues, greens, reds, pinks, oranges and other colors. My mouth filled with saliva. A loud tone used in a hearing test filled my ears. The tone kept getting more and more intense, like nothing I'd ever experienced, and it got painfully loud before it began to subside.

Things were happening too fast for me to think clearly. I began gasping, quickly exhaling, trying to clear my lungs. And I felt extreme nausea. And that is when my bladder and bowels let go at the same time. I knew something serious had snapped inside me. I did not have many experiences to compare it. About the closest experience to what was happening to me, I recall now, was when I tried to lift a heavy metal chest and had felt my bowels letting go in my trousers. Just the back strain from that time had put me out of work for six months! But now my bowels felt more uncontrollable than from lifting something too heavy for me. This time, I felt as though I was having a fatal overdose (OD). I already knew the symptoms of an OD: respiratory failure, cardiac arrest, a stroke. I recalled the time that one of my best friends, someone I will call Merrilyn, OD'd. It happened at her place in Boston's Allston neighborhood, a district of the city inhabited by drug consuming college students, who were tenants either from Boston University's campus dormitories, or the many apartment buildings stretching west into the Brighton neighborhood, or south into the town of Brookline.

Merrilyn and I were business partners. We dealt coke to college students and did quite well. Years later when I learned that she had OD'd on the street, unexpectedly, in the company of friends, in front of her apartment no less, I was not surprised. I was one of the three men in her life. When I learned of her death, I and a few mutual friends met to see her for the last time. Together we pooled enough money to give her a decent funeral and cremation. Not one of us, however, knew how to contact her family. She was a recent immigrant from Argentina still learning to speak English when she OD'd on the streets of Boston.

But now I thought that I was the one about to OD. I needed help, I thought, but I was aware that Wolfie didn't know a thing about CPR (Cardio-Pulmonary Resuscitation), nor how to administer emergency medical aid for someone having a heart stoppage, as I believed then was happening to me. He couldn't help me, I grimly told myself. And I knew that he would abandon me if I died. I imagined newspaper stories of my death through my painful ordeal: reports that I was found dead in the bedroom of the house. Norman would find me dead. And he'd have to notify the police and my family. Maybe, the news story about me then would mercifully state that I had suffered a heart attack, to spare my family embarrassment. Perhaps the truth that I OD'd wouldn't be broadcast or circulated in the press. As though in death I should care what people said of me: just then I was in no shape to really worry about how my obit was written.

The rush in my head now was like your being abruptly awakened from a sound sleep, only to find yourself high up on a high wire without a clue as to how you got there. One moment I felt my brain afire, the next I was on a precipice, hanging in the wind above a steep water fall in a cold sweat, dangling by my finger tips and my fingers giving away. I was in a free fall to oblivion, my life flashing on a screen in my head.

Until the 1980s I lived without a fall. I was one of the biggest dope dealers on the streets of Boston. I was also a rape survivor. And it seemed that I was about to die.

In the past, even though I had my share of close shaves, I'd gotten into Grad School selling drugs all the while. And now, my refusal to get out of the drug trade was going to end my life in a way I had never imagined. As Wolfie's stuff took control of me, I silently prayed, knowing any moment that the end could come in a flash of light or perhaps a black nothingness. My thoughts spiraled around in circles, memories of my life of wine, fast cars, and "fly" (loose) women passed before my eyes. I'd been too lucky, too lazy, and too wise. Nobody could tell me a thing. After all, my situation was different from everybody else's: Wasn't it true, I asked myself, that I'd never been caught by the law? I was living proof, and anyone who knew me would have agreed, that dealing illegal drugs as an "unlicensed pharmacist" didn't necessarily mean that your fate was to end up in the gutter, prosecuted in court, or sent to jail. I was living proof that dealing could give you all that most people would wish in life. But I had failed the cardinal rule of most dealers: don't consume your product, unless you know the effects beforehand, or you could wind up just as dead, or hooked, as some of your junkie clients.

As time passed however I realized that the longer the clock continued to tick with me not dead, the better my chances of survival became, as long as nothing else happened inside my body. My heart then began to pound so hard it felt like it was trying to break out of my chest. That's when I lost consciousness. And I didn't regain it until I felt a wet cloth slap my face.

I opened my eyes, and I saw Wolfie staring at me. He was trying to revive me. He wiped my face with a cloth.

Gradually, my breathing returned to normal. I'd been given another chance, not a second chance, but one more out of the many I would squander. For all that had happened to me, which should have scared the hell out of me, I was hooked on the possibilities of what I could do with the drugs.

Wolfie spoke then, telling me that my eyes were shut all of the time I was under the hit. He had used me as a guinea pig, packing the bottle with resin, cocaine base and rock to see how it would affect me. Now he knew what he had done to me. Naturally, I wanted to strangle him, and I might have, but for my friendship with his uncle. And he apologized for experimenting on me as a lab rat. I realized that I was as much to blame as him. He hadn't after all held a gun to my head to try the stuff.

In l965, marijuana became the cocktail of my generation, the drug of choice of the hippie movement. Troops on leave from Vietnam to the States were able to obtain it from the South Vietnamese. And the ones mustered out of the war after completing a tour of duty brought it back in enough quantity to spread it around the entire country without any serious legal penalties. Pot spread to campuses, to slums and corporate workplaces alike; and it soon became a rite of passage for college freshmen and high school seniors. And it didn't just appeal to young adults. Soon enough, pupils in junior high schools began to smoke it as well.

Of course, not everyone indulged in weed. Some people drank cough syrup that contained codeine to get high. But my peers and other young adults began to mostly use drugs as a supplement to alcohol, especially beer. All during the sixties, however, as the price of drugs on the street dropped, many kids turned away from liquor, it being more expensive to get drunk than to get high.

And intoxication often left an unpleasant hangover. So "the bud," as we called pot, became the rage as an alternative to liquor. And for the "get high" crowd filling the discos and music concerts, pill popping to get a "buzz" followed close behind in popularity. Besides selling pot, dealers engaged in a brisk business distributing "bennies." A growing market developed on the street for the ones called "black beauties," large black capsules filled with a white crystalline powder known as methamphetamine, which could keep you awake for days.

A lot of the drugs coming my way then were new to me. I had no idea what the dangers of taking certain drugs entailed. The emphasis was on the speed at which they got you high and the duration of the high. Some drugs were said to go better with alcohol. Few studied the fine print about them in the scientific literature for warnings about using them. Prescription drugs were considered safer because they were prescribed by doctors; and in our young naïve minds they had to be safer. One truism I held about the risks involved in drugs was that everyone should be free to choose his own risks, whether riding in a stolen car or taking drugs. Mine was to sell drugs, make a little money, and get high. Call me an unlicensed pharmacist. But I never thought of myself as part of any health profession.

While still living at home, I decided to learn how a new drug on the street, called "speed" affected people. I got my chance to test it when a family friend offered me a black capsule of "speed." And early one evening, I took a capsule and washed it down with water. About a half hour later, I felt the high strong and steady. When the rush settled into my psyche as a steady buzz, I watched television, until bedtime.

After I'd gone to bed, I anticipated going to work the next day. But as I tried to close my eyes I found that, much to my horror, my eyelids wouldn't stay shut! I couldn't force them to close. I couldn't even blink. I felt my heart beginning to quicken and pound harder in my chest. Every now and then I found it hard to breathe. And so I lay awake tossing and turning until daylight.

In the morning I was exhausted. I had no appetite. My "high" seemed over. But later at work that morning, when I drank some water, my "high" kicked up again. And it lasted all day. I had no appetite at lunchtime. But later I would catch myself grinding my teeth.

When I finally got home that day, I hit the bed feeling drained. I was lacking any energy, an unusual behavior on my part. My mother found me in the bedroom and asked me whether I was ill. It was not until the following morning that I felt back to normal.

When I described to a friend familiar with "speed" what had happened to me, he explained that drinking water extended the effect of the drug. "Speed" also interfered with one's ability to sustain a "hard-on," the opposite of what Viagra does today. It was all new information to me. But a lot of drug information was based on anecdotal experiences, undocumented testimony, and unverified hearsay.

Now my experience with "speed" was useful information but it was two days too late for me to learn that it was not for me. I'd just learned my lesson the hard way. And as I soon would discover that when I took "Meth," I was unable to have sex, so I never took ""speed" again. One didn't go with the other. I also discovered that when you sniffed it you were choosing not to have teeth. In the long run, because it damaged your gums, "speed" was a hell of a choice for fun!

"Speed" highs were not in my best interest as a dealer, any more than getting drunk was. I didn't want to become my own worst customer. My mother always asked me when I tried to defend stupid behavior: "If 'so and so put his head in the fire, would you do it, too?'" If I weren't stupid enough to take joyrides in stolen cars, I surely wasn't about to risk my health consuming something that didn't work for me; I wasn't interested in taking anything that was going to leave me at the mercy of my customers. In l965, having reached the age of 21, I was old enough to drink and vote, and in my mind I was also old enough to smoke marijuana. But I've never believed that kids should be able to use drugs. I didn't sell dope to teenagers, which doesn't absolve me of selling drugs to people who did resell the drugs to kids. It was something I learned to regret most about the trade.

From the perspective of a dealer, however, kids were unreliable customers. Another reason not to sell to them was that the kids never had the kind of cash I was asking. And I didn't sell anyone drugs on credit. Still another reason was that kids would easily snitch on you in the event the cops caught them with the drugs.

In any event I didn't need teenage customers. In l966, the automatic student deferments from the draft ended for college age youth. This was almost an intentional government blunder, as it boosted the anti-war protest movement. Now a slim majority of students who seemed ready to accept the Vietnam War so long as they didn't have to enlist now were involuntarily dragooned to fight it. An American troop buildup was underway. And as Vietnam's fighting escalated, it took more and more young American lives: not just every month, but every week, and sometimes every day in a week. And many times on the evening newscasts, the tally of GIs killed rose to five hundred or more in a single day of combat. Images of body bags and the young faces of the dead inside them enraged ordinary Americans, more and more mothers, fathers and students. No administration argument seemed more powerful for the prosecution of the war than the unspoken argument against it in the mounting number of casualties: the wasted lives of the young sacrificed for a war that seemed unconnected to protecting this country. The end of student deferments for the draft triggered protests on the campuses throughout the nation. And the demonstrations spread soon off the campuses into the streets and halls of government.

In February, 1965, I received a notice to appear before the Draft Board in two weeks. My classification had changed from 2-S to 1-A, which placed me at the top of the list to be inducted into the Army. To say that the letter filled me with dread would be an understatement. In fact it scared the hell out of me.

I was taking night classes in business administration part-time and taking just enough classes to get me a deferment. Now I was in a panic! At the time, the words of a popular song began to reverberate in my head: "Please Mister Custer, I don't want to go!" There was too much hypocrisy in the war for Vietnamese freedom when African Americans didn't yet have that freedom. Most blacks opposed this hypocritical war as I did. And learned scholars on campuses and local politicians held the same view: the war had no legitimacy according to our Constitution. But I wasn't a pacifist or a coward. I would have gladly gone down South to fight against the racist crackers oppressing us. That is, I would have joined the army to fight racism had the government asked me to do so. But the cry of "Freedom Now" for the Vietnamese didn't apply to African Americans in the South. In America, the war was in Vietnam for Vietnam freedom from Communist oppression. But I knew that the USA was there for purely selfish reasons. The reasons had nothing to do with freedom for anyone but whites in America. Even if that were not the case, why fight for the Vietnamese? And I'd ask myself, why should I go off to fight for freedom for people I didn't know or care about? People of a foreign country! It didn't make sense! Then President Lyndon Baines Johnson once had promised that he wasn't going to have American boys fighting for Asian boys! But, then: why the draft? It scared me every waking hour. And I was even more fearful at night thinking about what waited for me there while I tried to sleep. In my mind's eye, I imagined my flag-draped coffin after I had been killed in Vietnam. And after I was buried, what next? Would I have struck a blow for the freedom of a cracker to put his foot on a black American's neck?

Confederate battle flags still flew in the deep South in front of white mansions. Or the same symbolic flag of the fight to enslave black people was on the bumpers of cracker pick-up trucks, a shotgun mounted in the rear windows. A popular film, "Easy Rider," used the flag image as a racist symbol for murderous white rednecks in a pick- up truck. At a climactic moment, towards the end of the film, the redneck bad characters shot the sympathetic pot smoking northern bikers. In reality, white southern homes mounted the Confederate flag on their lawns and state parks. They gave the flag the same place of honor that people in the north reserved for the Stars 'n Stripes. It seemed to me that the Confederate flag represented freedom for Southern whites to once more enslave and humiliate black Americans.

To me the Confederate Battle Flag will always be a racist flag. It was flown to defend slavery of African Americans and racial oppression. And I could not fight for people who flew it in the Vietnam War. I believed then and now that had I been killed fighting people who had never oppressed or harmed me, people who were fighting against my white American enemies, then I would have died for nothing. And I would have deserved to die. I seldom saw any flag but American flags flying in front of black homes in the South, although, in truth, I had not seen much of the black South.

The selection of kids through a lottery to serve in the military seemed like a crooked game when it was biased by race and class. It seemed that if you weren't white or from a middle-class family, you were a prime target for the draft "lottery." And you had few options for paying a lawyer to win a draft deferment. I knew many white guys from affluent middle-class families in the nearly all white Boston suburbs of Brookline and Newton who escaped the draft lottery. The official Uncle Sam's Draft Board letter addressed draftees with one word, "Greetings." And that one word would send a kid to Vietnam to fight and die as surely as a death sentence from a judge. The guys trying to escape the draft got their parents to pull strings with draft officials or federal politicians; and in many cases they paid off people to get deferred to the Navy or Air Force Reserves, the Coast Guard, or the National Guard; and getting into those military forces meant that you didn't go to Vietnam. President George W. Bush, Jr., for example, took that kind of deferment. He served in the National Guard based in Alabama, which meant that weekends he could whore and get drunk in New Orleans, Louisiana. He did not have to fight in Vietnam with a high risk of returning home inside a body bag. More and more of us learned of the class bias in deferments. And more and more of us working-class people became cynical when we saw wealthy guys like Bush escape the draft lottery to fight in Vietnam. American casualties from the fighting rose each week, as the war escalated and seemed unwinnable. And more and more of us didn't believe the war was worth the risk of dying in it.

I knew that there would be no deferment for me unless I could prove to a physician that I was unfit physically for military action. I learned from friends that there were a lot of medical doctors doing a brisk business certifying healthy young men as unfit for military service in Vietnam; that is, certifying them military deferments for a steep bribe. Well, I couldn't afford that option. The day that I made inquiries about draft deferment options for me at the Board, such as the National Guard enlistments, or even the Navy, a white female clerk gave me the bad news. She was a heavy fat woman who spoke with a "Southie" accent, the accent of a resident many black Bostonians associated with racist South Bostonians. At the time South Boston was the center for opponents of public school integration. (And Southie's leaders like former Boston School Committee Chairperson, Louise Day Hicks, defied federal judge orders to integrate Boston's public schools. Hicks tried to galvanize whites throughout the city to oppose busing black pupils from all-black schools in Roxbury to all-white schools in white neighborhoods. The issue wasn't the racial makeup of the schools so much as that all-white schools were newer and better equipped from the common tax revenues controlled by Boston's white school committee headed by Hicks. Racial integration would mix both races into the superior and the inferior schools, and Hicks wasn't going to have white Southie kids attending inferior black schools.) The white clerk answered my question without a second look at me. She told me that there were only openings in the Army and the Marines for people in the greater Boston area. I didn't ask anything more. But I knew that she was lying through her teeth.

Despite what hypocritical "armchair patriots" (among them, President Bush, Jr., former Vice-President Dick Cheney, and Conservative Radio Talk Show host Rush Limbaugh), would have later generations believe, there were then more young people against the war than in favor of it. Conservatives today spin the history of the Vietnam War by distorting it as a military defeat for the USA. They would have young people today believe that the Vietnam War was supported by a majority of Americans. But it was a political victory for the American majority at the end of the 1960s. And the black community was particularly hostile to the war, which was an opportunity for major disruptive social protests and political concessions from the white establishment.

Drill instructors (D.I.'s) at Fort Benning, Georgia were said to be especially hard on black men from Boston and New York. One of my friends, who had deserted the Army, told me of an especially brutal "cracker D.I." who had barked at him during push-ups: "Push your way back to Boston!" I wondered if basic training in a southern state was another way of the Army expressing a hidden racist message. Yet I was determined to do my part, if I had to serve, and try to get an assignment as a clerk typist or some other position behind the lines. My mother was mortified at the thought of my being sent overseas to Vietnam.

In those days, the war was graphically reported on the nightly news, seven nights a week. None of the news was pretty. I decided to try to get out of being drafted. My parents and I held a meeting with our family doctor. We decided to get a medical deferment for me, on the basis of a disabled knee. To that end we began to organize the paper work and obtain x-rays of my knee. We concocted a petition for my physical examination at the Army induction center at the South Boston Fargo Building. My attempt to evade service wasn't exactly a "con job," because I really had a damaged knee from an old motorcycle accident. But I was taking no chances on being inducted. The following morning, I arrived at the induction center at 8 a.m. and spent hours filling out forms. I also took a qualification test for non-combat positions in case I was drafted. After lunch, I spent more time in rigorous physical examinations among fifty other inductees. When I was asked to squat on the floor, I protested that I couldn't complete the action, because of my knee problem.

The doctor was skeptical of my claim until I showed him my medical papers. He looked through the documents and instructed me to take a seat. I knew doctors had a thing about criticizing other doctors. My qualification test came back and I found out that my score placed me for consideration to enter either Military Intelligence or the C.I.D (Criminal Investigations Division). Either of those two positions would have guaranteed me a relatively safe position out of the line of fire. Knowing my propensity for being where the action was, I would probably have ended up working with the CIA's Air America in the Golden Triangle. It was late afternoon when I had my final interview with the doctor in charge. And when he suggested I should have surgery on my knee, I asked him whether the Army would be willing to pay for it. I knew full well that the Army wouldn't. When he confirmed that I would have to pay for it, I was overjoyed. I knew then I was free to go home. I wanted to scream out loud right there and then I was so happy! But I kept my feelings to myself. I was now free to continue on with my life.

That Spring I traded my motorcycle for an MG Roadster. It was a gold-colored hard top, a two-seater, flashy and what those in the know then called a "pussy magnet," that is, a car for attracting and picking up women. The roadster signified my transition to another level of operations on the street. The trade was becoming too dangerous for someone operating off motorcycles, which drew unwanted police attention because of the noise and because few people had them where I operated. I didn't want to push my luck with needless exposure. Besides, riding in sports cars had become the "in" thing for the hipsters of my generation. English-made Triumphs and MGs were two of the most popular cars for dealers after the Volkswagen Beetle.

Early that summer I started a job at an underwriting service company in Brookline. I shall call the firm the Retail Credit Services, although that was not its real name. It was a Georgia based company located in Coolidge Corner in Brookline, an affluent town with large numbers of Jewish residents.

A suburb bordering the Fenway neighborhood on the western edge of Boston, Brookline ran along the lower part of Roxbury where I lived and Allston and Brighton facing Cambridge and Watertown on the other side of the Charles River. But Brookline had an entirely different ethnic mix than Boston. It had a much higher average household income; and it had no significant numbers of African American or Hispanic families living there. It was mostly all white, with a high percentage of affluent upscale Jewish families and wealthy other whites among its residents. President John F. Kennedy's family once had a home there when he was a youngster. The building that housed the Kennedy family has been preserved as a national landmark. My working in Brookline, then, gave me new opportunities to learn business, both legal and illegal, at the company.

Retail Services completed local credit reports and made property inspections for large insurance companies in the greater Boston area. It had offices in all of the states and extensive contacts with court and police agencies. It was a company that mirrored some of the generational changes through some of its employees in the drug culture, the free love lifestyles, and the hip beatnik values infecting the youth of the country. It was a window through which I viewed the world outside its offices until the end of the sixties.

The contacts I made at this job led me to a path of intrigue far beyond the experiences of most of my colleagues. My supervisor was a young white man only a few years older than me, and he said to me the first day that I'd been selected for the job because a lot of the white investigators didn't feel safe going into the predominantly black neighborhood of Roxbury. The great Hispanic and Caribbean migration to Boston starting in the 1970s had not yet begun. And the new immigrants of color had not filled up a part of any neighborhood, as would happen in the 1980s onward in places like the South End, Mission Hill and Jamaica Plain (or as some called it, because of the rapidly growing Hispanic immigration there, "Jamaica Spain.")

Up until my coming on board a number of the older white males in the office hadn't had any experience dealing with blacks on other than a superficial level. Small wonder then that their written files and reports seemed to reflect deeply ingrained biases and ignorance of minority neighborhoods.

I read report after report in the company's files describing black communities filled with crime, a slum with dilapidated buildings and high auto theft rates. Sadly, much of that was true, as it was true of white South Boston street crime by a white Irish mafia. But Roxbury was redlined by insurance companies on their residential insured maps, "Negro," which was "blank" and clean of insured lines. In contrast, "Southie," which was controlled then by the notorious killer still then on the FBI's Most Wanted List, the mobster James "Whitey" Bulger, was not redlined. Neither was the Mattapan section largely inhabited by Jewish residents redlined, nor their tenement property in and around Blue Hill Avenue's Grove Hall, where reports of "Jewish lightning" (arson) were regular items in the community grapevine.

Requests for house and auto insurance in black Roxbury were routinely denied. City maps showed block-by-block home, auto and life policy lines at home and business addresses, but around black neighborhoods one found encircled in bold red ink "Negro." Needless to say, there were few if any policy lines written inside the red circles.

The company declined recommending policies routinely for most persons, automobiles, businesses or homes in Roxbury or Dorchester as a matter of policy. It was also company policy to write unfavorable recommendations on people having marital difficulties, in divorce or in separation.

A few weeks after I was hired, I decided one day to get my hands on pot. And in my free time I began hanging out in Harvard Square with white "beatniks." Once home from work, I changed my clothes from suit and tie into my hippie outfit, jeans and leather jacket, so I could fit in better with the street crowd in the Square. Melvin Toon, my best friend from high school, was already a Harvard Square regular. I started tagging along with him, and through him I began meeting all kinds of people, dealers and potential customers. Soon we began stopping by the apartment of a white dealer several years older than us. It was at his place that we would often go to drink wine and smoke reefer.

Often we found a steady parade of young loose white women there hanging out for fun and excitement. One night, I decided to leave work to catch the bar closings in the Square. I had been working until after midnight because I had a larger than average work load the next day. I made the rounds with Toon, but that night I quickly tired and wanted a good night's rest. So I called it a night and after we made a brief stop at his friend's place to see whether there was much else going on, I went home.

The next morning, while I was putting my caseload together in the office, a courier delivered our daily *Boston Herald* newspaper to the office. Right away the front page caught my eye as I looked through the mail. The headline read: "Drug Raid in Cambridge!" There a photo jumped out at me from the page. It was of my friend and several of his visitors inside his apartment in the glare of police flashlights. They were under arrest for illegal drug possession.

I couldn't have been more relieved at that moment that I had left the place before the raid. I wondered if the police had surveillance photos of me. I was sure that the police had a photo of Melvin going to and from the building. The names of the arrested were in the article. But Melvin's name, much to my relief, wasn't among them.

Of course, at that time marijuana arrests were headline news. If I had been arrested, I would not only have lost my job, but I would have faced a felony charge in court. This would have also meant ending up in the company employee reference files with a drug arrest under my belt. The company's news researcher was an old timer who cut out news stories and made up reference sheets from the papers. I had sensed early on the job that he was watching me like a hawk, so I knew I had to seem clean around him. He came from Charlestown, another white neighborhood then quite hostile to blacks.

My problem with him was that my work quota of fifteen completed file reports each day was hard for me to deliver. And I believed that there was no way I could make the rounds to 15 residences and businesses to inspect them all in an eight hour day. But I also knew that I needed the job. I had to come up with a solution.

Necessity, then, gave me an idea to complete the report load each day. Instead of going out into the field, searching for addresses, interviewing and inspecting places to get oral statements from the residents, I snuck phone calls to them out of the office. Unbeknown to me, I learned right away from scanning our submitted reports that some of my fellow workers had the same idea, for it was humanly impossible for many of them to cover as many inspections on their reports in one day. But filing fake inspections seemed the only smart way to meet our workload.

At the time most of the households in the inner city were working class, with both heads of the house working full-time. The only times I might make a visit to a residence was when the residence had no telephone. But I began to invent statements, much like the rogue New York Times reporter Jason Blair, who also made up his news reports.

In my reports I became effective at making up statements from fictional neighbors. It was not difficult to write a convincing report after verifying that the subjects lived at addresses that the office could independently verify through old and often outdated records, even when the subjects had moved elsewhere. I was fortunate none of my reports were called into question. I knew of cases where some inspectors I worked with had written up statements from dead people as the drivers of automobiles in accidents!

My fictional inspections were nothing new in the company. I had to get the reports filed, after all, in a two day deadline for clearing the cases. Otherwise, you'd find yourself under a stack of paperwork, which could pile up. This was also when I heard the term "shitcan" used for the first time.

"Shitcanned" described the fate of cases that were a pain in the ass and couldn't be cleared. Nowadays, we'd use the term "trashed." We worked in the morning at the office dictating reports, and we were usually on the street to inspect property by twelve o'clock every day. Usually we didn't return to the office until after six o'clock, when most of the other staff had gone home. Or we reported to work the next morning. As I became more involved with my co-workers, we often ended up at someone's place around lunch time. After hanging out for a while, we went our own ways. I'll never forget the time I went to a co-worker's place and saw stacks of old cases piled up like a decade of unread newspapers. When I asked him about them, he laughed and said the cases went back about two years. I was not even the best at "gaming" the company.

I was working still at the office for a short time when the first woman was hired as an inspector. We shall here call her Raven. She was to be the first of many to come. She was single and into the same things as our tight little circles within a circle, that is, smoking the bud! I was the only black person working in the office of forty whites. But I wasn't intimidated or nervous in their company. Becoming a part of the crowd wasn't too difficult for me. I had years of experience socializing with whites, going to schools with them, and I had grown up in Boston's Roxbury, then the most racially diverse neighborhood in the city when whites there still outnumbered blacks and other people of color. And I'm one of those people easy to get along with most people.

I was the one, who, as a white friend of mine used to tease: "The lad could fit in like Flynn. He had to put up with a few black jokes in the beginning. But that was all right. He learned to dish it back." I understood white people to the extent that I'd grown up with them as friends and neighbors. I liked some of them and disliked others. My attitude was no different in the office. Before long, I began to socialize with white co-workers, who had their own apartments in Brighton and Brookline.

For the most part, I was living a middle-class life when I was at work there, but leaving it for a working class neighborhood in Boston after working hours. These were the times when "the weed" was plentiful and came in numerous varieties: "Acapulco Gold," ""Panama Red," "Jamaican Brown," and "Mexican Green." It was easy then, as well, to cop hashish and magic mushrooms. Sometimes one came upon someone dealing mescaline and "Orange Sunshine" acid, but that was when LSD and other hallucinogenic drugs were still rarely sold on the streets.

It was the plentiful availability of marijuana that cut across all racial, social, and political divisions, for sharing a joint, a brotherhood of "the weed," brought the members of my generation together, peacefully, and that development frightened the older ethnic and racially divided generation in the city.

Now the thought did occur to me then: What if our coming together in a joint fest led to an alliance that might change or challenge the political or social agendas of the white supremacist establishment? A solid majority of my peers were against the Vietnam War. Many were opposed to racism and constraints on us such as sexual discrimination, poverty, and police brutality. We had issues that united a majority of young people across ethnic, racial, religious, gender, and class lines. We were united in our opposition to the same things.

And as the war and civil rights protests continued, it was only a matter of time before we'd turn peaceful protests into violent street riots. Unknown to us, however, the Federal Bureau of Investigation was steps ahead of our radical turn to violence. FBI director J. Edgar Hoover, who was well known for his anti-black, racist humor and his conservative politics, had his agents busy compiling dossiers on black activists as well as anti-Vietnam War leaders.

Following the end of student military deferments, radical groups like the Students for a Democratic Society (SDS) and the Weathermen ramped up their campus protests. They disrupted government offices, even torching local draft boards on federal property. Radical vandalism triggered police crackdowns on all student protests. And the FBI assisted local police to suppress any protests on campus or in the black slums.

We now know that the FBI and the Pentagon ("Operation COINTELPRO") devised a plan to interrupt and create a climate of mistrust among white radicals and black activists. The FBI and other government agencies used undercover agents connected to the Army and local authorities, such as the state and city police, to infiltrate those groups.

Toward the end of the sixties, many sophisticated radicals forbade illegal drugs in public forum meetings and any discussions of planned violence, as a precaution that the meetings were monitored by the police. Everywhere the watchword was caution in speaking over the phones or freely reporting on protest meetings to strangers.

Although I was spending more and more time around white people, I continued to maintain relationships with my black friends and often brought the two groups together. I was surprised how easy black women seemed to get along very well with white men in most social situations.

In my experience, young black women viewed white women as rivals for black men. And the black women I knew expressed intense hostility for "Miss Jane or "The Plague" as they referred to "white women" in code. Although it was rare to see a white man openly dating a black woman, one saw a growing number of relationships between a black man and a white woman. Such couples could be seen at nearly every party and social event. The sexual competition between white and black women for black men, in the new racially integrating campuses, was so clearly a point of racial hostility and friction that black coeds and black male-white woman dating was covered in an issue of "Life Magazine."

Cultural attitudes about race were the first to rear their ugly head at this time. One of them was the black attitude that whites had no natural dance rhythm and blacks did. So at interracial parties, black women there gave white guys dancing on the floor usually a passing grade, while a black fellow, without rhythm, got a lower mark.

Call it reverse racism. blacks and whites were friendly but still reserved even among radicals. They didn't really socialize much.

The reason I didn't relax around whites was that I believed that if I forgot racial differences, nine times out ten I'd hear black jokes or insensitive racial remarks about blacks from the whites. Whites of that period generally held racist views that a majority no longer hold today.

There's a saying that captured why I never relaxed or engaged too much in socializing with most whites: "How can you call yourself a friend, when you don't know what causes me pain?" One of my white co-workers, Alan, who came from a white neighborhood in Mission Hill, the part of Roxbury bordering Jamaica Plain and Brookline, was an exception to my experience. He had none of the prejudices towards blacks of his white peers. In fact, Alan admired many black celebrities; and popular black music was his favorite music. He had all of Aretha Franklin's albums. But more interesting to me was his awareness of the racism in the office. He went out of his way early on in our relationship to warn me of the" two-faced" covert racists in the office. And we became good friends. What I liked most about Alan was his down-to-earth honesty; that he wasn't trying to be something he wasn't, that is, what in street slang, we'd call "a wigger." There's no bigger turnoff to black people like me than a white phony who makes a bad attempt to imitate Ebonics.

Alan said to me one day that I spoke like someone who was brought up in the suburbs rather than in the black community in Roxbury. He sounded a bit disappointed. And I didn't know how to respond to the statement. It put me on the defensive, because I was only being myself. The comment forced me to acknowledge my mother's influence on my personality and values. She expected me to dress properly and act presentable in public, to avoid slang and to use correct diction and pronunciation.

Most blacks and whites in my old neighborhood respected my mother. Many holidays and evenings she would invite neighborhood children into our apartment to give them snacks. At other times she might give some of the needier ones clothing. Most of my peers addressed their parents by their first names, and most of their parents, even the white ones, addressed my mother as "Mrs.," a sign of respect in those times when whites generally called blacks by their first names. It was as though blacks did not deserve an adult title, perhaps a lingering cultural meme from when we were the slaves of white people. I would prefer to believe the whites addressed my mother as "Mrs." because of their good manners, and their respect for my mother. Because of her, of course, I developed a sense of pride in my family's good name. And because of that pride, I shunned associating with the worst "bad asses" in the neighborhood. Admittedly, however, in many other respects, I was as much a "bad ass" as they were.

Hanging out in Brookline and Cambridge, I came across old friends from high school, among them my Roxbury neighborhood and old friends from my more recent "bikey" days. Many were involved in all sorts of illegal things, car theft, housebreaking, store robberies, and shakedowns. But I considered myself above petty crimes. And I sought out respectable and law-abiding friends in Brookline when I had the chance.

I still used my generational vernacular at times, especially slang which often meant the opposite of what we said. If something was called "bad" it actually meant that the "bad" was good! "Fuck," another slangy obscenity of ours, became our favorite word of choice. It could function as a noun: (e.g., That was a good fuck!) It could function as a verb :(e.g., I'm going to fuck you up!) It could be used as an expletive: (e.g. Fuck you!) or as an adjective :(e.g., He's a fucking asshole!)

Our heroes on the silver screen were Sidney Poitier, Jane Fonda, Steve McQueen, Jack Nicholson, Clint Eastwood, Charles Bronson, Warren Beatty, Raquel Welch, Rita Moreno, Karen Black and Faye Dunaway. Many of the movie stars besides Jane Fonda were not afraid to address many issues important to our generation in their films. Michael Douglas, for one, was making a mark on the TV screen and Al Pacino, for another, was living in Boston, staging plays at the Charles Playhouse, in the South End. Student radicals and hipsters influenced Hollywood, which made films using our language and sexual mores. Conservative opponents of our lifestyles called such films as "Easy Rider" and "Days of Rage" nothing but "smut."

In July there were race riots in Brooklyn, Manhattan, Chicago and Cleveland. But they were nothing like the race riot in the Watts neighborhood of Los Angeles that same year, not, that is, anywhere near the costs in terms of loss of life and property. Over a hundred people lost their lives in the Watts riots.

Significantly, a Chicago riot then affected the agenda of Martin Luther King. The riot was a bitter defeat of his attempt to shame the city known as the most racist in the North. Looting and anti-white violence in the Chicago race riot exposed a criminal element among the black neighborhoods. And that diminished general public support for Rev. King's peaceful non-violence protests.

In two days of July, 1966, rioting in the black neighborhoods and a highly publicized verbal attack on King by a prominent black minister led to a white backlash against the Civil Rights leader. Mayor Richard Daley called out the National Guard and a massive police presence to quell the riot. The city's white reaction put a lid on legitimate civil rights protest marches.

On July 31st, King attempted to march to a white neighborhood in the company of about three hundred and fifty protesters. And there they were met with chants of "white power" from white counter demonstrators. The protestors met a barrage of rocks and. The cops had to rescue the King demonstrators.

The straw that broke the back of the open housing crusade occurred when King was hit on the forehead by a rock on August 6, 1966. That was it for non violence for many blacks. This incident signified the first defeat of the civil rights leader in a Northern city and the movement never recovered from the loss.

In November, one of the biggest stories took place in Massachusetts, the election of Edward W. Brooke, to the

United States Senate. It brought nationwide attention to the state, giving it a reputation as being progressive and liberal because Ed Brooke was the first African American to be elected to the Senate since Reconstruction, more than a century ago.

Brooke started out as a Democrat, but after he was unable to get support from state Democrats for an elected office, he switched to the Republican Party. Brooke was already a media item for his inter-racial marriage, a rarity among his peers. He met his wife during World War II while stationed in Italy. And he ran for his first state office as a Republican while he lived in Roxbury, campaigning with his Italian-American wife and two daughters to enthusiastic receptions in largely Italian neighborhoods, East Boston, the North End and Revere.

Although some Democratic operatives tried to use the race issue against Brooke, the public didn't fall for it; and he won a resounding victory at the polls. Brooke's election was a feel good moment for Massachusetts. Ted Kennedy escorted Brooke to the floor of the United States Senate to be sworn into office. The public elation over Brooke's triumph was tempered in the city of Boston where a court fight brewed over de-facto segregation in the schools. The Boston School Committee and some members of the city council were to blame for the situation.

Blacks have never had much political power in Boston. For the better part of a century, City Hall was under the patronage of Irish and Yankee polls. And despite the city's reputation as the so-called "Athens of America," the quality of public education, with the exception of the exam schools, was substandard in nearly every respect.

Boston was a small town racist city with a world class reputation because of its colleges and medical institutions. In a 2008 survey Boston was chosen by the participants as the number one city for public rudeness in America, and it copped the award for having some of the worst drivers in the world.

☙ ❧

Chapter 3:

Inner Circles

At the beginning of l967, with my life in the trenches of Brookline, things continued to get better as I made more contacts in the area. I was twenty-four, living well above many of my peers and making lots of money. One of my business contacts was a new acquaintance. I shall name him George, a Brookline boy who had his own insurance agency at Coolidge Corner, the local shopping area. I got to know him when I sought his help on a case involving one of his clients. I couldn't "shit can" the case because my supervisor knew about it. When I visited the address to confirm proof of client residence, I wasn't able to find his name on any of the apartment building mailboxes.

The phone was unlisted. Agency instructions on the case said not to interview the client. George's insurance agency address was listed on the form. It was only a block away from the office. Although there was a policy discouraging us from contacting the insurance agents, I decided to take a chance and walked over to George's office one afternoon. He was helpful, informing me that the applicant was on vacation. I filled out the report in his office. We became friendly after that and I was able to use him as an unnamed reference with some applicants he knew from Brookline. I didn't know it at the time, but George was going to have an impact on my life in a way I never expected.

I was now spending time in Cambridge, hanging out with a different crowd. It was no longer fashionable for me, in my new circles, to dress and behave as a "beatnik" look-a-like. My new crowd was more into dressing up and going out to night clubs. They worked hard; they consumed; and they wanted the best for their young lives. Like them, I took on the role of a capitalist consumer with money in his pockets.

It was also the year that I scored for the first time in the office with a woman I'll call Barbara. She was a part-time secretary who lived in the area. She had a nice body and short black hair. I was eager to seduce her. I made plans to hide my interests from our office supervisor, someone I'll call Alice, who almost caught me making a play for Barbara. I had to use all kinds of ploys to keep the affair a secret but it was mostly a case of keeping my personal business private, not a fear of losing my job.

The affair with Barbara began badly. I slipped a note on her typewriter, assuming that she was away from her desk on a break. I wrote on the note that I was attracted to her and that I would like to talk with her outside the office. Luckily, I left the note unsigned. When she didn't return to the desk, I watched in horror as Alice picked up the note. She headed into the assistant manager's office with the note in her claws. I knew she'd be keeping an eye out for the culprit.

Two days later, I saw Barbara in a coffee shop as I was leaving work and got to talk with her then. It turned out that as a part timer she was out of the office loop on many things. She hadn't heard about the note. We hit it off and I offered her a ride home. When she started to respond to my seductive moves in the car, I decided to pull over to the curb. Later I could hear myself thinking: "There was something off about her."

Sure enough, after we necked for a while, she squeezed my dick in my trousers. Right away, I knew it wasn't accidental but we couldn't continue our tryst because my car was too small for any action, and then she remembered that she had to meet her mother at work.

A few days later, we ended up in the bedroom of her mother's apartment and I got down to business. When I got into her, she squealed too loud for my comfort in her apartment. It was hard for me to give my all or to relax while wondering whether her neighbor could hear us or if her mother would suddenly burst into the room with my black ass buck naked on top of her pale white daughter screaming for more.

She was a "space shot" who gave nicknames to human sexual organs. For example, she named her vagina "Pink" and my Johnson "Little Boy" while we were getting down. My alter ego kept saying all the while I was jamming her that "She was a ding- dong bitch!" Anxious as I was during the sex, it still gave me a charge. In the weeks that followed, we made out several times in her mother's apartment but we never dated.

Barbara was Jewish. She had been seeing a Palestinian student named Mohammed all the while she was seeing me. I didn't realize how unusual her dating situation was until the June 1967 Six-Day War. Eventually, I lost interest in her and moved on to other women.

That spring, there was a new group of people in the office, all of whom I shall give fictitious names: a guy named Bennie from New Jersey, Mark from New York and another black guy, Don Howard from Maryland. There were also Ricky and Dean from the state of Maine. Several women also came on board.

Bennie was an ex-cop from New Jersey who dressed like the fictional detective Mike Hammer. He impressed people like Alan as a Nazi Storm Trooper. Bennie was stocky, nearly six feet, and he wore his hair in a blonde crew cut. One day Bennie caused a stir in the office by wearing a gun in a shoulder holster. He explained that he had a private detective's license and a gun permit. Still, the manager told him to leave the gun at home when he came to work.

Mark was a New York Jew, who looked and sounded like the stereotype of Jewish ambition: aggressive, chatty, witty, and amusing. He acted out the ethnic image mostly when he became consumed with realizing an idea, driven by some goal to the point of an obsession.

He wore glasses and was slightly overweight. He also had what some people called a Jewish nose. He was a very nice guy, and one of my closest friends at the company. Mark's drop-dead gorgeous wife Fifi wore short mini-skirts and high heels. Before long she would start accompanying us to parties and other events besides company functions. For someone who looked like a dead ringer for actress Ali McGraw, she was down to earth and very sociable.

Don Howard was married but with no children. His wife Sissy was open and friendly to me, but Don and I were strictly business associates. Don and Alan liked the same kind of old R&B blues music, and they became good friends going out together with their wives.

Dean , from Maine, was a sharp looking fellow who dressed in expensive suits and drove a green MG convertible. We became good friends, often amusing ourselves with jokes about the office politics, their characters and oddities about them. Many evenings, Dean and I went out to different clubs in Boston looking for women to score.

Ricky, Dean's roommate, was more into the L.L. Bean kind of fashion. Ricky came from northern Maine, Belgrade Lakes. When I was no longer pursuing Barbara, I passed her over to Ricky, who had complained to me that he was having trouble finding a woman.

One afternoon, I was hanging out in Harvard Square, when I came upon a friend of a friend who had just bought a Shelby GT 350, a special edition of the Ford Mustang fastback. It was attracting a small crowd in the

Square. It had two cables attached on both sides of its chassis, an air scoop on the hood, and the combination made the car look as though it could race so fast that the hood had to be locked down.

Right after that, Melvin married his high school sweetheart Merle, and so another of my old gang was no longer able to run with me. He made a good choice for a mate, an attractive girl, who had always been one of my favorite people. She and Melvin had a son. When later I heard through the grapevine that the two divorced, I was sad for them. But I was even sadder when I learned of her death of a heart attack in Florida, June, 2010.

Not long after Melvin's marriage, I started hanging out with a guy named Leroy from Central Square in Cambridge, whom I had met a year before in the Back Bay near Symphony Hall at the old Hayes Bickford Restaurant on Huntington Avenue. The Hayes Bickford served fast food and full meals at its self-service counter open 23 hours a day. Since it only closed each day for an hour between 5 and 6 A.M., it became a favorite city hangout of night people. And in the wee hours of the morning, I encountered pimps, drug dealers, Mafiosi, petty thieves, night shift workers, cops on the graveyard shift, vice detectives, late night party goers, sports celebrities, journalists, students, doctors, nurses, hospital workers, travelers, and insomniacs. Situated on the corner of Gainsborough Street and Huntington Ave, the restaurant faced the Huntington Theater. Jordan Hall concert and lecture hall was diagonally across the street on the opposite corner of Gainsborough Street.

Hayes Bickford was a favorite late night donut, sandwich, breakfast plate and coffee spot for me as well as the concert and theater crowds. At one time or another I ran into just about every politician, local celebrity and judge in the Hayes Bickford's. When the chain restaurant closed its doors in the 1980s, city newspapers published nostalgic interviews with some prominent patrons. A McDonald's restaurant now has replaced it on the site.

Leroy and I stayed friends for many years. Whereas Melvin was the supreme master of the dating pickup no matter the race of the woman, Leroy was his close second when it came to black women. Although I dated white girls, I always made room for black girls.

My car was picking up rust spots and I wanted to buy another ride. It seemed at the time that everyone in the office had a decent car, except for Dean's roommate Ricky and me. I decided to try for a Shelby Ford. I was still living at home and figured that I would be able to afford a new car.

I went to a dealership and filled out an application for a loan. It was turned down because of my age and lack of a credit record. The salesman suggested that my father might sign as a co-signer. That didn't work because of my father having recently purchased a home, he couldn't qualify.

The salesman tried to steer me to an older model of the Shelby, but I didn't like the car as much. I've never liked convertibles; there were no fastbacks available at that time. The stingray was sleek and had a three hundred and sixty five horsepower engine. It was silver colored and could take on just about any car, except a 427 model Corvette, a Cobra or a Ferrari on a straightaway. I decided to shop around for another make of car that was fast and had style. With my limited budget, I ended up settling for a three year old Corvette convertible. Driving it, I became one of "the bad asses" of the street. I was faster than fast. The car would float above the highway at a hundred miles per hour and whine like a fighter plane. It was also a magnet for chicks. I had the one car that could outrun the cops and easily disappear at night.

One of the techniques I learned about vanishing from a cop chase was to turn off all my car lights, take the first exit after hitting the gas pedal, and keep my foot off the brakes so I wouldn't have brake lights. As a technique for escape, it was an obvious danger to drivers and pedestrians.

I went into "double-hock" to buy the car after being given directions on how to do it by a friend of my father's in the finance business. This meant getting a loan for half the money at a finance company and the other half at a bank or credit union. The finance company loan would be listed as personal, with the bank loan being listed as an auto loan. The bank would hold the title until paid in full.

I insured the Corvette with George, using the address of a friend who lived in Wellesley. He only charged me a twenty dollar fee for handling the paper work but he could have made at least two hundred bucks on the deal! Insuring a car in the suburbs has always been cheaper than insuring it in Boston.

We weren't worried about getting caught by the insurance company for using a phony address to insure my car. The insurance company, after all, was one of Retail's customers and a client that I handled. George and I had become very good friends by now. I think he enjoyed teaching me about the insurance business. In some ways, being three years older than me, he seemed almost like an older brother.

Eventually, one of George's associates needed information; and he was willing to pay for it under the counter which was illegal. George contacted me and I checked the reports on file. We knew that all of the files weren't accurate. If a file's informants weren't listed by name, chances were that the file was made up.

The amount of "hearsay" information in some of those reports could have gotten the company in trouble. A lawsuit might have resulted in some cases, because the company files often contained false personal information about clients and their credit.

To my way of thinking, I wasn't doing anything wrong by helping George. It was the right thing to do. Friendship superseded business. In the back of my mind was the thought that someday we would be doing other projects together and the best was yet to come.

☙ ❧

Chapter 4:

The '60s

At the end of the sixties in Boston, I recall attending live concerts that featured Miles Davis, John Coltrane, and the Beatles. Many cities offered such free concerts and opened public basketball courts to cool off racial tensions among the volatile youth of the inner city.

Mind altering drugs—substances with unpredictable effects like LSD—hit the streets, but I was not yet dealing them. The Vietnam War created a growing resistance among college students, and fear of the draft, a fear that motivated street protests, rebellion in the streets, despair in some and a frustration in others with traditional politics. That fear also drove many kids to sexual promiscuity which facilitated a demand for pot, cocaine and alcohol. The market for distributors like me soared.

By July, the American troop count had reached nearly four hundred thousand men. A childhood friend, who joined the Marines two years earlier, returned that summer. There were many other youth not returning except in body bags. Not all the casualties were poor minorities. Increasingly, the majority was from the white middle-class; and they were college students drafted out of the classroom. Some of them foolishly took a year off from classes. Others simply dropped out of college. Or they became part-time students while engaged in full-time work in the mistaken belief that the draft board wouldn't drag an enrolled college student into the army. All of them, of course, duly received notice from Uncle Sam to report to the nearest induction center, and not to forget to bring a toothbrush and a change of underwear.

Many of them were shipped off to the war that very day from the induction center, once they had passed their physical, mental and background checks. Many of them never returned home alive. Meanwhile, newspaper headlines featured on the front pages the photos of local boys, the weekly casualties of the war. They had once been the kid next door, the paperboy, and the hoops star, the kid who played baseball and sat next to you in class - young kids drafted out of high school or taken out of college, kids rushed to Vietnam to fight and to die for something no one could explain or defend with any clarity. Now, too many of the kids were our honored dead. During that period, I often went through obituary photos of several of my buddies in 'Nam who were among a list of casualties. The grim news left me with none of the gung-ho for "the war" that they said they had on their first leaves.

My friend the draftee, however, didn't want to talk much about what had happened to him over there. Sadness alternated with anger in his voice when someone mentioned the war, causing him to brood. Once I recall, we were talking about a friend killed in Vietnam whom we knew when he abruptly shook his head. He began grimacing from some hidden pain, as though he was about to break out in tears. Then he turned and rushed away from me. Immediately I knew better than to approach him whenever he left us like that. There was no telling for sure, but his mood change filled me with fear for my own safety. I dared not approach him at those moments. Clearly the wiser and safer course for me was to let him be, to wait until he came back. Then, I'd change the subject.

As a soldier, he didn't appear to be the same person I had known as a kid. He had, for instance, a harsh tone quite uncharacteristic of his former self in his descriptions of killing Viet Cong. Sometimes he'd describe body parts and killings of prisoners in gruesome details that always made me feel uncomfortable. Although we stayed in touch long enough for him to be the best man at my wedding, it was the last time we met.

Years later, I rented a video about the war which featured an interview with a black marine who had fought in the siege of the U.S. Marine base at "Khe Sanh." He stated that the soldiers fighting from the trenches had to sleep with their faces covered to avoid having a piece of an ear or nose bitten off by voracious rats which came out at night. That marine's story often came back to me when I recalled my friend.

Many Vietnam vets came back home to meet scorn and ridicule from peace demonstrators. And weekend warriors who avoided combat, as George W. Bush Jr. did during his domestic service in the National Guard, were contemptuous of Vietnam vets. But the weekend warriors also supported the Vietnam War hawks. What irony! What blatant hypocrisy! The same right wingers who complained that peace demonstrators didn't respect or honor the Viet Vets were often the same ones who scorned Viet Vets as losers. Now many of my generation in 2010 forget how those older vets shunned homecoming Vietnam vets. To vets of WWII and the Korean War, the Viet vets lost their war, and they were mostly misfits, drug addicts and cowards.

Black vets, of course, had to shoulder the additional burden of confronting racism in Saigon. Many areas of the city's red light districts, according to news reports, became off limits to blacks, as friction between blacks and southern whites often led to fights. (Leave it to redneck "Whiteys" to carry racial shit with them to the battlefront of our country's wars!)

It was particularly galling to me when on television one of the armchair generals declared that the black soldier had proven himself in Vietnam, as if blacks had to prove anything. Blacks have always proven their loyalty to America. It's America which has had a problem staying loyal to black Americans. Vietnam vets and other blacks weren't trusted by the establishment no matter what our politics. We were used by politicians on both sides of the aisle for our vote. We seldom decided national war policies; and in the 1960's, we often found ourselves on the other side of the door of white legislators deciding it.

I remember a conversation with a middle-aged white cop at a Boston Peace demonstration; and he said to me that he was against the war just as much as me, even though he could never identify with peace and civil rights leaders or demonstrators. I realized then that the war had set so many people against each other that the possibility of members of our police forces joining opponents of the war was remote. Appealing to the police, in fact, to join in a protest march seldom occurred to me, or to the peace activists I knew.

That July 23rd, race riots erupted in Detroit, Michigan and Newark, New Jersey. I remember lying on the beach listening to the radio with my future wife Marilyn, whom I was dating at the time. The rioting in the mainly black neighborhoods seemed so far away that I felt detached from the outbreaks of violence. Over six hundred people were killed in a few days of rioting. But they were abstractions to me, anonymous casualties. I didn't know the dead. And I didn't feel anything for them. Besides, I had a pretty girl on my mind most of the time, "Marilyn," an attractive redhead from Vermont. I had met her at a party in Boston's Allston neighborhood. She wore wire-rimmed glasses, and she had her long hair in a ponytail.

We hit it off right away. What a sense of humor she had! But she had never dated much before me, nor dated an African-American. Not that she was a hick, but she was innocent, trusting, uninhibited, and generally comfortable with herself and strangers. On the other hand, she didn't patronize me, nor treat me as a symbol of anything. I was simply a guy attracted to her. And for some reason she seemed attracted to me. Like Alan, there was nothing phony about her.

Not many weeks later, I met her parents in Rutland. I can say unequivocally that, as parents of my past girlfriends go, they were both pleasant and welcoming to me. Although they were divorced, they each had a stake in valuable land on Killington Mountain before it became a world class ski resort.

As I recall, I have never had any problems with parents of the women I've dated. My problems usually came from my dates, because I had a habit of juggling more than one romantic interest. I had no problems at all with Marilyn's family. She had two sisters, one older, one younger, and they treated me very well.

At the time, Marilyn worked as secretary to the president of an exclusive women's college on Commonwealth Avenue in the Back Bay. And she lived alone in her own apartment just around the corner from my office in Brookline.

Her favorite jazz artist was John Coltrane, whom she had discovered long before I did. We complemented one another as a couple. She had her feet firmly on the ground. Hers was a steady routine, life focused on the nitty-gritty. Unlike me, she didn't take many risks in her life. I was ambitious, sometimes impulsive, and I played the odds. I confess that I was also seeing a dark-skinned black woman with a model's face and body. I shall name her Michele, though that was not her real name. She worked at the customer service counter in a department store in the Roxbury Mall where I happened to work twice a week as a store detective. She wore her long black hair in a bun.

From the first time I saw her, I wanted to have her and we started sleeping together after work but I never took her seriously. She seemed sexually insatiable, a nymphomaniac. I soon concluded that I would never be able to satisfy her needs.

Twice a week in the sack with her was more than enough for me. We never went out in public and our affair lasted only until the end of the Christmas season. Even though both women enjoyed smoking reefer with me, I knew enough about women and jealousy to keep them apart.

By the spring, I also began going out with Connie, a petite little blonde from Norwood. I took her to the company party that spring. As an interracial couple, we generated a lot of inquisitive stares among my white co-workers. By then, however, I had become a member of a group of non-conformists in the office. Inter-racial couples didn't bother them and I didn't care what the rest of my office thought of my dating white women. Already the first of several scandals had occurred in the office and I was in the middle of one controversial situation that was making trouble for us.

It began from a small thing which ought not to have caused anyone trouble but for the stupidity of one person. A mailroom boy from Brookline had been selling reefer to several of the inspectors on a regular basis. One night after the staff had gone home, one of his customers questioned the weight of one of his packages sold by ounces. A dispute erupted and became heated. I believed it was going to lead to blows. I decided to intervene before that happened. I convinced them to let me judge the packages of pot on the mailroom scale. Unknown to me, the next day someone squealed about the incident to one of the old timers and he threatened to report the incident to the management and the police. Calmer heads prevailed on him not to stool on us to the Brookline Police.

He must have informed Zack, one of the managers, because Zack fired the mail boy and put me on probation for my job. His decision effectively locked me out of the office after hours unless a supervisor was there. I often closed the office after working hours. Zack apparently wanted to punish me in part because he suspected that I stayed late to conduct personal business. He already knew that I violated a company policy regarding the use of company telephones for personal use. Like most of the other workers, I used office telephones for private calls. Sure, I used company phones to complete our case loads in the evening, when many of the applicants were home. But I also used them to sell pot or coke. Zack stopped my dealing after hours from the office. I was in a dilemma. I needed the job, but I also needed to deal pot to maintain my expensive lifestyle.

I survived my probation period for a week without getting fired and my lockout in the evenings didn't last very long before I was back in my old spot: All thanks to Zack, a middle aged balding guy with five kids, one of them in college, and a large mortgage on his new home in Brookline. At a company softball game, he informed me that he was taking me off probation. He said that he'd let me stay in the evenings on the "QT." But I had to agree not to use company phones for anything but company business. I made a deal with him not to bring drugs with me to sell or to use in the office. But you can't have the yin without the yang. Zack was about to experience the trials of managing the Boston office in the 1960's culture infected by youth cynicism, where the traditional work ethic was suffering badly.

The turn in my fortunes at the office came in July. That day, I heard a cry for help from the door of the ladies' powder room. A number of us rushed into the room to find Raven, a co-worker, on the floor next to a sofa in the outer entrance of the room. She lay there face up, as stiff as a board. At first, she appeared dead.

One of the office assholes whispered to me that she was a junkie because she usually wore long-sleeved blouses, and that she had finally succumbed to a heroin overdose. But she was still breathing and much to our collective relief she was alive. We helped her onto the sofa. Slowly she revived. When she opened her eyes, we questioned her as to what happened. Haltingly, she said that she was still groggy and not sure what to tell us. Minutes later, when she was fully alert, she described how Bob, the assistant manager, entered the foyer and tried to fondle her while she was resting on the sofa. I didn't believe her story, but Alan did. Bob denied that he ever touched her. The next day Alan confronted Bob with Raven's allegations, threatening to beat him up after work. When Bob complained to Zack, the executive officer, Zack fired Alan later in the day, in the face of Bob's denial that he had done anything to Raven,

I still didn't know what to believe. It was a "he said, she said" situation, with no other witnesses. At the end of the week, Bob informed us that he was being transferred out of our office to another office location, but he didn't say where.

The following week, our supervisor Alice came into the office carrying a wet piece of paper, which she described as a "dripping document." She claimed that she found it in the ladies' bathroom toilet with Raven's initials on it. How that report got into the toilet was very odd. But I never was privy to the report's contents. All that I could surmise was that it seemed damaging to Raven because I didn't see her again in the office. And when I asked Zack about her, he said that she had been fired for the document that Alice found. He didn't tell me what was in the report either. I'll never really know, although I suspect she was let go as retaliation—perhaps, for falsely accusing Bob. I missed Raven. I had been hoping to seduce her. Now, because I didn't know where to find her, seducing her was out of the question.

In August, FBI director J. Edgar Hoover launched the super secret COINTELPRO program, the purpose of which was to expose, disrupt, spy upon, misdirect, and neutralize Black Nationalist organizations, hate groups and subversives. Undercover FBI agents began fanning out across the country to enlist provocateurs and spies to infiltrate any suspected organization. COINTELPRO remained a secret until the Freedom of Information Act of the 1980's was passed, and the public then learned about it from activists. We also learned that while the government was tracking down and disrupting many civil rights protests, serious crimes—homicides, robberies, rapes, and drug related assaults—were increasing.

CB ED

Chapter 5:

Out in the Cold Again

"Hey Joe, where you going with that gun in your hand?"

--Jimi Hendrix

On January 31, l968, the Tet Offensive exploded on America's television screens. North Vietnamese regulars and Viet Cong forces attacked virtually every major city in South Vietnam on the eve of the lunar New Year. Many of the South Vietnamese soldiers were on furloughs to celebrate with their families.

Although the Viet Cong and North Vietnamese forces lost over 45,000 men and the number of prisoners US-led coalition forces captured was nearly 7,000, the bold Viet Cong attack showed that the war was not only going to be longer than a predicted few years, but that it was a quagmire. It was playing out as the North Vietnamese commander General Giap predicted. It was wearying the American public of continued support for it. And it was galvanizing, dividing, and polarizing our country into warring political factions. Many college students began to work to elect as President a U.S. Senator named Eugene McCarthy. He was not only the first and the most vocal Democratic Senator to come out publicly against the war, but he became a challenger to President Johnson in the New Hampshire primary.

I put a "McCarthy for President" cloverleaf sticker on the trunk of my Corvette. Although I benefited from the protests in my dope deals, even I had reached the point where I was willing to march against the war. One evening I noticed a black line drawn across the McCarthy sticker. I was furious. I wished that I had caught the person who did it. If I had come upon him or her in the act of defacing the sticker, one of us would have ended up in the hospital.

Around this time, Bennie became friendlier than he had ever been to me. He invited a few of us from the office to his place. It was the first time I had seen an apartment without anything more decorative than a calendar on the wall. His place had the personality of a cheap motel room.

Because of Alan's assessment of him as a Nazi, I decided to keep my distance from Bennie. I was extremely naïve, of course. For if Alan's claims were true in the slightest degree, Bennie wouldn't have befriended me, much less have worked in an office run by Jews. I never did discover what Bennie really thought about politics. But in hind sight, obviously, I believe now that

Alan's calling Bennie a "Nazi" was for Bennie's conservative politics. And as Alan was a liberal, he meant that Bennie's conservatism amounted to the politics of hate and other ills associated with extreme right-wing views.

Bennie got me side jobs working for a private investigator, a former Secret Service agent. After that, we became friendly but we never hung out together. I don't recall ever seeing Bennie get high. I suspected that he was a heavy drinker, but he seemed to keep to himself mostly after work.

Barbara, another co-worker, had a Chinese girlfriend whom she introduced to me, a young woman named Shelly who lived in Brookline. Shelly was from Rhode Island and she belonged to a wealthy family. She worked in a doctor's office. We began to spend time together at her place; and I slept with her once. We smoked a lot of reefer together and had endless discussions about the world. I confess that the Quaaludes she supplied me with were the principal reason I spent time with her. I resold nearly all of the free 'ludes' she gave me to make extra money.

What many people found attractive about the "ludes" were their cooling or calming effect on other drugs like speed. It also boosted one's sexual sensitivity and relaxed one's muscles. And it numbed the body to pain. Those of us who indulged in "ludes" often joked about the aches and pains we felt the next day after bouncing off the walls all night.

Once I almost cracked up my car because of 'ludes.' I discovered that I had a low tolerance for the thick pills, so I usually took a half of the pill. Otherwise, I'd find myself unable to walk, let alone drive. The drug caused a slow motion effect on my motor control, so that my attempt to step on the brake pedal could take as long as ten seconds. And that was far too long to avoid an accident. Usually, people who "fooled with 'ludes" were hip enough to stay indoors while they were high. It was too dangerous to go out on the street right after popping a 'lude.'

The Tet Offensive by the Viet Cong began as a massive general assault against American and South Vietnamese troops on January 30, 1968. It resulted in a military defeat for the Communists. But it also was a political defeat for President Lyndon Johnson. One by one his political allies began to desert him. And in March he lost one of his strongest media supporters. Beware the Ides of March!

Walter Cronkite, a popular television evening news anchor at CBS, was long a supporter of Johnson's Vietnam policy, but in early March he returned from a post-Tet visit to Vietnam full of doubts. And in his nationally broadcast report, he declared that our war against the Viet Cong and their allies, the North Vietnamese Communists, was unwinnable. He openly called our Vietnam War a military quagmire. And his opposition to the war turned many other Democrats against Johnson.

On March 12th, Senator McCarthy finished a strong second in the New Hampshire primary. Clearly,

President Johnson had a battle on his hands for the nomination, until Senator Robert "Bobby" Kennedy entered the race for the presidential nomination four days later.

Kennedy's candidacy split the anti-war movement. Some called Bobby an opportunist for waiting until McCarthy had run against Johnson to declare his candidacy. Others felt that Bobby offered an alternative to McCarthy who fought a popular impression in the published commentaries that he was a one issue candidate

On March 3l, l968, President Johnson announced a bombing halt and made the statement that he would not be running for re-election.

Although Hubert Humphrey, the vice-president, had decided to run as a candidate, he was not expected to prevail over Robert Kennedy. Despite his stellar record as an advocate for civil rights in the 1950's, when it took courage to stand up for black civil rights, his record did little to persuade black America that he was a better choice than Bobby.

Richard Nixon became the standard bearer for the Republican Party. Many of us hoped to see him defeated once again. The possibility of a second defeat at the polls by a Kennedy must have been a nightmare for Nixon. Early primary polls showed that Bobby would certainly carry the battle to Nixon's Middle-American strongholds. We were beginning to dream of Camelot again. But on April 4, l968, Reverend Martin Luther King, Jr., was assassinated in Memphis, Tennessee. My recollection about where I was when it happened has remained a blank. I can only remember my parents being upset at the news bulletins on the radio and television following the tragedy. I remember saying a prayer when I heard the news. But the question ringing in my head for a long time was: Why? Why was King assassinated? Why him? King was one of the few black men in America who would turn his cheek to the white aggressor. What would happen now that he had been taken away from my people?

Even though I hadn't always agreed with his tactics, I knew that his death was a big loss for the civil rights movement. And neither of King's lieutenants, Reverends Jesse Jackson nor Ralph Abernathy, seemed to me quite able take his place in the movement.

The one Protestant religious leader who appealed to as many Americans as did Rev. Martin Luther King was Rev. Billy Graham. But there the similarity ended. Like Martin Luther King, Billy Graham had Southern roots. But the Southern experience has always been different for blacks and whites there. Graham disdained interracial dating; and his racism militated against his becoming an advocate for equal justice and civil rights for non-whites in white society. Graham's racism came to public light in the 1990's, in recordings of his conversations with Richard Nixon. There the public heard Graham express bigotry to Nixon, and the tapes revealed that he shared Nixon's anti-Semitism.

Until Graham saw a way for his ministry to increase its financial appeals to blacks, he behaved as many white televangelist Christians: he shunned the Civil Rights struggle. As a rule, white Christian evangelists of the times, with few exceptions, were never involved in King's protests owing to their close ties to the white supremacist power structure. Unlike King, Graham chose the company of the rich and powerful, no doubt tailoring his opinions to mirror theirs, such that he even took a trip to Vietnam at the request of President Johnson in support of that war.

King, of course, was outside the mainstream political power circles, and he spoke truth to power, regardless of the person's power or position. Excepting King, I do not recall while Lyndon Johnson was in office that any of the spiritual leaders in the civil rights movement came out publicly against the war.

Most black Americans were never separatists. They still wanted a place in the American dream. They hadn't completely lost faith in the system and were unwilling to go back to Africa or live in an all black region set aside for them in the American South, as many whites still hoped.

It was around the time of the King assassination that word spread about a secret concentration camp for black Americans. The rumor was of a place that would hold most of the country's blacks in the event black rioting got out of hand. It seemed like just a wild rumor at the time, totally off-base. But I became less skeptical about it when a friend from Germany named Reiner told me about his father, a former officer in the German Army. His account of the World War II camp seemed like the one allegedly for blacks. There was, however, no other credible evidence of the camp for blacks other than rumor.

A couple of nights later, at a party, a number of white people came over to console me about what had happened to King. They felt as though King's assassination was a personally terrible tragedy. But not all whites felt that way about King.

At another party in Needham, in which some people from Retail Credit were in attendance, Mark told me that a group there had made all kinds of racist statements about King. Many of them were off-duty cops of the host. It so happened that I had arrived at the party with Leroy and friends while the whites were making the remarks. Mark said that our arrival had hushed the racist talkers. Depressed already over King's death, I didn't really need to know that incognito racist cops were among the party. But I was not happy either when I realized that I had been stood up by Connie, another irregular date. And Marilyn wasn't with me. Perhaps, as I recall now, she had gone away for the weekend. In any event, I was feeling very lonely at the time.

I supposed that Connie might have been seeing her ex-boyfriend. I remembered then the times we were in bed together and she'd start crying out of the blue over her ex-, a guy she called "Charlie," which pissed me off, even though I was jamming her all night long. Actually I knew her "Charlie," who played in a band called "The Bacchanalians." We got along pretty well. But I never knew whether he knew that we shared the same woman. I lost contact with him for forty years. When I ran into him again, we talked about old times. I didn't have the heart to ask him about Connie. I was still afraid to reveal my relationship to her. A month later, I learned that he passed away shortly after our reunion.

I ended up at Mark's apartment in Chelsea that night. It was late after the party ended, so I decided to take him up on his offer to sleep there overnight. He and Fifi had become quite accustomed to joining me at numerous parties with both Marilyn and Connie. But Connie had spent more time with us. Since Mark had become a close friend, I settled down on a sleep sofa. About an hour later, Fifi awakened me. Suddenly, she was beside me on the sofa, her hair brushing my face. I smelled her fragrance and was swept up in the rapture. She turned her face to me and I found myself staring into her eyes, deep, dark and mysterious in the moonlight.

"Move over!" she said. Man, oh man, I didn't need to hear more. She was wearing a short negligee. The moonlight created a striped pattern across her body, as it streamed through the blinds of the sliding glass door of the patio. I moved my mouth onto hers and she opened her lips under mine, flicking her tongue against my teeth. I ran my fingers along the edge of her thigh reassuring myself that I wasn't dreaming. Her skin was smooth, soft, and warm to the touch. I knew that I wasn't dreaming. I would remember this woman in my dreams for some time after that night.

I slowly explored her with my fingers, lost in her scent. She smelled so enticingly delicious, I wanted to bite her. All of her was beautiful. I wanted to treasure every moment. Touching the top of a breast with the tips of my fingers, I felt Fifi shift her body exposing two lovely melon size breasts. Kissing them I felt their nipples harden like two raisins.

"What have I done to deserve this," I silently asked myself as I concentrated on the pleasant task at hand. She was so pliable that she seemed able to arrange herself at will, conforming to my silent commands as we made out. Then, she grabbed my dick, lifting her ass to take me deep inside her dewy mound. We sighed together as I touched bottom. "Gawd damn!" What ecstasy! "My, my, my!"

We thrust together as she continued expanding, taking more and more of me inside. I wanted more of her as we moved toward climax. I tried to hold back. It was impossible. All the time while I was enjoying Fifi, my head was filled with bubbles of pleasure: Why me? Why was I so blessed? She seemed like a wild dream.

Then, it was over and she left the room. I heard the bathroom door close.

There was no way in hell that I would have risked losing my integrity by attempting to move on Fifi. I was a better friend to my friends than to hit on their wives. I valued my friends. And I wasn't about to risk losing them over sex with their girlfriends or wives. I had learned the price of betrayal of a personal trust long ago on the streets. Plus, with Fifi, I had never detected any sexual interest in me per se. She seemed to like me because Mark did. And had I put a move on her, I believed then that nothing would have happened for me except having my feelings hurt.

So her jumping on me in the middle of the night was totally unexpected. I learned later from Mark that he had sent her to me out of kindness. Open marriages and free love were common among a lot of users and hippies. Perhaps Mark felt sorry for me not having a date, having seen me bummed out by my broken dates in Needham. Over the years, there would be many women in my life: Women of all colors and cultures would come my way. But Fifi would forever stand out from the crowd in my memories of physical pleasure. She and I never talked about what happened and it never happened again. We continued to hang out until Mark and Fifi returned to New York the following year. Those were the days!

On June 5, l968, Bobby Kennedy won the California primary after losing a couple of primaries to Hubert Humphrey, his victory cut short during his victory celebration that very night. Sirhan Sirhan, a disgruntled Palestinian American, shot him to death in the kitchen of the campaign's celebrations at a Los Angeles hotel. The tragic politically inspired assassinations of 1963 were repeated in l968, and another progressive leader of my generation was gone.

I recall browsing through a bookstore at Coolidge Corner that June evening, listening to the music that the store was playing on a local radio station. When the station interrupted the scheduled program to report the second Kennedy assassination, I cursed out loud. I was in shock, as were many fellow shoppers in the store. Many of us felt disgusted and enraged.

Bobby Kennedy was an irreplaceable loss. He listened to anti-war and civil rights protesters. He reminded us of our duty to stand up for the less fortunate. Sometimes, he made me feel a twinge of guilt at my lack of commitment to a cause: I can never forget his rhetorical question: "If not now, when? If not me, who?"

A broad coalition of Americans supported Bobby's bid for president. He did not appear at the time to be under the control of a political machine. And he was no longer in Jack Kennedy's political shadow. He made a sacrifice when he decided to run for President, when he might well have retired to a life of safety as a Senator.

Many of us wanted him to take us back to the "New Frontier" waiting just beyond the horizon. We didn't have the experience to chart a path across the turbulent waters. Bobby seemed to be the one to lead the country out of its divisions. Many young people felt that he would never have let us down.

In the anti-War and Civil Rights communities, there were calls for a revolution in response to Bobby's assassination. But it was only talk. The radicals and protestors, with a few scattered splinter groups of militants, didn't have the guns or the stomach to act on the revolutionary voices calling for a violent control of America. Many political radicals with the fighting experience to wage a revolutionary war came home from 'Nam spiritually, psychologically, and physically dysfunctional. The Vietnam vets who had been radicalized politically were in no shape to fight anyone. Besides, the main issues radicalizing them to support other demonstrators were for adequate military benefits and job preferences—two issues easily used to co-opt their support against the other protesters. And for peaceful protests, there was nobody of national stature with the experience or broad political appeal enough to galvanize a national consensus behind civil rights and anti-war causes.

The nation mourned Bobby's death. His funeral at St. Patrick's Cathedral in New York in 1968 left a bitter taste in my mouth. National television networks broadcasted the funeral, with the train carrying the senator's body, Kennedy family survivors, and his closest supporters from New York to Arlington National Cemetery in Washington, DC. As the train rolled slowly past the spectators, I envied those standing alongside the railway corridors to pay their respects. Along the way, several people stood in a rail bed; several others lost their lives when a train going in the opposite direction hit them. Death never takes a time out. Many of my friends and I wondered what might have happened had Bobby lived? We then anticipated a violent summer.

At the 1968 Olympics in Mexico City, two gold medalists Tommy Smith and John Carlos raised their fists in a black power salute at the podium. American spectators loudly booed the Olympians. Back home, the American Olympic governing body took away their gold medal prizes. They were unable to compete in official track meets in the USA. I remember one of my bosses at the Retail Credit office saying that while they had a right to express themselves, they could have chosen another place to do it. In making a symbolic gesture of support for black equality, they provoked a widespread racist reaction among whites that I am sure was unintended.

But the unintended consequences for many blacks like me were what such a casual unconscious white racism meant for me and Marilyn.

Marilyn and I took a trip to Philadelphia that summer. We were a mixed couple in a city hostile to interracial relationships. I wanted her to meet some of my relatives as I had met some of hers. Philly was an odd city on race. The powers that be there promoted it as progressive and tolerant of social differences and the city tourism office pointed out that most of its work force and neighborhoods were integrated. Yet, as I well knew from Boston's ethnic enclaves, people can live next door to each other for years and never interact socially.

To borrow a contemporary phrase from the military policy on gay soldiers, Philly, was a "don't ask, don't tell" kind of city. Many blacks there favored separate enclaves from whites. They didn't seem to understand that separate but allegedly equal lives limited their economic opportunities and tax benefits from their taxes. As a minority, blacks stood to lose politically where decisions on spending taxes were made. Separate but equal status was a delusion, for a minority by definition was unequal to a majority making political and economic decisions according to numbers of recipients. All the same, blacks wanted the right to live on the same street or work on the same job as whites. The goal of equal treatment was enough to satisfy blacks with a segregated status quo. Integration with whites was never our goal. We agreed with the 1960's published opinion polls of white attitudes on race. By a large majority, whites polled said that they didn't mind living in a segregated white community, and neither did blacks. In Philly, few people cared that the city had a racist police commissioner named Rizzo working with a black mayor named Goode. That the two officials stood for opposite positions on racial equality in City Hall did not mean racial equality in my mind. Still, in local government, Philly was more tolerant than Boston. And that was true in other areas as well.

Visiting my Uncle Jake for the first time, for example, I was astonished to see women driving streetcars. Boston didn't have women driving buses, trains, or streetcars until the 1980's. It was not altogether an absolute victory for women, but more along the lines of a compensation for other forms of gender discrimination in the same workplace. My uncle joked that women were allowed to operate streetcars because the tracks would keep them from driving off the road.

Marilyn and I had a pleasant Philly visit that weekend in July. We decided to go to a beach in New Jersey called Wildwood on the Jersey shore. My cousin Marvin and his girlfriend were with us. I'll never forget that day. As the four of us walked along the boardwalk, blacks and whites stared at us. Marilyn and I, of course, were the attraction. Even a black cop and a white cop both gave us the evil eye. Marvin decided to fuck with me and held back a few steps, so it would appear that Marilyn and I were alone. That's when it really got stupid. One of the assholes on the walkway tried to peek down the front of her bathing suit right in front of me. Having never experienced such harassment in Boston, despite the racial animosity in some parts of the city, I was more than perplexed. I felt deeply humiliated, all the more so because I feared to protest. Marilyn, however, behaved with aplomb, cool as a cucumber, shrugging. She gave the goofball a look of disgust that told him where to go, and kept her stride. I was proud of her.

I decided to enter U/Mass Boston in September of the next year. To pay my tuition meant giving up my Corvette. It had been an exciting car to drive on the highway. The car had a speed maximum of 170 miles per hour; I never tried to reach the max for fear of losing control. But once, when I was alone on an empty road, I pressed down hard on the accelerator until I hit 120 m.p.h. I could not afford that expensive car on financial aid at U/Mass. I knew that there would always be a chance to get a new car, but I wouldn't always have the time to get an education.

In January 1969, the number of U.S. troops in Vietnam reached 543,000 men. I began to hear stories about rookie lieutenants being fragged by their disgruntled troops. Fragging meant that one of our men had thrown a fragmentation grenade into a tent, while someone was inside.

ଓ ର

Chapter 6:

The Winding Road

"The long and winding road that leads to your door"

--Paul Mc Cartney

My experiences in Boston gave me an outlook on life that was very different from those of my cousins and relatives from other places. I was less tolerant of racial discrimination than most of the older generation of blacks. Growing up among whites—that is, having felt equal to them in Boston—gave me confidence that I could achieve my goals regardless of white racial discrimination. In Boston, I never felt that my race would be an insurmountable barrier for me, as it had been for my parent's generation under Southern white imposed segregation laws. Some blacks in Boston of my generation had militant nationalistic and violent views about whites that I did not share. Other political problems went well beyond racial issues.

The Democratic political convention for President in Chicago, for one, worked against our ability to deliver a radical Presidential campaign candidate for the party's nomination. White working and middle-class women, Southern white women, white men from small town America wearing ill-fitting suits and VFW ribbons—none of them were going to vote for Julian Bond, the only black candidate, or the radical anti-War candidate, Minnesota Senator Eugene McCarthy. Radical presidential preferences were unacceptable, and not just viewed as unelectable by a majority of the white delegates. But the Chicago convention was the only chance radicals had to influence the choice of the Democratic candidate for President. Vice-President Hubert Humphrey, we were sure, would have been better than segregationist Alabama Governor George C. Wallace or Richard M. Nixon.

Unfortunately, Humphrey allowed Johnson to muzzle him on speaking out against the war as a condition for the president's support. His loyalty to Johnson caused resentment in the ranks of the antiwar movement. Many of them considered Humphrey a sellout. And many began to riot in protest outside the convention hall and on the streets. The rioters destroyed public property and attacked the police. Mayor Daly responded forcefully to suppress them.

There was no question that Mayor Richard Daley wanted to teach the demonstrators a lesson. Following King's assassination, he gave his Chicago cops free rein to put down riots with lethal force, resulting in many innocent lives lost. I felt little doubt that Daley's cops were repeating their response to suppress the riot at the Democratic Convention. Thankfully, mainstream civil rights organizations, moderate antiwar groups, and some of the delegates did not attend the Convention. Rumors abounded that the Yippy Party, a motley collection of street people sponsored by Jerry Rubin and Abbie Hoffman, were going to riot, but they were also mostly a no-show during the riots. Members of the Communist Party, who had jeered Abbie Hoffman on Boston Commons, never took the center stage outside the Convention halls either. Although the Communists were against the War, they were continually blaming the upper class for our problems. For example, when Hoffman took the stage at the Boston rally and said: "John Hancock wasn't a fucking insurance salesman, he was a revolutionary!" most of the crowd cheered wildly, while the few boos for him came from Communists. This competition among the most extreme radicals intensified leading up to the Convention. When the daily protests turned violent in Chicago, Daly's cops started beating demonstrators every day in skirmishes at Grant Park. The violent police response provoked a national backlash. And on the last day of the convention, Wednesday, August 28, l968, about ten thousand demonstrators showed up.

That evening, when protesters attempted to march toward the convention site from Grant Park, the cops waded into the group using tear gas and billy clubs. On TV screens across America youthful protesters chanted "The whole world is watching. The whole world is watching," as police beat them. As the cops went on a spree beating innocent bystanders and newsmen, hundreds of people in the vicinity were injured that night. A Walker Commission, later investigating the outbreak, called the incident a "police riot."

When Vice President Humphrey was nominated for the presidential nomination, he condoned the actions of Mayor Daley's police outside the convention. It turned out to be a close election. Nixon had always seemed a rightwing monster, and his vice-president, Spiro T. Agnew, seemed a fraud. In November, Richard Milhous Nixon was elected president. And he had long memories.

With Nixon in office, I lost interest in politics and threw myself into work and play. Not many months later, while I was working one evening in the office, I overheard one of the file girls talking to someone else about a person who'd been killed in an accident. I don't know to this day why I got into the conversation, but when she informed me that the victim was George, I was shocked.

George had been killed in a head-on crash with a drunk driver, she said. My memory of the nights that followed is vague. I clearly recall getting in my car and driving several blocks up Harvard Street to the Lally Funeral Home in Brookline where his wake was held. The other driver was a Vietnam vet, also killed in the crash. George's wife was in the car, but she was only injured in the accident.

Recalling George, as I drove to his wake, I suddenly felt immensely sad. I regretted how I would not ever see him alive again. That it began to rain did not help to relieve my depression. I entered the funeral home hatless, but I still had the sense to wear a raincoat. As I write this, my memory fails regarding many other impressions at the time. I recall entering the funeral home, climbing stairs to the viewing parlor, and my last impression of George, lying still, looking pale, and feeling cold to my touch in his coffin.

I don't know how long I stood there. After a few moments, I started to sob. I recall two of his brothers coming over to me. I hadn't known them before that evening. I exchanged a few brief words of sympathy with them and it was all that passed between us. Moments later, I was back in the car, staring through the windshield. I would always be leery of drunken drivers and their destruction of life and property. Maybe the fear of a fatal auto or motorcycle accident was one of the reasons I never picked up a drinking habit.

In the following weeks, I moved into Marilyn's Beacon Hill place, a second floor apartment on Revere Street. It was modest and infested with roaches. I recalled having used sulphur candles in Roxbury to successfully exterminate roaches in my apartment there so I lit the candles to get rid of them in her apartment. The smell in the place was so intense from the sulphur that we had to stay at a friends' for a night until the smell dissipated. When we returned and aired out the place there wasn't a roach alive. The candles had killed everything that was alive there.

During one of my Beacon Hill explorations, I ran into an old friend named Harold. We had both attended dancing school as kids to learn tap dancing. Harold was going by the nickname "T" and had been living on Beacon Hill for some time. He introduced me to a number of people on the "Hill" including John, an engineering student at Northeastern University and his girlfriend, Linda, whom I recall mostly because they owned a pricey KLH Stereo system. John kept the stereo player in a locked chest filled with cinder blocks to keep it from being stolen. I lost touch with them, but Marilyn and Linda got along very well and became lifelong friends.

I also met a fellow named J. O. through T. who would become a lifelong friend of mine. He was a dealer from whom I could buy my reefer at a good price almost anytime. As I've always gotten a charge setting off explosive devices, J.O. also provided me with Fourth of July fireworks. He was a very successful dealer and hustler, my ideal role model.

Through John and Linda I met Scottie, a black commercial pilot who flew a Lear Jet out of Logan Airport. He was the owner of a Corvette, a year old powder blue fastback. That spring, when Scottie asked me if I wanted to take a ride aboard his Lear, which was used to carry airmail out of state, I put him off. I was too frightened at the prospect of a plane crash.

Scottie came from New Jersey and had learned to fly jets in the Air Force. He impressed upon me that there were a good number of black pilots who could fly jet aircraft. Racial discrimination by commercial airlines left them little prospect of being hired. Such pervasive racial discrimination was alive and well in some professions until the eighties. I learned from Scottie that racial discrimination aside, even blacks like entertainers James

Brown and Sammy Davis, Jr., who owned private planes, didn't employ black pilots to fly them. It puzzled me then as much as it did when Scottie told me about Brown and Davis, and I doubt that either man could give me a satisfactory explanation of why they didn't hire black pilots.

Scottie was at the top of his career, a very demanding one, because you can't afford to make mistakes in a Lear jet. I amused Scottie once when he visited me by playing "Eight Miles High," a number by "The Byrds," which began with the sound of a Lear Jet warming up before takeoff. When I wanted to shake up the neighborhood or when a group of drunks were making a racket at night, I'd put the speakers in the window and turn up the volume, simulating a plane flying low through the neighborhood. It did wonders to silence the drunks under my window. Scottie told me that he once flew low over the street where his parents lived in New Jersey late one night. He said the wash from the jet rattled the houses in the neighborhood causing a small panic. He didn't get caught, however.

He also introduced me to something called by an unknown acronym "MDA," also known as "the love drug," in a small brown capsule taken orally or dissolved in liquid. Some people used it as a vehicle to the fifth dimension, or "date rape." MDA gave a pleasant buzz, which lasted for about two hours. It could be used to experiment with creative pursuits or to facilitate getting in the mood for lovemaking. It gave me a tremendous sense of well-being and was different from an acid trip, which could return, unexpectedly, in hot flashes. Several times I used MDA as a creative stimulant when I was writing songs and poetry.

Scottie meanwhile kept pressing me to take a ride aboard his Lear jet. I felt that I could not be evasive; I needed to give him a definitive yes or no answer. One of the old timers in the office who had a pilot's license eventually talked me into flying with Scottie. He put it to me that it was a once in a lifetime opportunity and I would regret not taking it when I had the chance. He was proved to be right.

One spring night I arrived at Logan Airport, at the executive aircraft terminal, where Scottie and I met for the ride of my life. I went with Scottie and his co-pilot to visit the weather center in the building to check out flight conditions. Once onboard, I watched them go through the pre-flight check of equipment. A little after eleven, a truck arrived and the plane was fueled up. Scottie explained to me that jets don't fly on gasoline, but kerosene.

Soon, we were in the departure line with other aircraft on the field. The other planes were large commercial airliners and each one took off separately. Just before our turn came, Scottie explained that we'd be flying at 40,000 feet in military airspace well above Commercial airliners which at that time flew at a ceiling of 20,000 feet. I was buckled into a jump seat behind the pilots as the two engines whined to maximum power and we shot down the runway. We left the ground in seconds and began a vertical climb to the heavens. It was nothing like the feeling of flying in a passenger plane, which was slow in comparison to this bird. The Lear jet was originally built as a fighter plane.

After we leveled off, I looked out the window and was blown away. Not only could I see a two hundred mile long strip of lights stretching the length of the Mass Turnpike from Boston to New York, but the other passenger planes flying twenty thousand feet below us. The hum of the engines was loud in comparison to the quiet of a passenger jet. But it didn't matter to me. It was like looking down on a living map of the East Coast.

Our first stop was New York City, where we landed and left a mail bag full of letters and packages. We took on another bag of mail and flew from there to Pittsburg, where we repeated the procedure. From Pittsburg, we went on to Cincinnati, Ohio, where we stayed over for half an hour. I called my aunt from the airport to say hello. I had seen her only once since I had ridden my motorcycle to that city in l963.

The co-pilot was doing most of the flying in order to build up his hours in jet aircraft. Scottie handled most of the takeoffs, however. In Ohio, the co-pilot offered to let me taxi away from the hangar, but I thought he was joking. I had no desire to fly a plane. I had not the faintest idea of how to fly one. I kindly declined his offer. I wanted to live another day.

What was neat about flying the Lear, I supposed, for Scottie, was that he didn't have to wear a uniform! His Lear cockpit was a very informal setting. Scottie told me that sometimes the FAA made random flight checks using questions to make sure that a qualified person was at the controls. Later, I heard that John had taken the controls for a few minutes when he had flown on the Lear. Sometimes, even now I wish I'd tried it. It must be similar to the feeling of taking the controls of a freight locomotive or a subway train - a lifelong memory for those brave enough to take the controls.

Sometimes now, when I'm looking up in the nighttime sky and see a small red dot rising from the direction of the airport at a sharp vertical angle, I'm reminded of my trip aboard the Lear jet. It was a hell of a ride. If I were to rank it along a measure of thrills for me, it only took a back seat to oral sex.

One evening I went to the radio station, WMEX, for the Jerry Williams broadcast program with the actor Peter Fonda, star of the film "Easy Rider." Fonda sat in the studio with a small audience answering calls from the listeners about the film shot in parts of the South and featuring drug dealing. He wore a dungaree outfit, a beard, cowboy boots and dark glasses. It was as if he didn't want to be recognized. Few people approached him after the show. The price of fame, I guess.

A few weeks after the radio show, I finally saw "Easy Rider" which featured Jack Nicholson in a cameo role. I felt a surge of outrage at the Southern crackers depicted in the movie. It was the talk of the office. In a way, it validated my fears about traveling by motorcycle through West Virginia, on the way to Ohio, in the early sixties.

That fall Bennie increased my work in the nether world of private investigations. I immersed myself into the culture. And Bennie threw a lot of reports my way. I became proficient in the art of shadow surveillance and tracking down the subjects of skip-trace inquiries, people who disappeared after running up a bill on a credit card or failed to return a credit card.

Workmen's compensation claims were a gold mine. I could make a day's pay for two hours work on some of those cases, staking out subjects who were believed to be faking an injury in order to collect money. I remember one case where Bennie and I waited on a side street across from a Boston bar. We had a tip that our target stopped at the bar before going to work. The plan was for us to tail him by car to his job. If he took a bus or subway train, I was to get on the conveyance and follow him. The subject knew what Bennie looked like. Suddenly, a cab pulled up in front of the bar and the guy jumped inside. The cab took off with screeching tires before we could get underway. The bastard had outfoxed us. It was the first and last time I ever saw the man. I don't know if the insurance company ever caught him.

It was through Bennie that I met his employer, Walter. He owned a private investigations business in the same building that George had his insurance office. Walter was so into being a private dick that he legally changed his name to James Bond, the name of the fictional spy. His private office had steel bars set in the door frame like the entrance to a bank vault. It all made him a more interesting character than the fictional Bond. And what surprised me most about Walter was that he had a federal license for a machine gun, which he kept in his office. I could not imagine where he would legally be able to use it in his work.

During my association with the agency, I was to learn the value of private information. In some instances, it can be priceless. Creditors are the most active seekers of information about their clients. A damaging piece of information can be used to determine whether to give a person credit or turn him down. Access to the right people or to the wrong people could even be used to change a damaging report. It often came down to who you knew, that is, learning who at the credit office needed money on the side and was willing to take a bribe to change a person's credit report.

In the information business, contacts within the police force and the court system are critical. Our system is designed in such a way that a corporate officer can escape jail by hiding behind his company. In other words, a company can assume liability for the liabilities of its owners. And while you can fine a company, you can't put it in jail. Money talks louder than words in the criminal justice system. Why else did only two people from Enron go to jail for the white collar robbery there?

At that time in my life, I wanted to get a gun. Actually, I wanted to become a cop. Many of the guys I grew up with, some of them hard-core thugs with criminal records, somehow became cops. But I was too short at that time, being all of 5'7," just below the 5'8" required by the Boston Police Department, and I couldn't pass the swimming test. Things were different with respect to credentials for hiring a police officer back then. If you weren't a certain height, you could be excluded from the police force. That requirement was not lifted until affirmative action came along and the height requirements were found to be discriminatory, especially against women.

I decided to stay where I was for the time being. I continued to learn about the gray areas in the field of private investigations. There were all kinds of tools that were utilized by people in this trade. I found out about the secret inventories of gadgetry that were standard tools of the trade. For example, there were bugs that could be used to listen to conversations in a private home. We had the same telephone handsets carried by company workers that could be snapped onto a phone line to eavesdrop. We had telephones with lights that could reveal a wiretap. There was also a secret office at the phone company where you could get private phone numbers by posing on the line as a state trooper. Some of us used these tools, some didn't. But they were available in the information business. And I had few qualms about breaking the law or using them.

More importantly, I learned how to use my eyes and my peripheral vision, an ability that would prove useful to me in the future. Many people, I've found, are unaware that our eyes are attracted to movement. Even the smallest movement attracts our attention. This probably goes back to the prehistoric days when early man had to be on guard against the many predators who wanted him for dinner. It usually happens unconsciously. You just find yourself looking at a tiny insect. It's a part of our early warning system.

Dean, my co-worker from Maine, had been asking about going out with my sister, but I couldn't guarantee him a chance. She was in college and was pretty busy. Plus, she was recently separated with two children. His sister, as it so happened, was going to Boston University, which wasn't far from the office. I called her up one night and took her out to the movies. That was all it took. We did the deed after the movie. I only saw her, however, a couple of times thereafter. I learned that it's hard to date a good friend's sister, when you're doing other women on the side with him. But that's how busy I was with my liaisons on the side. It seemed in those days that everyone was fooling around. I even went out with one of my younger brother's elementary school teachers, who were older than me.

Dean was a little pissed off with me when he found out about my fling with his sister. Not for racial matters, for we knew each other too well, but he didn't like getting beaten to the punch with my sister instead of me getting with his sister. I promised to fix him up with a black woman as soon as possible, as the best I could do to even the score. But that wasn't to be.

Janet, a file worker, soon thereafter talked Dean and me into going to that March's St. Patrick's Day parade in South Boston; I hadn't noticed her until she proposed the parade. Although she had been with the firm for almost a year, she didn't seem remarkably attractive enough to make me notice her. In fact, I considered her rather drab. When she invited us to the parade, she became an enchantress, at least to me, overnight. Before my eyes she developed a body with super legs, a sexy woman looking wild. Although she wore bland clothes to work, she dressed in a flashy miniskirt for the parade. Later, I would try to get to her. But she was hooked on Dean.

For the visit to Southie, we followed a protocol. We left our cars in Brookline and took the Commonwealth Avenue streetcar to the Red Line train at the Park Street station. Janet and a group of her friends accompanied us. A couple of the guys with us were football players at Boston College. Whatever planning had been made for my safety was very tight. We ended up in front of the D Street housing projects, where we linked up with another group from the projects. One of the guys in that group was black and had lived there for some time. We made up a goodly size crowd and I felt safe and secure. There was no trouble. The expected race riot with drunken Irishmen never happened.

That summer I returned the favor by inviting them to a rock concert featuring Smokey Robinson and the Miracles at the Columbus Avenue ball field, in Roxbury's South End. It was attended by a mostly black crowd. Janet, Dean and several of her white friends stood out in the pool of black concert goers. They were never in any danger of racial animosity. And the only violence was a small brawl among the spectators. None of my guests, as far as I could tell, was in any danger.

On July 21, l969, the astronauts reached the moon. It was the highlight of the year's good news in the U.S. but the pride most Americans felt about the space achievement was overshadowed by the person taking credit for it. President Nixon basked in the glory that should have been shared by my president, John F.

Kennedy, for he had started the project. The times had changed, sadly, with Nixon in the White House, even though President Kennedy's promise to have Americans first on the moon had come true.

Many people were going back to school in l969. As I made a conscious decision again to return full-time to college that spring, I began making plans to apply for the fall session at the Boston campus of the University of Massachusetts. A lot of my peers realized the necessity of getting an education and there were plenty of government grants and loans to make that possible. It was the smart thing to do.

One missed opportunity for my advancement in education came to my attention through Marilyn. I learned that Harvard University had an enrollment program for minority students. And she felt that I might be able to qualify for the program if I could bring up my SAT scores. Only my mind was made up to enroll at the University of Massachusetts (UMass) and frankly, I didn't have the desire to go in that direction. If I knew then what I know now, Harvard's minority enrollment program would have been my first choice. Instead of a Harvard catalogue, I purchased a thick college preparatory book and began studying from the first page to the last for UMass. I also attended a summer program for pre-freshman students to prepare them for college.

The biggest news of the summer after the moon landing was the upcoming concert at Woodstock. As the hype went, Woodstock was the place to be. I waffled about going until the last minute. Although I could have attended the concert, I had my misgivings based on the news predicting trouble and traffic: the word on the top 40 radio stations was that traffic on the roads leading to the festival was so jammed that people were hiking to the grounds from distances as far as twenty miles, even before the music had started. I decided to stay home and go to the next one. The naysayers' predictions, in any case, were already enough to keep me away. Rumors about illegal drug use and the potential for a major riot filled the press, which seemed to parrot the Nixon Administration's stance.

Several hundred thousand young people came together on Max Yasgur's farm on the weekend of August 15-17. And many people, parents included, held their collective breaths. The potential for the riot of the century was very real. We knew there were going to be massive amounts of illegal drugs on hand, for drugs and a rock concert went hand-in-hand. That was a given. A rainstorm over the weekend, unfortunately, caught a lot of festival goers by surprise. The storm turned the large concert field into a quagmire.

Those of us who hadn't made the trip were kept informed by the rock and roll music stations and the national news about what was happening. Actually, most of the news was fairly positive. The only disaster turned out to be the mess on the ground. Everything else was peachy. There was no fighting or violent behavior tolerated by the participants. Even, network comedian Johnny Carson joked on his late night show that if the parents of the youths had been crowded together like their kids, drinking their alcohol, there would probably have been an adult riot of major proportions. When Carson parodied the slurred speech of a drunken parent, his audience exploded in laughter. The cops on the scene, realizing that the outcome of the festival was in their hands, didn't try to make any drug arrests. This spirit of cooperation went a long way toward making the environment as safe as possible for everyone.

The anti-drug lobby put out a false story through its friends in the media outlets that two young men attending Woodstock went blind after dropping acid and staring at the sun. That was the best lie they could come up with and it was soon discredited. This would be the beginning of a crusade of half-truths and lies against drugs that has lasted to this day.

I received an acceptance letter from the university at the beginning of summer and sold the Corvette. I was moving on to other things. When I graduated there would be opportunities to buy whatever kind of car I wanted.

That spring, I got married to Marilyn in a small ceremony at the Trinity Church at Copley Square. My friend from the war was my best man. I was now driving an old Volkswagen convertible. Her parents came down from Rutland, Vermont with one of her sisters. Both sets of our parents got along fine. I invited a couple of people from Retail Credit and a few friends from Beacon Hill and Roxbury to join us. Marilyn invited a few of her friends as well. We had a breakfast reception at a hotel in Cambridge. But much to my regret, Melvin and Leroy never showed up.

It had been a decade of wonder, but most of our dreams were shattered by unforeseen events. My generation was now ten years older and wiser. Still, we kept mostly to ourselves. We traveled in groups to parties, nightclubs, movies and concerts. We had our music, our clothes, our communes, and our lives. These were the things we still controlled. We didn't have the power to elect any of our peers to office. We couldn't change the drug laws. The only changes were happening inside our heads. Since the mid-sixties, many of us had begun giving up on the political system. "Turn on, tune in, drop out" was a timely slogan for far too many.

I then quit my job at Retail Credit and I took out a loan through the Small Business Administration to start a small investigations company. I went into business with Don, my friend from work. My contacts in the insurance business enabled me to obtain letters from two insurance companies promising to give me cases. My mentor-friend from the Registry I presumed could help me get a private detective's license through his name. When I next spoke with him, he told me that a "Statie" (state trooper) investigating his recommendation had a hostile attitude to my request. To make a long story short, my plans never came to pass. The companies required that my business be covered by an expensive liability insurance policy. Moreover, the state police required that my friend would have to leave his job if the license was granted.

Because of a conflict of interest, he was still moving toward retirement and the risk of giving up his job for a new venture wasn't worth it. After having rented an office, I then had to let the matter drop. Luckily, I was forgiven the ten thousand dollar SBA loan by the government.

Later, I would discover that in order to start a serious business, it would have taken at least five times the SBA loan to succeed. I soon found a work study job through U/Mass and I put everything else on hold.

☙ ❧

Chapter 7:

A Man's Best Friend

Marilyn and I moved to my old neighborhood in Roxbury just around the corner from my parents. We had purchased a female Doberman Pinscher puppy to safeguard the apartment. She was one of the best dogs I'd ever owned and I trained her by the book. A few weeks later we were owners of a new Toyota station wagon, a wedding present from Marilyn's mother.

We had a family of sorts. Phaedra, our pet Doberman was our baby. I felt better having her in the apartment with Marilyn when I was working at Holiday Magic. Dobermans always get respect on the street. They have a strong sense of their presence. What was unusual about Phaedra was her delight in racing up to a stranger in the park and veering away from him at the last moment. The pedestrian would often freeze in panic. She seemed to be grinning with her sharp teeth as she raced about.

Phaedra was naturally protective and I noticed that whenever a stranger was talking to us, she would come over and check him out. Then, she'd go back to what she was doing. What we liked most about her was her temperament which was mild rather than aggressive. To the surprise of strangers, she loved to be petted and most strangers were all too happy to pet her.

Phaedra loved to run in the woods of Killington, Vermont, where Marilyn's family owned land near the ski slopes. At that time, the developers were just beginning to build chalets. One day Marilyn, her mother and I were walking along an old logging trail at the base of the mountain when I heard the sound of an animal making a bleating sound similar to that of a lamb. There was no other sound except the sounds of the forest. Some of those trails went on for miles.

Marilyn's mother then asked me to call Phaedra back to us and to hold on to her collar. She listened for a moment before we resumed our trek through the woods. Then, she told me to hold Phaedra close to me because she recognized that the sound was from a bear cub.

One thing Phaedra picked up on her own was the tactic of immediately establishing a perimeter around our space by charging into the woods to flush out any bird or animal that might be hiding nearby. Sometimes, I'd hear the crash of a deer leaping through the brush that was caught off guard by the tactic. I'd always call her back for once a dog has tasted deer blood, it usually keeps attacking deer and a dog that attacks deer causes the authorities to put it down.

One day, as we were down at a beach near Plymouth at low tide, Phaedra dashed into a stretch of water which prompted a rock crab to leap to the surface. After gripping it in her jaws, she carried it to the beach. Following that incident Phaedra began to charge into the water to see what would happen.

Early in the summer, we mated Phaedra with a male Doberman from the bloodline of a champion named Baron. I hoped to get a red puppy from the litter but nothing is guaranteed in dog breeding. That fall, Phaedra had a litter of seven puppies. All were healthy. There were five males and two females. One of the males was red. Sometimes, it seemed that when I really wanted something to happen, it did. In six to seven weeks, we had a vet crop their tails and give them the required health shots. We sold four of the puppies, each one for two hundred dollars. The male's owner got the pick of the litter. I decided to keep Red and his brother Epic.

Anyone familiar with my family remembers our dogs. I kept a mixed breed Doberman named Dobie at my parent's house sometime earlier. Dobie's mother had mated with a neighbor's German shepherd in the same Waltham neighborhood where I bought him. Dobie was a smart dog who lived with my family before they bought a house on Oakburn Ave. We lived behind the school I attended until the fifth grade. My mother could direct Dobie to walk an elderly friend of hers to her home a couple of blocks away and he'd do it.

I recall now that the dog snarled and snapped at the husband of my mother's best friend, which struck us quite at odds with Dobie's friendly disposition to other strangers. The man was so scared of Dobie from then onwards that he refused even to be left in a room with him. I was puzzled by Dobie's unusual behavior. Later, however, I discovered that the husband had raped two foster sisters in his wife's care. He knew better than to try that mess with my sister. I was convinced that the dog sensed a threat to us when the man was present.

I passed my summer pre-freshman program with one of the highest scores in the English part of the SAT exam so I decided to major in English. As I set my sights on a journalism career, I joined the school newspaper as a cub reporter.

Late in November, Bennie contacted me and told me that someone from the government wanted to speak with me about a deal in the works. He accompanied me to a lawyer's office downtown and left me there. The "lawyer's" name, as I shall call him here, was Coan. He showed me his I.D. from the Bureau of Alcohol, Tobacco and Firearms. We got down to business right away. Apparently, there were guns being sold in Roxbury to certain criminal elements. Then, mentioning a name to me that I recognized as someone I'd heard about, he asked what I knew about the person. I surprised him when I said that my "ears" on the street identified the man as an undercover black Federal Bureau of Investigation (FBI) agent, who owned a business in Roxbury. Coan also recognized the man's name, not as a G-man, but as an informant or a snitch for the law. His response was news to me. I realized then that this guy had been using the FBI as his front: He had people on the street believing he was an undercover agent. It served as his protection for being an FBI informant. I suspected then that he was probably working for the Alcohol Tobacco and Firearms (ATF) police as well. Nobody with any brains wanted to fuck with an FBI agent, or the ATF, of any federal law enforcement agency. But Agent Coan proposed that I work a sting operation by buying some illegal guns and testifying in court against the sellers as a private citizen. I didn't get it. I asked why not use an undercover agent. But he responded that it could be viewed as entrapment if he did that. I then proposed to work as an agent for the ATF. Could he get me hired, I asked? I was reluctant to get involved in his operation as a private citizen, which might mean going into a witness protection program. And I didn't plan on leaving Boston or being a victim of an assassination. An unspoken rule between cops and crooks is that you don't retaliate against a cop for doing his job. Nobody likes a snitch! We couldn't reach an agreement, so I went home. I wasn't about to make Marilyn a widow.

In October, the Vietnam Moratorium Committee organized one of the largest antiwar demonstrations in America on the streets of Boston. It was a memorable experience for me at the corner of Arlington and Boylston Streets that day. I looked up Boylston in the direction of Mass Ave and saw a moving wave of people as far as my eye could see. The most amazing thing about all of those people marching for the Vietnam Moratorium was their silence. The marchers were so quiet that the sound of their shoe leather could be heard hitting the pavement as they walked past me at the corner of Boylston and Arlington streets.

I expected live coverage of the march by the local TV stations. After all, this was one of the biggest demonstrations in the country. But the local TV stations gave little more than lip service to the event, leading me to realize that they didn't have any balls. The lack of coverage convinced me that the media often acts as the fourth arm of government and as a shill (shield?) for its corporate advertisers.

Before John Kerry became a U.S. Senator (D-Mass.), he was among the speakers at the demonstration. After he became a U.S. Senator, I saw him walking alone one night on Columbus Avenue in the South End near the Hard Rock Café. I was in the company of an old classmate from U-Mass, who was working in the Secretary of State's office. I remember Kerry engaging in conversation with my friend, and then placing his hand on my shoulder, as though we were old friends. At the time, he was in the news for his statements questioning Affirmative Action as a remedy for addressing discrimination. Eager to get a quote from him, I asked him how many blacks were on his staff. He was taken aback by my question, and he didn't have more than a couple of blacks employed in his office. He mumbled something about there was a lot of work to be done. His response to me was evasive and politically correct. But it also showed how little he understood racial discrimination. Already his vapid response seemed to me that he was running for President. I was disappointed in him, then, as a leader. The 2004 presidential election and his bid for the presidency later proved my estimate of his ability correct. Having lost Ohio by a margin small enough to be challenged, he was yet unwilling to demand a recount so he lost the election, but he lost, as I believe now, for good reason. He seemed afraid of crossing the Reagan and George Bush, Sr., administrations.

In the 1960s, the U-Mass-Boston campus was located at the corner of Berkley and Columbus Avenues, with the administration building at the corner of Arlington and Columbus streets. The school library in the old building with a medieval castle facade was on the opposite corner. This site was only a block away from the Public Gardens where anti-war demonstrators and speakers denounced the Vietnam War. Many of my classmates were older students and Vietnam vets. We looked like a scruffy lot and dressed military fashion. Our standard uniforms were made up of jeans, boots and army jackets. I fit in fine.

I had completed the first semester at U/ Mass and had made the Dean's list when I got a call from someone who called himself an old friend. His name was Eli. He said he had an opportunity for me to check out.

☙ ❧

Chapter 8:

Holiday Magic

"Don't let the green grass fool you"

—Wilson Picket

Eli attended high school with Melvin and me. He was a member of the "Aladdins," a singing group consisting of two other students at the school. He was so good as a natural singer that he was ready for prime time performances or a record album. Now we all liked to sing American songs, but Eli also sang calypso music of the Caribbean. And although Melvin belonged to another singing group, he also sang for Eli.

Eli and Melvin also belonged to a clique on the university campus which ran most of the student activities. I was half-in, half-out, of that group, too, as though I were a charter member. Few memories stand out, but I remember clearly Eli getting thrown out of school. It happened over an unprovoked assault in the cafeteria. As I recall, one of the black students eating there pulled a prank on Eli in the cafeteria. In a case of mistaken identity, Eli retaliated against an innocent Jewish student nearby, breaking the student's jaw. It was a mistake Eli was to regret, because he was expelled right afterwards. And I do not believe he graduated anytime soon, or whether he graduated at all.

I still continued to associate with Eli. I admired him for his voice, his dance steps, and his self-confidence. He had qualities that I didn't think I had. A lot of guys in those days wished they could dance like him. When he returned to Boston in l966, he had finished his required military service as an Army MP, so he missed the most dangerous years of the Vietnam War. Almost immediately he found work as a store detective downtown in the Jordan Marsh Department store. I had worked there after school as a clerk. Eli was very impressive and persuasive to many of us younger guys around him. All it took was for him to talk to me about a future in security work to get me to take his advice after I graduated. And it was Eli who taught me how to smooth talk women.

When Eli coveted your girlfriend, he was notorious for pulling what was then called "a back door" on you. He had already pulled a "back door" betrayal on me with a girlfriend right after I met him, years earlier. At the time, I wasn't very attracted to the girl. When he took her away from me, I didn't miss her. That is, until he did it to me again with another girl! I learned the hard way how devious he could be in the seduction of women. I'll never know how he became such a lothario. Married and divorced twice, he played the field recklessly. One of his two previous marriages had been to a Jewish woman, but she had hidden their marriage from her family all the time that they were together. It was a time in the country's history when it was socially risky to marry outside of one's race. Black and white couples were prosecuted in some jurisdictions for publicly dating, for having crossed the unspoken but almost universal color bar in the country. And even though Eli had fought to keep the country safe from its enemies, his marriage daily exposed him to white racist taunts, assaults, and social ostracism. His marriage, needless to say, couldn't and didn't survive, given his wandering eyes and the social hostility to inter-racial couples.

A few months after Eli's divorce, he introduced me to two pretty young women who worked at Jordan Marsh. He was going out with one of them named Helen, a girl with dark hair whom I recall wore fancy stockings. The other one named Mary had short blonde hair. She also had a friendly disposition, and we "got down" on our first night's date. But Eli and Helen often went out together, something Mary and I did not do. Sex was our main interest, yet it was not enough for me. I wanted to take a girlfriend out on the town. I was tired of hanging out in Mary's apartment, with nothing to do but what comes natural there in the sack.

One evening, while waiting for Mary to come home from work, Helen and I were alone. There were candles burning and we were smoking reefer. Suddenly, the apartment door opened and a white guy in his thirties came into the apartment. I was shocked into silence. He ignored me with the joint in my hand and asked Helen what was wrong with her roommate. He said Mary was downstairs on the front steps crying.

At first I thought it was a drug raid. Had she turned us in? Helen turned to me and explained that the guy was her landlord and left me to go downstairs. When she returned with Mary, the two of them went into Mary's room without saying a word. After a few moments had passed, Helen came out alone. She was very upset. With her voice breaking, she sat down next to me and told me the true story. Eli had been seeing Mary behind our backs. He had also put a guilt trip on her by telling her that he couldn't leave Helen. I learned that Eli was "banging" both of them behind my back! It was hardly the actions of a friend! But I shouldn't have been surprised. Eli had stolen his second wife from one of his alleged best friends.

I was speechless at the time, as Helen started crying. I put my arm around her in sympathy, but the gesture only caused even more tears. And she began to shake. When she buried her face in my shoulder, she began to recover from her disappointment. Suddenly she turned her face up to me; she let me kiss her on her mouth, and soon we started kissing in a lip lock, our tongues exploring deeper and deeper. Soon, we were out of our clothes and fucking. The passion was exquisitely intense. It was some of the best sex I experienced in my life. Before I left, she told me not to tell Eli what happened.

After I arrived home, I called Melvin and told him what had happened. I asked him if he thought I should tell Eli what had gone down. He told me I should tell him, because Helen was going to tell him no matter what she promised.

The next afternoon, I called Eli and told him I was driving over to his place. He said okay. When I arrived, I told him what had happened. He said little and picked up a blackjack from the table. He looked at me calmly and began to tap it against the palm of his hand. Had he swung it at me, I would not have defended myself even though I was blameless. He must have had second thoughts about hitting me. He silently considered what I had said, and then shrugged, as though he didn't care. I left his place in one piece. We never talked about it again. Both girls ended up quitting their jobs. And I never saw them again.

Now I believe that I was the one who got played. Melvin knew right away what the deal was with Eli. Our girlfriends were fair game to him, but his girlfriends were not fair game for us. A few weeks later, as though nothing unusual had happened, Eli married Cathy, an assistant buyer at the store. She was a tall, attractive brunette from a wealthy banking family on the North Shore. They were an unusual couple, given his humble working class background. It was Eli's third marriage. I wasn't, of course, invited to his wedding. Years later, he married for yet a fourth time to a much younger black woman whom he met at a sales recruiting center.

One evening Eli invited me and Marilyn to attend the sales company's presentation. That was the night I was introduced to a company that would change my life, Holiday Magic. The presentation was at an office building on Brighton Ave in Allston. Holiday Magic was a cosmetic company. It sold its products door-to-door and at home parties through a sales force made up of "Holiday Girls." The company had been in operation for a couple of years at the time. It had a corporate structure like Avon Company, but it offered franchises like McDonald's. Eli was working for someone in Holiday Magic who owned one of its franchises, that is, he profited from the sales people in his franchise group. When a sales person made a sale, a percentage of the sales went to people on the management chart above the sales person. The man in charge of Eli and others was a general distributor named Ron, who held the rank described as "General" on the sales chart. That night "General" Ron explained to us that we could make a lot of money.

Ron wore a flashy suit and gold rimmed glasses, his uniform, I suppose, if flashy clothes can be called as such. He wore an attitude on his sleeve. I didn't care for him from the "git go," and the feeling was mutual. In retrospect, only because I'd known Eli for years did I go to the Holiday Magic meeting with Ron. Otherwise, I would not have wasted my time that night. The event was in a room with an elevated platform in front of a row of chairs. Things started promptly at eight o'clock. Ron greeted us and he called the night an "Opportunity Meeting." There must have been about ten people in the small audience. The meeting started when another man in a black suit, whose name now escapes me, joined Ron at the front of the room. Although I can no longer quote him verbatim, I distinctly recall the gist of Ron's message. In a nutshell, the message was: Mediocrity in a person was by choice. A person's success was also by choice. Unfortunately, most of the people in that room would probably never get anywhere in life because they didn't realize they had a choice between mediocrity and success. That message was clearly intended to beg the question: How does one choose success?

After his introduction and a short film showing male distributors endorsing the program, Ron explained to the audience that a general distributor could make $3,000 for every new general he recruited into his organization. One who had a group of 20 Holiday Girls selling $50 in product per week each could make up to twenty six hundred dollars a month.

Marilyn was cool to the idea of getting involved. She was skeptical, above all, of Ron's claims of profit margins each month for distributors, but I became hooked by the testimonies of people making money quickly and without a great deal of effort. Ron said that it took $4,500 to become a General distributor who made 65 cents of every dollar sold. The position below that was Master distributor who made 55 cents of every dollar. To become a master required an investment of 4,500, for which the company gave you product at a wholesale price of $3000. The markup price for sales was double your investment. You could in theory make a killing, as the saying goes, even after paying Ron his wholesale price.

I became convinced that I had hit the jackpot with Holiday Magic. I asked myself: Where was Melvin? Why wasn't he at the meeting? Where was everybody else? The profits were too good to be true. We were in a group of people, all of them taking in the filmed evidence before us. I trusted Eli. I was convinced also that my main man, as we call friends we admired, the one and only Eli, was too clever to be involved with any enterprise in which he wasn't making money.

The positions below Master were also outlined, along with their profits. Organizer, the next in rank, bought into the business for $130, followed by the Holiday Girl, who came on board for $13.99. These two positions gave you a thirty per cent discount on the products. At the time I only had enough money to come in as an Organizer, but I felt that I'd become a General in short order. Working for Holiday Magic, I planned that evening to get rich.

What distinguished Holiday Magic products from others, it then seemed to me, was the fruit scented products, soaps, lipsticks, perfumes, powders, shampoos, and other fragrant cosmetics: among them were Strawberry Frappe cream, Cucumber wash, and Mint Scrub. The scents smelled like the real thing: expensive high quality perfumes. I purchased a bunch of sample packets that evening. I began carrying them in my book bag and I gave them out as samples to potential customers everywhere I went. I also began recruiting Holiday Girls, as a part-time pursuit. As the distributors began to grow in number at the center, the main office in California sent a group of what would be called "IGs" or Instructor Generals to guide and motivate us.

In a matter of weeks, however, trouble broke out between Ron and the other general distributors over a rent hike. Ron had leased the building in his name and wanted more money. The company got involved in the dispute and pulled rank. The "IGs" took over the center and most of the meetings. As part of their program, they had an interview with all of the distributors to determine who they were going to work with. Tom, Eli's partner, said that the "IGs" had been big money-makers and had been chosen by the company to help their distributors become successful. We were told that the "IGs" would do our closings for us, if and when we brought people through the door. It didn't work out quite like that.

I found it easy to bring people through the door, adapting what Melvin had taught me about picking up girl prospects. But I had problems getting most of them to sign-up. For some reason I was the one who had a fear of getting them to sign, in closing the deal with Holiday Magic. Eli and Tom didn't work with me very much for reasons I didn't comprehend. Later in life, I would discover that some men have a tendency to sexual rivalry, and can be as jealous as "bitches."

I brought so many people through the door that the "IGs" mentioned me to the home office. Nobody could top my recruiting ability. All the same, I couldn't keep anyone for myself until I won a promotion to the rank of a Holiday Magic "General." All too soon, I discovered an obstacle to my advancement: All my recruits for the company, according to my contract's fine print, were under Eli, and a good percentage of all my sales and the sales of my recruits went to him. I was in effect working for Eli! So he had got me again! I was furious!

It also turned out that the "IGs" weren't always successful at closing. When asked at a meeting how I recruited, I found it hard to explain. I had approached

Eli and offered to become a partner but he wasn't interested. He was more skilled at closing deals than me. If he had worked with me, we could have had one of the biggest organizations in town.

One day Melvin suggested that I tell Eli that I'd gotten a writing contract with Motown Records to see his envy. Melvin began acting excited about the news to get a rise out of him. Imagine my disappointment as Eli merely turned and looked at me. The expression on his face was "Big Deal!" He didn't even try to seem envious, or offer a tepid or false compliment. If such an event had happened to Eli, I would have been excited for him. What I've come to understand about human nature is this: When someone considered a friend is unexcited about another's good fortune, it often demonstrates either jealousy, or ill-will.

The teams of "IGs" were an interesting group. One team included a New York money-maker named Dave Smile, a Jamaican, who drove a Rolls Royce. With Smile was an Israeli woman, Nava, and Gene, a white guy. The pale, thin Gene wore glasses, a dark suit and tie, and he looked like an accountant. But the three of them together presented an intimidating image.

During my interview with a new IG, a black man from Ohio, I was given his definition of someone who keeps his word. He spoke to me in somber tones and said: "I believe in keeping my word. If I said the wall outside was white and it was black, I'd go out and paint it white. That's how much I care about keeping my word." Did I believe in keeping my word?

Years later, I would use these words to make a young girl cry. At that time, I would have few friends and be headed to the hospital. I would also be on the road to redemption.

When we talked about one of my prospects named Peggy, who had said during an interview that she didn't have the money to become a Master distributor, the "IG" said to me: "I don't care if she has to go out on the corner and sell her ass. She's gonna' get that money!"

As I became more deeply involved with the company, I began to take on that same cold- blooded attitude. Meanwhile, some of the distributors began to act jealous about all of the people I was bringing to the meetings. Even with my recruitment, much of the profit from their sales went to Eli.

There was the perception I sensed in my colleagues that I was also making good money, although it wasn't true. It didn't matter what was the truth. Perception was everything. And public perception, together with ignorance, helped to draw people to the program.

There was nothing more pitiful than a General with no one in his organization. Recruitments were essential to success in Holiday Magic. Some guys and gals in the program had given up their full time jobs to work there, which, in hindsight, was a big mistake.

As the year unfolded, it turned out to be a period of mixed blessings for me: I was making a little money with Holiday Magic and my organization was beginning to grow. But as the months passed I was unable to achieve the position of "Master." I was still a poor student living on loans and grants and a few reefer sales. In addition, I did little jobs on the side for the detective agency, thanks to Bennie. My home life was so-so. I began to detect unhappy tones from colleagues whenever they had occasion to mention Marilyn's name. The ones who had met her enough times to know her views on Holiday Magic were aware of her critical attitude to the company. I was aware of what this meant for me at the company. One of the things I realized was that Marilyn's attitude would not help my position at the firm. The bosses at Holiday Magic, unbeknownst to her, seemed to deduct points for promoting male workers whose wives weren't involved with the company or who appeared unsympathetic to their husband's career prospects.

Truth to tell, Marilyn was doing more to keep our house together than me. Yet I'll never forget the adage used by one of the "IGs" at a meeting which addressed the issue of a husband or wife who didn't support the program: "If thy right eye offends thee, pluck it out." I'd begun to fall for the hype. Soon, I began spending a lot of time at the center away from Marilyn. A crowd of single women passed through the workplace as temporary office workers, temps that gave me opportune excuses to visit their homes on company business. Many such visits were personal, as in extramarital dates, and at such times I was right at home. But Marilyn and I enjoyed a brief Christmas vacation just before the New Year came along.

As the year came to an end, President Nixon called for another military draft lottery to raise the number of draftees that very December. According to Nixon and

Kissinger, it was going to be l975 before the war came to an end. They never revealed the true date as to how long their much publicized "secret plan" to end the war would take. Nixon had been attacking the anti-War movement in his first year of office. His political opponents on the left of the conservative Republicans were still 76 million strong. It was only a matter of time before we flexed our muscles. 1970 was going to be a year of transformation.

☙ ❧

Chapter 9:

The Beat Goes On

"Let's go round again"

—The Average White Band

Lordie! Lordie! I hated Richard Nixon as much as I would a gang of Nazis in the White House! Nixon reminded me of a prissy but cruel schoolmaster, a dictator determined to bring a group of unruly students to heel. Being that I was a member of the student body, a leader whose opinions other students respected, I was determined not to cooperate in the process.

During those frenetic days of the early 70s I felt myself being pulled in different directions. Sometimes I felt like the character in the old TV drama "I Led Three Lives," the story of an undercover informant for the FBI who joined the American Communist Party. The lead character of the series - an informant, a husband and a Communist Party member named Herbert A. Philbrick—was as duplicitous as I was in posing different public roles to different people. Suffice it to say that I went to the dark side of my nature in the 70s in my new roles. In one dimension of my two lives, I was husband, student, anti-war protester and salesman of Holiday Magic products. In the other dimension, I was a drug dealer. I carried samples of drugs along with Holiday Magic samples in my book bag. Going to college, of course, helped to keep my feet on the ground, that is, from becoming a politically suicidal idealist. Being at the center of local anti-war demonstrations helped me from exclusively living off the drug trade. I realized that becoming a capitalist success often meant ignoring the injustices around me.

On the Holiday Magic front, I had gone as far as to fix up one of my "IGs"—a much older and lonely, gentle father-figure—with a girl in my organization named Evelyn. They started dating. I felt as though I had ended up doing Philbrick one better. Not only was I a salesman, a husband, a student, and drug-dealer, but I had become a date-maker as well.

The twist about that role is this: The girl was a mature and attractive young woman who could handle herself in a May-December relationship. I don't remember who brought her into the business, but she had informed me earlier that she liked sleeping with older men. And she wasn't faithful. The same night that I introduced the two of them over dinner, I had her in the sack at her place. Not only that, but as we relaxed in her bed, she bragged about her sexual skill in pleasing me. She even said that

I should be appreciative of her generosity because what she'd done for me—a blow job as well as sex for nothing—was professional sex worth at least two hundred bucks. I took her at her word. But I never paid for it.

On the college front, things were more chaotic. Classes were being cancelled for teach-in seminars on campus. Some professors were more sympathetic than others to students who took part in anti-war demonstrations, so they cut them a break on class work.

In May, four students in Ohio and two in South Carolina, respectively, at Kent State and Orangeburg, South Carolina, fell mortally to National Guard and police shootings. The public and student campuses erupted in outrage, sparking nationwide protests and prompting the University to disregard professors who suspended classes at area colleges for a protest rally.

In one local protest, there were 50,000 students in front of the state house at a rally on the Boston Commons. It was an angry crowd. They began calling for the flag in front of the state house to be lowered out of respect to the fallen students. The State police hesitated to do so at first. Sure enough, after a few intense discussions in the State House the flag came down. The governor quickly and wisely decided not to resist the protest demand for a symbolic gesture of solidarity with student anti-war protesters elsewhere. That evening, there was a police riot in Boston after a standoff between police and anti- war Northeastern University students in the dormitories on Hemenway Street. The students were throwing debris onto automobiles from the roofs of the buildings. A platoon of Tactical Police Force (TPF) cops showed up in a bus with their helmets and long clubs. After breaking into the dorm buildings, kicking asses, and working their way to the roofs, they showered the traffic below with debris and cinder blocks.

This was a time when cops engaged in brutal unprovoked assaults. In attempts to cover their butts from lawsuits, many frontline police officers trying to break up a demonstration routinely taped their badge ID numbers to avoid identification. They sought to cover themselves with anonymity in the event the beaten demonstrator, or victim, later sued the police for brutality, in an unprovoked assault or for excessive unlawful force. Not one Boston cop involved in beating protesters, as I recall, was ever brought up on charges of police brutality.

Most of the academic year, our professors lectured us on the war and civil disobedience lessons, substituting teach-ins for many classes. By the end of the first semester, I had a B+ average in my classes. I had written a few articles for the student paper, and yet, I had enough time left over to make a new friend on campus.

She was a woman from Norwood. Her name was Sally. We met frequently in public places, and she hung out with me but wouldn't get down. I was very attracted to her but she was hard to figure out. Perhaps she was so fascinated with my craziness when I was with her that she found it hard to stay away. Sometimes, I'd just grab her and kiss her. She protested that I was a married man and ought not to do that, all the while repeatedly saying that she wouldn't make love to a married man. Other times we'd walk along the Charles River like lovers. She kept her word about not fucking with a married man. None of my tricks to seduce her worked.

She had short blonde hair and was reasonably attractive, but not as attractive as Marilyn. As long as I was seeing a woman who I wouldn't be ashamed to be seen with in public, that was good enough for me. What also worked against me was the fact that Sally didn't get high. Sometimes, I'd drive her home. Once she invited me inside to meet her parents who didn't react too badly to me. Her older brother was also home, an old colleague who worked at Retail Credit when I was there. She was surprised to learn that we recognized one another. It seemed a small world then.

One day she finally broke down and decided to give me what I wanted. It was completely unexpected. The place she directed me to drive her was a vacant wooded area in Norwood. We seemed to be alone and although I went so far as to partially undress her, I could not shake a fear in my head of danger ahead. It kept me from going all the way.

In truth, I had the feeling in the woods that someone was watching. Sure enough, when I glanced about, I spotted a Metropolitan District Police cruiser through the bushes, just across the road from us. The cop was looking for something or someone in the trees. I was very lucky, because I already had my pants half-way down, and he was looking the other way. I never told Sally what caused me to pull back but I never got a second chance with her, either.

At the time, I was also seeing a black woman named Shirley who lived in a nearby town but who visited Boston at every opportunity during the year. She had a pretty face. We had actually met and begun seeing each other since the early 60s. In fact, years earlier, she and I had been at the same place when the Metropolitan District Police (M.D.C.) almost caught me with my pants down.

At the time, she had already been married for a couple of years, but she had no qualms about getting down with me. She contacted me whenever she was in town and continued seeing me until the mid-1980s when she suffered a stroke down South.

I finally became a General distributor for Holiday Magic in the summer of 1970. No doubt my promotion was enhanced by Marilyn's former landlord whom I persuaded to invest thousands of dollars in the business as a partner. Not long after that happened, I got my first $3,000 check. It made my day. I was a confirmed General who was black and in the black. I then enlisted a sergeant, "Donald" in the Metropolitan District Police (M.D.C.), into the business. In 1967, he had given me a jump start in my Corvette after an asshole had run into my car after following me too closely on a street near Revere Beach. The driver might have done it because a white girlfriend of mine was riding beside me in my car. When the police arrived, he tried to blame me for the accident. Of all the nerve! I was indignant; moreso because in my eyes the police body language seemed hostile to me. They obviously were upset by the sight of an interracial couple. In my experience, this was a general white, hostile attitude toward interracial couples.

It didn't matter that I was innocent of any romantic relationship with her. And I knew that it wouldn't matter to them that I wasn't even fucking her. The white M.D.C. cops behaved quite unfriendly to me. One of them asked me, but not the other driver, was I drinking. No matter, I stood my ground. I protested that I had not been drinking alcohol and that I was not at fault for the accident. Next, my passenger and the other driver began having a loud shouting match until the cops quieted them down. The girl with me was just a good friend. I was with her because I was trying to get together with her cousin.

When the police stopped the shouting match, I acted. Not saying a further word, I wrote down the other driver's information. It was obvious that I wasn't drunk and that the other guy had hit me. The cops had a quiet conversation with the other driver as I took down his information. When it was time to go, my car wouldn't start because I'd left my car lights on while the engine was off. Luckily, my friend Donald, the M.D.C. sergeant, pulled up and seeing my dilemma, helped jump start my car engine.

Donald was my first and only general in Holiday Magic. Still, I had come close to breaking even in the business. My organization was working pretty well and I was having a good old time. My life with Marilyn was a different story, however; and Eli was part of the story, for he hadn't changed after all. One evening, I was at the center and I had to return home for something. I hadn't seen Eli all day. When I pulled up to the house, there was Eli's car in front. He knew I was at the center, so he could only have been up to one thing. How does that song go? "Who's making love to your old lady while you were out---?"

One thing I failed to appreciate was Marilyn's integrity. I didn't appreciate the rarity of finding someone like her who would do the right thing regardless of being wronged by the type of man I'd become, as reflected in my involvement in Holiday Magic. Something I did appreciate from Holiday Magic was a course I took called "Mind Control." I use it even now.

It enabled me to go to my special place in the fifth dimension after the drug MDA had disappeared. I also learned the technique of problem solving through the use of water. It involves drinking a glass of water, but silently repeating the message "This is what I must do to find the solution to my problem" while drinking the water. Before going to sleep, frame the problem in your mind. The solution will come during sleep. It worked for me, but not for Holiday Magic.

In l972, the U.S. Attorney, in a criminal warrant from a District Court in California, shut down Holiday Magic as a pyramid scheme. My experience at Holiday Magic was a bumpy ride in more ways than one. All along, I had behaved like a dog in heat. I had gone through a number of women at the center like a buzz saw. Holiday Magic offered parties and orgies like the ones allegedly at Hugh Hefner's Playboy Mansion.

In the fall of l970, Scottie showed up at my door with a new Corvette. It was a gold-colored coupe with an L-51 engine. I convinced him to let me drive it downtown to pick up Marilyn after work. He was living in New York

City but was in town on his way to register his car in New Hampshire. He then allowed me to drive it to New Hampshire the next day. It was a powerhouse. I could feel the engines surging. It was all I could do to keep from driving it over sixty. Scottie had stayed over at our place for the evening. Marilyn and I had gone to sleep when I was awakened by Scottie trying to get in bed with us. It was laughable. I couldn't get angry. I thought he had too much to drink and didn't know what he was doing. I told him to go back to bed, turned over and went back to sleep.

Nothing else was ever said about the incident. Even though we presented ourselves as sophisticated about sex, as "Anything goes!" and "Do your own thing," for us that meant it was okay to experiment with open relationships. The sexual highway was wide open to different arrangements. Nevertheless, Marilyn and I never switched partners nor did a threesome while we were together.

My old friend Norman Greenbaum came out with a record called "Spirit in the Sky." I never bought it. But I did buy the Chicago II album. It was one of the biggest albums of the year. Crosby, Stills and Nash released "Ohio," the song about the Kent State shootings that same year.

Later in the year, Scottie came back on a visit and told me that he had gotten busted for flying in a load of marijuana in a rented plane. He had lost his job flying the mail. He'd been accused of taking passengers aboard the Lear Jet and keeping the fares but this was more serious. Apparently, the feds were tracking him on his drug pick-up flight from Mexico to the USA, and they were in the airport tower in New Jersey waiting for him to land. Scottie wasn't that stupid. Suspecting a bust, he flew away from the airport until his fuel was too low to continue, and he ended up ditching his plane at another airport. The feds were able to track him by radar and located the position of his plane. They were waiting for him on his arrival. He didn't have a chance to get rid of the grass. He was arrested not far from the crash scene by the feds and state police. Out on bond when I saw him, he told me that the feds were making his life miserable. According to him, the case would be held over his head for at least another year. I didn't see Scottie after that. And I never found out what happened to him.

That November I began receiving skip-trace calls from the finance company looking for the Corvette. I wasn't very helpful.

The spring of '73 would signify my crossing to the dark side. I was well prepared to make the move.

Chapter 10:

A Radical Change

In the spring of l973, Marilyn and I separated, but I had instigated several temporary separations with her during my time at Holiday Magic. Now the split was permanent. And we split up our possessions equitably. I found out later that Marilyn had been counseled by my mother to make the final decision. Mama was unhappy with my behavior and my refusal to work things out with a marriage counselor.

I got to keep the car, the Toyota station wagon that her mother had given us. The two puppies and most of the furniture, including a brass bed, also stayed with mc. Marilyn got the stereo and our dog Phaedra. Her father came down to move her. We packed her things on the truck. Then she was gone. Forever.

I didn't feel like rejoicing; and besides, everyone in my family seemed to blame me for our split. Actually, in hindsight, they were right. I was a fool to have caused the breakup. I believe that not one of the women I'd been seeing at that time could hold a candle to Marilyn. Sure enough, most of the women I was fooling around with amid all the drama—distributing dope and sneaking around—faded away. My extracurricular relationships had all been based on mutual pleasure, the excitement of the moment, all of it short-lived. I had gotten it in my stupid mind that I should be able to fool around in my marriage because Eli, Leroy, and Melvin had been able to fool around in their marriages. But all of their marriages broke up. Had we, I asked myself, all gotten caught up in a fucking contest?

What is it about the past? Sometimes it can keep you from moving on when you let it. Two things about the past seem true: You can't change it or deny it. Well, you can try to deny it but if you've done wrong, you can't fool yourself for long about the obvious logic of consequences from choices you've made. Nor can you hide from yourself.

In the 70s, most of the momentum for meaningful social progress initiated by four dynamic political leaders—King, JFK, RFK, and Malcolm X—had slowed to a crawl. Once they were forcibly removed by assassination, there was a chorus of voices like those of the notorious Tower of Babel that pulled people in different directions. "Go for yourself" became my rallying cry. Or, the old standard: "Turn on, tune in, drop out!"

A number of us had guns. During the busing crisis of 1973, there was a run on Federal Identification gun owner cards, which allowed the bearer to purchase a shotgun, rifle or tear gas. And it wasn't all that difficult to get a pistol permit if you owned a business or knew the right people. I was surrounded by licensed guns that were carried by many of my friends in the drug business. I also carried a small canister of tear gas with me on my travels.

Still, guns weren't for shootouts with the cops or rivals on the streets. They were there for protection against a rip-off. There was no urban warfare, at the time, as there is today in some places in the streets, such as drive-by killings of innocent bystanders. Gun violence then was mostly associated with the drug trade; and I seldom met someone involved in a shoot-out. For most of the summer of l973, my time was productively and safely engaged as a home pest exterminator. When I quit that job, I started a night job at a brake manufacturing plant in Allston. That job lasted a few months, until I realized that there was asbestos used in the plant manufacturing process. One night, when I went to the bathroom at homes, I seemed to smell asbestos in my stool. Whether that was the case or not, I decided that night would be my last night working at the plant! The summer passed quickly to fall.

One evening early that autumn, I was in my apartment feeling sorry for myself for being alone when my telephone rang. Someone whom I'll call Bennie was calling with a proposition for me. I knew that some of our friends from Beacon Hill had suddenly started selling reefer. I wasn't sure of the source for the distributors. I decided that Bennie might be able to enlighten me.

When Bennie arrived at my place that night, we got down to business. He made me an offer that, as the saying goes, I couldn't refuse. There were fifty kilos of marijuana involved. He asked me if I could sell what amounted to a little over a hundred pounds. Of course I could do so, just between the people I knew from Holiday Magic and U/Mass. I knew I could get rid of the stuff. The purchase price was ten thousand bucks! But where, I wondered, could I keep that much reefer? For me, the easiest answer of all was my parents' basement. Despite having batches of pot called Epic and Red in my own apartment, I knew I couldn't take a chance keeping a large quantity there.

A year earlier, I had grown two six-foot tall marijuana plants in a small garden behind my apartment building. Even though the garden wasn't visible from the street, it had caused me a lot of trepidation. I was always aware that someone might discover the plants by accident.

This was cheap Mexican Reefer, I gathered, that would soon be in short supply if Nixon had his way. He'd already declared a war on drugs, which commenced with the notorious "Operation Intercept" in the summer of l973. What I hadn't considered at the time was the end result of Nixon's operation, which cut off the flow of cheap Mexican marijuana and opened our neighborhoods to a flood of cocaine.

Not long after I agreed to take on Bennie's assignment, I got a job at a bank, South Shore National, in Quincy. I was referred to them through a friend of Bennie's who owned an employment agency. I was assigned to the Installment Loan department. It meant that I was again in a good job, and nothing that had happened to me so far could stop me from advancing up the bank ladder. I seemed unable to crash. I was driving an old car at this time. The Corvette was long gone. The Toyota station wagon had been sold, since one of its cylinders had frozen.

Bennie gave me the reefer on credit indicating that his sources must have had a hell of a lot of reefer to risk without collateral. I decided to move it slowly. The cost of each pound was one hundred bucks. I decided to charge two hundred each to start. There were at least two pounds in every package. By charging a hundred for a quarter pound, I could make three hundred on a package. But it was more efficient to sell pounds at the level where I was operating. The reefer came in red and blue colored cellophane wrappings. The packages could have passed for Christmas gifts. The weight was written on each package. Inside the colored wrapping was a compressed brick of green marijuana inside a sheet of a Mexican newspaper.

I placed the bricks inside a large carton and put them in a dark corner of my parents' cellar. My father had a work bench in the cellar. That was another reason to move the pot out of the house quickly. Before I made any move to do so, I mapped out a plan in my mind as to how I would get rid of the reefer without getting busted. When you have that kind of weight on hand, it usually means jail time unless you give somebody up and then you have to move out of town and disappear.

Having worked in the security business, I was aware of the many techniques used by the feds and cops to track and arrest people. I was also educated in the foibles of human nature like jealousy and being careless: dangerous factors in real life crime as well as in crime dramas produced by Hollywood film writers. I broke things down to a few simple rules to follow. First, I would never sell to teenagers, no matter how much money they had. Secondly, I would only have a working and middle class clientele, "no street people need apply" for drugs from me. Thirdly, and lastly, I would deliver the goods and offer a money back guarantee if the customer didn't like the stuff.

I also decided to treat people the way I wanted to be treated and to keep a low profile on the street. There was no reason for me to hang out at the clubs, spending money, and thereby raising the curiosity of police snitches. Although I had never sold drugs at this new consumer level, overnight I now became one of the biggest dealers in Boston. In the past, I pooled my money once in a while among friends to buy a couple of ounces of reefer. But now, with the larger amount of dope I was poised to distribute, I became the "go-to" guy for other dealers. It was almost like having a pile of money dropped in my lap.

Now I had always been a law abiding citizen. I had no criminal record, no criminal past. All the same, I came to the realization early on that just because you might break a law, it doesn't mean that you have to behave like a criminal. In no time, I had customers all across Eastern Massachusetts, a majority of them whites, the main reason being disposable income for drug purchases. They had the money to spend on their pleasures. Besides, I got along well with them and we shared common interests. We never indulged in bullshit talk on racial issues.

After I'd been at the bank for a while, I used one of my friends at work as a cut-out. He would play the man in charge, while I played the middle man. I used the term "the people" to describe the fictional group that ran my operation. I never let anyone know outside of a small circle that I was the man in charge.

I moved the weight in four months and bought a one year old 240Z sports car for cash. I also paid for the insurance in cash and registered it in Boston. On my first weekend with the car, I took it on a trip to Rockingham Park in New Hampshire, where the head gasket blew. It wasn't an accident. The person who sold me the car had filled the crankcase with STP instead of oil to keep me from finding out the engine needed an overhaul. Still, the engine in that car was so sturdy that I managed to drive back to Boston at fifty miles an hour.

When I got back to Boston, I arranged with a male friend of Raven's to leave the car parked near his shop in South Boston before reporting it stolen. I didn't have time to play games with the seller and I wanted the engine rebuilt by the insurance company to which I'd paid a sizable amount of money for complete coverage.

After the car was found and repaired to my satisfaction, I had an auto engine which would last longer than the body of the car itself. I had the work done by a Jamaican mechanic at a Datsun dealer. Later, when the mechanic changed jobs and began work at a high performance garage for foreign cars in Waltham, I visited him at work. He also brought me new customers at his job.

When I had finished with that load, another man I met through Bennie, a man named Carlos (though that was not his real name) gave me forty pounds of his reefer to sell. A former New York cop named John (an alias, also here) owned the "Limbo," a West Indian restaurant on Washington Street at Dudley Station in Boston's Roxbury neighborhood. It was none other than Bennie who introduced me to him.

The "Limbo" restaurant was like a clubhouse for our little gang of four. There was also a steady stream of stolen goods: clothing like leather coats, fur jackets, suits, and sweaters, passing through the premises. Those were glorious days for hipsters like the one I was becoming. I could also barter for items by brand name like stereos and TVs in exchange for reefer.

My job at the bank was boring as hell. I wanted to get into a management training program because of my college experience, but it wasn't enough. There was another black guy named Gene who was related to a Patriots football player in the program. Unlike me, he was a college grad. I began making plans to go back to school now that I could afford it.

Unexpectedly, Urban Renewal came to my neighborhood near the end of l973. It offered me a Section 8 housing grant for cheap rental digs. Under the program, I could move to either an apartment at 808 Memorial Drive in Cambridge, or a new building still under construction at 101 Tremont Street in Brighton, just across the Newton line. Both places were in pricey real estate locations. At the same time, my parents bought another house on Mount Pleasant Ave in Roxbury. I could have lived with them also, but my decision to live elsewhere was a no brainer. I gave my dog Epic to my parents before I moved out. Blessed now with the good fortune of having a cash cow to pay for my wants, I was lucky also in where I could live: It was neither stupid luck, nor "niggah" luck—just plain good luck. I began to consider which of the two places to live would best suit me.

Because I knew too many people in the Memorial Drive complex, I decided to check out the building in Brighton. It was still under construction and I got to see the apartments before they were completed. The two floor duplex apartment I chose was located on the top floor of the building next to the rear grounds of a rectory. It was like living next to a small forest, a place for me to chill out. After I moved in, I felt as though I was living life at the top, as though I lived where one might expect to find an executive at the bank as a tenant.

It was a quiet street, a peaceful neighborhood. One time, however, a gang of neighborhood drunks got rowdy in the woods near my building. They seemed to be just bored local college or high school kids out for mischief. In any case, they began to interrupt my repose that night after I had a long day working at the bank. I was very tired, longing for a good sleep. So I took out a slingshot that I'd bought from a buddy named simply under his initials, J.O., who lived on Beacon Hill. I put a large M-80 firecracker in its pouch and shot it into the woods. The boom echoed for miles and the kids scattered. There were no more incidents henceforth.

Once more, I was surrounded by silence and peace. No one bothered me there. I even recall joining my neighbors on the Fourth of July, shooting skyrockets off our apartment patios.

Mine was a pleasant residence in Brighton, just down the street from the middle class enclave of Newton. I was delighted to fit right in with my new neighbors. Among a small group of black neighbors, I also found two women who lived in an apartment building down the street from me; and as it turned out, one of the women dated a man from Texas who happened to be one of my pot suppliers. The other was a call girl who introduced me to one of her madam's clients. For some reason, I never banged either of the women. Perhaps it was because they seemed like sexless friends to me.

The period before I moved into my apartment would mark two turning points in my life. Both in their own way were positive developments. They involved two very different women.

At the time, I'd been seeing a Jewish girl named Rhoda for close to six months. She came from Philadelphia and had been chosen as a rabbi by her temple. She was a kind person, very likable. It was odd how I met her.

We met on a sunny, autumn day. As I recall, I had taken a hit of mescaline, preparing to jog along the Charles River. I had two new eight-month old puppies to jog along with me. My mesc' high made me feel like I was walking on air. All I could feel of the real moment was the late afternoon temperature, as it cooled my sweating skin. When I stopped running to catch my breath, I cut the dogs loose to sniff around. She walked directly towards me, a mysterious smile on her face, her arms crossed over her chest, bathed in the colors of the evening sun. It felt as though she recognized me. In retrospect, I realize that her behavior may not have been so much an attraction at first glance as that she may have been as high as me.

Certainly my drugs had me buzzing. And I was open to her. Without a word, I turned her around, placing my arm over her shoulders. We walked together like two lovers in silence. She was wearing a peasant dress, with her hair hanging loose on her shoulders. We made small talk. But it was not until several minutes passed that we introduced ourselves by name.

As it got dark, we returned to her apartment on Beacon Street. She had a pet cat which the puppies startled when we entered the place. The cat rushed out of the room into the bedroom of her roommate. A little later, it mustered enough courage to come out of the bedroom to reclaim its territory. Or perhaps her cat realized that my puppies were too young to bother with it. That evening I made love to Rhoda for the first time. "Do it!" was another of our slogans that promoted the idea of fast sex.

Coincidentally, I discovered that I knew one of her girlfriends, Dana, who was a call girl. It's a given in the drug business that sooner or later you'll meet fast, slick women. It also turned out that this woman was bisexual, as was Rhoda. It was my first time in bed with a bisexual woman, someone who, incredibly, later became a female Jewish rabbi! In truth, I couldn't tell the ethnic difference between Jew or Gentile women such as Rhoda in bed. All I knew was that she was very sensual.

One evening at a restaurant, Carlos gave me a large Coffee-Mate bottle that had been in a freezer. It was half full of coke. He asked me if I thought I could do anything with the stuff. I told him I'd see what I could do. I was unfamiliar with the white powdery drug. I had tried cocaine before, but it hadn't impressed me. When I took a sniff of his powder, however, it took me off in minutes. It was then that I realized the coke sold on the street to me must have been cut with sugar, flour, or another fake substance, for it gave none of the powerful hit of the stuff Carlos laid on me.

Initially, when I passed portions of his product around to some of my customers, I made a couple of hundred bucks. But I didn't make out as well as I should have. Eager to please, but cautious, I treated his powder as though it had been damaged by moisture, an inferior bargain for customers seeking a cheap thrill.

Rhoda and I enjoyed the same powder; and she showed me how to use it on our genitals to enhance sexual pleasure. She showed me many delightful positions and sensory moves during the time I saw her. I was to discover that she hustled on the side for an old Madam in Boston's Chelsea neighborhood, a predominantly white working class town. It didn't matter too much to me what she did on the side, as long as she took care of me. Still, our relationship cooled off after a while, perhaps out of boredom with a purely physical relationship. But Rhoda turned out to be a valuable friend when she put me onto a farm in Brimfield, Massachusetts where I could get pounds of reefer on credit.

A woman named Carol, on the other hand, turned out to be my worst nightmare around this time. I'd met Carol through a friend of Eli's, named Joe. They had a daughter together, but weren't getting along. Carol lived in an apartment in Somerville, the town sitting between parts of Boston and Cambridge. It was also the home of the Winter Hill Gang controlled once by the notorious Irish American gangster James "Whitey" Bulger. I ended up sleeping with her after she convinced me to take a whole Quaalude against my better judgment. After the act was over, she rushed me out of her apartment early in the morning. It was still dark outside and I was in no condition to drive. She didn't care. But what happened to me could have ended my life, for Somerville was no place for a black person to be found by "Whitey's" gang, on the streets drugged and disoriented.

All I remembered was getting into my car and driving away. I was supposed to return to Roxbury. When I woke up, I was driving in the early dawn on Trapelo Road in Watertown, also a town next to Cambridge, but with no idea how I got there. It was with God's help that I was able to turn around and head toward Boston, finally reaching my parent's house about forty minutes later. I collided with the rear of my father's car as I came to a stop outside the house. That's how much the "muscle" drug affected my motor control. Later that day, I was filled with rage against Carol. I knew that I was on the edge of strangling her and the idea of doing it kept coming back in my head. If she had appeared in front of me, just then, I would have gone after her.

For some reason, perhaps to vent my rage, I called a desk sergeant that I knew on duty at a police station. He listened to me as I told him the part of the story about a friend of mine being put out on the street, when he was in no condition to drive. I told him the guy was very upset. He used the bureaucratic language found in many police reports to describe the "incident" in police jargon. This brought me back to reality. I realized that despite all the reasons I had to justify the steps I wanted to take, the "incident" still boiled down to a black and white factual report that would only take my actions into account. When the Sergeant asked me the one thing I hadn't thought about: What if things didn't turn out the way I planned? My justification in the eyes of the law for assaulting or blaming Carol wouldn't matter to the law. I couldn't take the law into my own hands. I realized rather quickly that I couldn't act emotionally. I could end up being the "perp" in a police report. Without further ado, I thanked the sergeant and hung up.

From that day forward, whenever I was tempted to retaliate violently against someone because the person insulted, threatened or injured me in some way, I took a time out before I let my passions drive me: I willed myself to think of something else, at least for ten minutes, at least long enough to let my anger pass so I could regain self-control. I never lost control of my emotions again. It was my fault that I took something I knew I shouldn't have taken. I had to admit that she didn't pry my mouth open, and force me to take the drug. In the clear light of day, when I was thinking rationally, I decided not to contact her. And I never saw Carol again.

One day Bennie came by the house in Roxbury and asked if I'd let him borrow one of my dogs to take on a trip to Arizona. His trip had something to do with a load of reefer coming across the border. He said he was going to be traveling with a small group of people.

Epic and Red were my two Dobermans, and they had two very distinct doggish personalities. Red was the friendlier of the two dogs. He was my baby. When he was still a puppy, he whined painfully from ear cones used to make his ears stand up. But I made him wear the cones, in spite of his discomfort, for otherwise, his ears would hang down like a Beagle's. Later, when his cones were removed and his ears were taped together on top of his head, he'd rub his ears on my floor trying to get the tape off. He'd rub until his paws had made his ears raw and bloody.

Epic hadn't had any problems with his ears. So I would often find myself spending time with Red trying to make him comfortable. He was very gentle and obedient. The two of them were about ten months old at the time. I always believed that Red was a special gift to me.

I gave Red to Bennie because I knew that Epic wasn't as friendly around people. Plus, Red had taken a liking to him. On top of everything else, Bennie had gotten me into a lucrative endeavor that changed my life. Alas, a few weeks later, as I was working at a bank, Bennie called me and told me that Red was dead after being hit by a car. It happened near a motel on a trip to Phoenix, Arizona.

As he explained it, someone broke into his motel while he was out on business in the city. He had left Red in the room, and when the intruder entered the room, Red apparently gave chase to the person who opened the door. Obviously, it was not the motel housekeeper who entered the room; otherwise, the front desk would have informed him of the attack on the staff. Also, Bennie said he found blood all over the floor, probably left by the intruder.

I broke down on the phone, startling him. It was completely unexpected. One thing about Bennie was his inability to show compassion or regret. I don't know how he'd expected me to act. But I had lost a friend I'd raised from birth. Bennie never offered to pay me for the dog and I never asked him for payment. After all, I let the dog go with him. Even now I wonder what might have happened if Epic had gone in his place.

Some people thought I was lucky back then. I had all the women I could possibly want, a nice car, money in my pockets. But I knew that soon enough, while things were going great for me, the good times would come to an end. It had happened in the past. Sometimes, I would experience a small loss; other times, it was a much bigger reversal than the financial gains I had made.

One day as I was leaving a scale company at Neponset Circle, in Dorchester, I ran into a department manager from the bank. He was a nosy old man and asked me what was going on. I had gone there to buy a new scale to measure cocaine. The shipment of new scales hadn't arrived on time. I told him that a friend of mine who owned a restaurant needed a scale to measure his spices. A skeptical look crossed his face. I could hardly have told him the truth. Telling me that the owner of the place was an old friend, he dropped the conversation.

I never heard about the encounter from my boss at the bank. But it showed me how small the world really was. I was to find out that secrecy was an important component of survival. The other adage I believed in was: "Loose lips sink ships." And discretion, political silence, diversion of conversation, minding your own business—were all important ways to protect one's interests.

At that time, a marijuana embargo of the Nixon administration began to restrict the smuggling of a large part of the US supply of Mexican weed. The administration and the Mexican government sprayed a defoliant weed killer on Mexican marijuana fields, using a poison called Paraquat to kill the crop. When the American press began reporting on the program using Paraquat, many customers for pot became nervous and reluctant to buy or smoke any reefer from Mexico.

I happened to be visiting with Rhoda one night and complained about the lack of pot supply. The thing I liked most about Rhoda, besides the sex, was her habit of putting something aside for later. Many a time, we would run out of coke or something else and she'd bring out a little stash she'd put to the side for a nightcap. What Rhoda said surprised me. She told me about a friend of hers in the boondocks of western Massachusetts who had a supply of marijuana. Not only that, but she could get me five pounds on credit the following day. She made a phone call and told me to come around the next day. Sure enough, the following night, a hippie looking guy from Brimfield, the town in western Massachusetts, came to her apartment with five pounds of reefer in a sack. In the drug business, like any other business at certain levels, you can get credit. But you're expected to keep your word to your creditor.

People who sell reefer always make money because there's no way you can smoke it all. Unlike pot, the problem with a hard drug like cocaine is that it's a liar's drug. Just about everything you hear about it is a lie, from the quality to the promise to delivery on time. And people who sniffed the stuff could get in deep trouble. In the company of one woman, you could go through a hundred bucks worth in an hour.

The hippie gave me an address of a farm in Brimfield where I was to mail money orders. We sealed the deal on a handshake. Every week, I bought money orders at the bank in two hundred dollar amounts to mail to the farm in Brimfield until the debt was paid. It was as simple as that. While the drug business might have been a dirty business, it was still a business.

☙ ❧

Chapter 11:

Business Is Business

There was nothing so important to me in the drug business that I'd risk my freedom for it. I always kept my feet on the ground. I never sold to strangers, directly. Actually, my customers usually screened business for me. And unless there was a woman they wanted me to meet, they kept my identity a secret.

Of course it was in their best interest that nothing happened to me. After all, how many dealers took checks or gave you credit on drugs? How many would take a return on the product and give you your money back?

One day, someone I'll here call "Whitey," whom I'd met through a contact at Holiday Magic, called me from Weymouth in a rage and told me to take back the reefer I'd sold him. He added that he didn't like me or my car. This had been the first time I'd done business with him.

I couldn't understand why he was talking to me like that. I thought there was more to it than he let on. I drove out to his place and took the reefer back. No problem. But I was through with the jerk. Maybe, I suppose, his wife was giving him trouble. But I never found out.

Another time, I gave credit on a half pound to a black guy in Roxbury on his promise to pay me back on his check day. When I called for my money, he said, in a disparaging way: "That's not real money; its drug money!" It was his way of telling me he wasn't going to pay. After I called his apartment a few times the following week, his wife lied to me, saying he wasn't at home. The next time I called, I told her that "the people" wanted their money. I was trying to convince them that her husband was going to pay what he owed. She got scared.

Sure enough, the next time I called he answered; and when he began to scold me, saying that I had threatened his wife, I interrupted him. He was bullshitting, I said, hanging up on him so that he would not have an excuse to hang up on me or claim I was harassing him.

I avoided a lot of the pitfalls in the business, because I never let out more than I could cover on my own. In fact, I would rather have given a customer a little something for free rather than give credit, when I knew that he or she couldn't afford it. It was important not to make enemies who could set you up or "drop a dime." There was no sense in letting things reach the point where you had to have someone beat up over drugs.

Especially, when there were many other eager customers who couldn't wait to do trouble-free business with you.

I generally avoided socializing with my customers, which kept them from becoming too familiar with my business or personal life. I kept a black book of numbers and listed my transactions every day. As I became a multi-drug dealer, especially with the coke, I found myself dealing with call girls and pimps. Sometimes, I had sex without protection and got burned. Someone was always offering to give me a piece of ass in those days.

I was back in school by this time and was attending class on the Harbor Campus of U/Mass, in Dorchester. There were a lot of new friends to make in l974. This was a year of scandal and retribution. The chairman of the Ways and Means committee of the Congress, Wilbur Mills, one of the most powerful persons in Congress, had a mistress who was well-known in Boston as a stripper. When he came to town, he ended up in the "Combat Zone' in Boston. Local wags rumored that he was chasing down the local stripper named "Fannie Fox, the Argentine Firecracker," as she was billed in the strip joints. During this period, Mills drove the two of them into the Capitol's Tidal Basin in an early morning spree. According to press reports of the accident, Mills appeared clearly under the influence of alcohol. The news was in the national headlines for days before he resigned from his legislative positions. The scandal ended his political career.

Republican President Richard Nixon, too, finally resigned from his office in disgrace, after White House tapes proved he had obstructed justice in the Watergate Hotel burglary, an illegal break-in of the Democratic Party National office to obtain sensitive campaign information. Nixon's Vice President Spiro Agnew already had resigned October 10, 1973, after being caught taking bribes and not reporting the bribe as income. Gerald Ford replaced Agnew. Upon Nixon's resignation, Ford became President. One of his first executive actions was to pardon Nixon for any crimes he may have committed in the Watergate scandal. Former New York Governor Nelson Rockefeller became Ford's Vice-president.

The Central Intelligence Agency, under both Presidents Nixon and Johnson, later admitted to Congressional investigators that it had been conducting spy operations against domestic civil rights protesters and the anti-Vietnam War movement. While finishing out Nixon's term, President Ford declared an amnesty for draft evaders and Vietnam deserters in 1974-1975, for those young people either living in Canada, as most of them were, or the ones living overseas. The executive clemency was so they could return free of prosecution in the United States.

Vice-President Rockefeller had ambitions to succeed Ford as President on the GOP ticket in 1976 if Ford decided not to run again, which Ford did in a failed campaign against Democrat Jimmy Carter. An Attica, New York Prison Riot in 1961 had damaged Governor "Rocky's" popularity with a sizable number of young voters and black people. Rockefeller's liberal policies and his controversial divorce and remarriage had also hurt him politically within the GOP. The prison was a killing field for the New York state police who killed hostages and prisoners. International leaders as well as many Americans widely condemned Rockefeller for the massacres by the "staties."

During my first year living at my penthouse, I met Jackie, a blonde from South Boston through a friend at the bank in Quincy where I worked. She and I also attended U/Mass classes. She came from a large family. Although I never met her mother, I became acquainted with her brother Jack, a Vietnam vet also enrolled at U/Mass. The three of us got along well. After dating for a few weeks, Jackie and I began living together.

We took trips to Montreal in my Z car every few months. We also traveled to a fancy lodge in New Hampshire where my cocaine dealer, Carlos, and his fiancé rented a chalet for the weekend. It was large enough for six people. Carlos became my main supplier of the powder. A white guy named Joseph and I became his closest friends. We attended his wedding to his fiancé who had no idea what was going on, as far as I knew.

Once, Jackie and I made a trip to Montreal that I will never forget. We took my dog Epic with us that time and camped one night in the woods of upstate New York. It was a good time for us, hiking, and taking a ride in a seaplane near Lake Saranac. One day, we were driving in downtown Montreal when we came upon a tourist buggy horse collapsed on the street. A crowd of onlookers made up mostly of tourists gathered near the animal. I parked within view of the sad scene; and the longer I watched the pathetic animal harnessed to the buggy, the more the sight depressed me. When I saw that Jackie didn't seem as concerned as me, I blew up at her. I don't know why I did it. I was so infuriated at her apparent lack of concern for the horse that I even offered to give her money to take a bus back to Boston. She wouldn't take my money, however; and short of throwing her out of the car and creating an incident, I had no choice but to calm down.

As we were driving through a neighborhood near Old Montreal, Jackie told me that she saw a guy who could have been my identical twin staring at me as we drove past him. I immediately circled the block, but I couldn't find him. My twin had vanished but later that evening, as we were shopping at a bazaar in Old Montreal, I was stunned to come upon a shop window with a drawing of a man and a woman who resembled Jackie and me. Obviously, some anonymous artist had sketched us as we paraded through the streets of Montreal. So naturally, I could not resist buying the sketch. Later, after we broke up and Jackie had moved back to her mother's house, I dropped off the drawing and some other things that I now wish I had kept.

This was the time when great music blossomed and flourished on a large scale. We had The Spinners, The Tramps, The Bee Gees, Hall and Oates, Donna Summer, Earth, Wind & Fire, Kool and the Gang, The Average White Band, The Doobie Bros., Rufus, David Bowie, Paul McCartney, Michael Jackson, Stevie Wonder, Teddy Prendergast, The Whispers, O'Jays, Fleetwood Mac, The Isley Brothers, Curtis Mayfield and others. These entertainers could sing, play and perform. Their records had more songs that you liked rather than disliked. They gave you your money's worth and had something to sing that made sense. U/Mass had a celebrity series directed by the student council. Both Angela Davis and Stevie Wonder came to the campus to speak. It was our time to get an education and enjoy ourselves.

Jackie wasn't really interested in going to school as much as she was interested in getting high. I had a low tolerance for women who weren't into self-improvement or education. Not that I was a snob, but I liked to have intelligent, serious conversations with my friends. A female mate lacking basic social skills, in those days, could lower a man's esteem with his colleagues; a woman out of her educational or class depth and unable to fit in with other women at a party, could hurt her mate's social reputation. Today, of course, the reverse would also be true, as many a woman's career has been thwarted, upturned, or ended by the shenanigans of a husband or boyfriend.

For all my intelligence, a woman going out with me risked being burned because, as the hipsters would say, I was "stuck on stupid" with the hookers. Jackie got burned once with my dalliances, after I gave her a dose of the clap. After that, she started taking off on weekends.

I had a psychic named Grace whom I consulted during this time in my life. She told me that Jackie had started seeing other guys when she took off on those weekends to visit with her family. Grace had a good grasp of foretelling some events in my life and kept me aware of some people of whom I should be cautious in my dealings. Grace encouraged me to read several selections from the Psalms that she claimed would help keep me out of trouble. The first was from Psalms 31:4,

"Pull me out of the net that they have laid privily for me; for thou art my strength". The second selection was even more to the point. To paraphrase Psalm 35:26, "Let the slings and arrows of those who would destroy me be turned against them. Let them be ashamed and confounded together that seek after my soul to destroy it." I memorized these words and would often meditate upon them, whenever I was troubled.

ᘓ ᘐ

Chapter 12:

Girls, Girls, Girls

She was just seventeen, if you know what I mean

—Paul McCartney

One night in 1961, Melvin and I went to a club called Club 47 on Harvard Square to meet two young women. Melvin always seemed to get the girl he wanted. He had also taught me how to "rap." Sometimes, we would spend hours going over the answers to questions a new girl might throw at a guy in different situations. Once, Melvin had asked me why I thought that he had so many girls at his beck and call. I thought it over and answered that they thought he was cute. He explained that it came down to the way you talked and that looks didn't make all that much of a difference. Who got "the booty" to bed, in the end, was what counted.

I don't remember the name of the girl with Melvin, but she had been going out with a friend of ours. The girl who ended up with me was named Addie and we hit it off very well. Addie was an attractive young lady from New York City, who had looks and class. I didn't understand much about class at that time. But I knew she was different from most of the girls I knew. One thing for sure, a woman's presence, the quality that separates attractive ladies from plain women, is always too obvious to ignore. Addie wore a fashionable haircut, a kind of "Page Cut," which allowed one side of her hair to hang longer on one side of her face, almost covering one of her eyes. Occasionally, she brushed it back as we talked, so she could meet my eyes with hers. I found my eyes drawn to those little movements.

Speaking with a soft New York accent that might have sounded pretentious to the uncultured ear, I found myself leaning close to Addie in order to hear her over the din of the music. Her dark hair smelled like flowers, almost intoxicating. Before long, as the evening passed, my arm moved around her shoulders, seemingly on its own. We had become a couple.

I had borrowed my family car for this date, knowing earlier that I'd be dropping the girls off on the North Shore in Newburyport, where Addie and her family were vacationing. When we arrived at the house, she did something unexpected: She invited Melvin and me to come inside and meet her family. The home belonged to her grandfather.

She turned out to be an affluent W.A.S.P (White Anglo Saxon Protestant) living on Boston's north shore. I met her parents, her older sister, Abby, who was going through a divorce, and her grandfather. They didn't show any surprise or hesitation when we entered the house where a small family gathering had been taking place. Her grandfather was the one who grilled me, gently, about my full name and family address. Once we had been there a while, we felt as much a part of the gathering as anyone else. Addie told me later that her father had barely escaped getting trapped in the middle of a race riot in New York City a few months earlier. She also mentioned that most of the year her family lived on Park Ave where they worked.

One thing for sure, out of all the women I'd known since high school, Addie was the cream of the crop. I would never have dreamed to ask her to "put out" as a price of riding on my bike. About a week later, she came into town on the commuter train and I picked her up at North Station on my motorcycle. She was dressed for the occasion wearing culottes and sandals. We rode around Boston for a while and I ended up bringing her to my parent's apartment in Roxbury. She met my mother and visited for a little while. As we prepared to leave, I remembered I'd forgotten something and left her outside on my bike for a moment.

When I came out, she told me that a white Boston cop pulled up and angrily said to her that she shouldn't be riding with "a colored guy." She said she shouted back at him that she was free to ride with whom she pleased, and that he didn't intimidate her. He drove away in a fury. When she told me what had just transpired, I was enraged. I wished, then, that I could have identified the policeman. But he'd disappeared. In hindsight, for my own safety, it was just as well I had not been involved in the incident.

After that, we rode over to the Harley Davidson dealership, at Roxbury Crossing, where I bought something for the bike. There was a small group of bikers there who checked me out. One of my white riding buddies was with them. He didn't come over to speak and I didn't join him. We merely waved at one another. Later, I got the word from one of my "so-called" white buddies that a few of the white bikers were pissed off that I had a white girl on the back of my machine. I couldn't have cared less. I had all kinds of girls on my machine.

Most motorcycle clubs were either black or white at that time. It always struck me as strange that some white riders wanted to ride with black women when they rode with a black group. Yet, when they rode with a white group, they rode only with white women. Still, they got an attitude if black riders did the same thing.

On my second visit to Newburyport, Addie and I went to a concert featuring the folk singer Dave Van Ronk. I borrowed the family car again. As I got behind the wheel, in preparation for the ride to Beverly, she moved close to me. I leaned over and put my face against her hair, inhaling her fragrance.

"Hi" I remember saying.

"Hi, Marvin" She responded, in her soft voice.

Pronouncing my name as (Mawr-vin) accenting the "r" instead of using the Boston pronunciation Mah-vin) was characteristic of her class of people. I sneaked a glance over her shoulder to the living room window to make sure no one was watching. Then, I leaned over as she turned her face upward, kissing her. The kiss lasted about a minute, full of promise.

For some reason still unknown to me, I ran short of money at the ticket booth but Addie didn't hesitate to slip me a few dollars so I could cover us. It was no big deal, but it showed class on her part to me. Another determinant of class is when you assist a young lady into the passenger seat of your car and after you go around to the driver's side, she unlocks your door from the inside instead of sitting there like a wooden Indian.

One afternoon when Addie was away in New York, her sister Abby called me to meet her in downtown Boston, where she planned a shopping trip. Abby was a worldly, attractive, and sensual woman who was at least five years older than me. Melvin thought she might be up to something. I wasn't sure, but I wasn't going to pass up the chance to be with her. We met in front of Filene's department store. After accompanying her around as she made her purchases, we went to lunch at an expensive restaurant, where she paid the check. I believe Addie was making plans to attend Bryn Mawr, an exclusive women's college in Pennsylvania. The visit ended and Abby returned to North Station and took the train to Newburyport. Nothing happened but there seemed to be an unspoken message that I couldn't decipher.

I saw Addie again in Newburyport, before she returned to New York and we planned to go all the way the next time we met in a month. At the time, her girlfriend happened to be at the house. After saying our goodbyes, I drove the girl back to Boston. I had met her in New York on one visit there. Her boyfriend and I even partied together, hitting on different women, but he managed to seduce one of the women I was trying to woo at one party and I still resented him.

For some reason, on the way back, Addie's girlfriend and I got into an argument about her boyfriend, who had given me the shaft over the party woman. The incident had nothing to do with her or Addie, and I brought it up for reasons I still can’t explain. I even "hit" on her for the hell of it—a bad move, as I ought to have known, since she wasn't going to keep my attempt a secret from Abby or Addie, who would not be pleased or amused by it.

It was no surprise therefore when about a month later Melvin told me that I had blown it with Addie. He told me that the woman was angry and had told him and Addie about my move on her. It was a hard lesson. I spoke to Addie once on the phone and apologized. But she refused to see me and I never saw her, again. I knew I’d lost something special. One thing I would never find out was whether the outcome I envisioned of an interlude with Addie would have matched the pleasure and intensity of my tryst with Mark’s wife “Fifi.”

I was to experience that wonderful feeling of young love, again. It came, unexpectedly, not long after my loss with Addie, happening when I visited the NAACP office for the first time, on Massachusetts Avenue in the South End. I don’t remember why I went there but the girl behind the counter got my full attention. I was "thunder struck" by her beauty.

Her name was Meg and when I first saw her, I thought she might have been Spanish. Her skin was tanned almost brown. Her teeth were bright white, picture perfect. She had long black hair that fell past her shoulders. Her body was perfect with a nice round ass. Even her feet were pretty in her sandals. There was a mutual attraction that pulled us toward one another of its own volition. She turned out to be Jewish. We stared into each other's eyes to the amusement of the other girls in the office. It turned out to be her last day on the job. She was so fine. We talked for hours that day, until it was near to closing time. I couldn't wait to call her that night. Unfortunately, her mother squashed things over the phone when I called Meg that evening, full of hope. She was not going to be allowed to see me again. I guess I must have made a hell of an impression on her.

I was in a depressing funk for a couple of weeks. Melvin surmised what had happened as I walked around depressed and unfocused. He was forced to fire me from a part-time job he'd gotten me, helping him make window displays, at the jewelry store where he worked.

A memory of young love can endure in the mind forever. The feeling itself is so rare and it seldom comes more than twice. If you find that feeling even later in life, you are surely blessed.

There have always been women attracted to me, as I've been to them. Yet, like that buzz that hooks you with that first cigarette or hit of cocaine, it could have been easy for me to become a serial womanizer on an unending quest. But I never let my frustration lead me to the path of using and abusing women. It would have diminished me as a human being.

Sometimes, I got to know couples close-up and watched the verbal abuse and threats heaped upon women by their men for money, "fiending" on the white powder. There was nothing glamorous about living that way.

In my secret heart, there were times when I didn't feel deserving of love. While those years are known as freewheeling, wide open times of experimentation, there were always limits on certain types of behavior. For the most part we acted as our own arbiters of what was acceptable or unacceptable. Making a move on your girl's girlfriend or your friend's girl was never acceptable. The scarcity of 'real love' was one of the reasons that so many first marriages of my peers ended in divorce. 'Fucking friends' were in big supply. There was always the possibility of picking up a sexually transmitted disease in those days, when a lot of men who didn't know better found the use of a condom, unappealing.

After Jackie moved out of my apartment, I started going out with a girl I met through one of my married customers in the building. Gina was a sensual beauty who was into hair cutting and had opened a barbershop with her brother at a Cambridge hotel. When I arrived at the apartment to meet her, I grabbed her into my arms. She had 'temptation eyes' that flashed out at me. Her background included a sometime boyfriend, a black heroin addict who would pop up now and then in her life. Gina always treated me well.

Her brother, however, was a trip. He was a part-time "Soul" singer who didn't like soul brothers, especially those going out with his sister. He tolerated me and I did the same. Once, when I used Gina's shower, she cautioned me to be careful about leaving any body hairs in the tub because her brother might get upset.

One night I was on my way home at around two in the morning when I came across a black girl walking in the middle of the street. She was cute and said that a white guy had kicked her out of his car. I picked her up and brought her home with me. We got buzzed and I shared my powder with her. She gave me oral sex and I "banged" her. It was a good time. Having sex with a stranger wasn't a big deal in those days. The next morning she left me her phone number in New York.

A day later I was feeling hung over and drained of energy. I had no idea what was causing my discomfort until I felt my swollen lymph nodes in the groin area. It must have been a hell of an infection. I had a doctor on the side that Bennie had referred me to. I went to see him right away and was given a shot of penicillin. After I got back to the apartment, I called the girl in New York and told her about what had happened.

The next night, Gina came over and we had sex. I told her I hadn't been feeling too good. But I hadn't thought to mention that I'd only been treated that day. Then, the next morning I noticed I still had minor symptoms of the clap. I was forced to go back to the doctor for another shot. In the meantime, Gina had sex with her former boyfriend and had passed the shit to him. When I let her know the story, she was pissed off at me. I told her that I hadn't done it on purpose, we weren't exactly engaged and I had let her know as soon as possible.

Regardless, things cooled between us and she started seeing only her other guy again. Maybe it was out of guilt. Not long after that, I started seeing her younger girlfriend, Janey. Janey was a trip. She was only twenty-two years old and worked at the state office building with my former junior high gym teacher. I also discovered that she was friends with an old buddy of mine from the old Lennox Street housing project. He had been the life of any party in his heyday. Recently, I ran into him at a neighborhood reunion after having thought he was dead. Oh, how Boston can, at times, seem truly a small town!

Not long after I started seeing Janey, I met one of her older sisters, Elena. She had been the sheltered one in her family and had just broken up with a Jewish guy who'd been her fiancé. She started coming around as things cooled off between Janey and me. Actually, things were never that hot with Janey. I'd been too lazy to find a decent woman. Elena was a constant worrier and told me to be careful that her ex-fiancé didn't come after me; one of her friends had earlier warned her he had seen us together. Well, I didn't give a shit.

One day, I was with a friend of her family's at a garage in Watertown where the punk worked. I'd come by the place on purpose to see what would happen. We got a look at each other but nothing was said and he never made good on his threats. It might have been because I was doing business with his peers or any number of reasons. But he never fucked with me.

By this time, I was making contacts in the Newton-Waltham area and discovered that my reputation had preceded me in some circles. The truth about my dealings affirmed, Elena described how she learned through the grapevine that she had heard about me, an anonymous black dealer living then in Brighton; I was, someone said, a really nice guy. I was a dope dealer, for sure, but the description, she said, was always qualified with "No, he's really nice."

Although I believed that someone might have complimented me, the description was more like a woman's description of a man than a man's description of a man.

Regardless, Elena introduced me to a small group of her girlfriends for business. Most of my customers for the powder were women. I had three Madams, their girls and a small circle of pimps, who hung out at an after-hours joint on Western Ave in Cambridge as my fast money customers. Some weekends, I'd clear five hundred bucks for myself in a single night. Any girl I wanted in those circles, I could have. But I had begun to abstain from casual sex.

Janey and I started going downhill after we went to Philadelphia during the summer of l976, because I wanted to see the fireworks there and get away from Boston for a while. My relatives hadn't acted too friendly when I showed up with Janey. She was a big contrast in looks and personality to Marilyn, not as relaxed or warm to them. Melvin got on my ass and insisted I sing along with the James Brown record "I'm Black and I'm Proud" when we were alone in the car, the implication being that were I proud of my race I wouldn't be with a white girl.

On the way back to Boston, Janey took over the driving and I crawled into the space behind the front seat and went to sleep. After about an hour, Jane woke me up. She was moving at about thirty miles an hour and said there was some guy following us. I looked through the window of the fastback into the red lights of a Connecticut state police cruiser.

After I had her pull over to the side of the road, I got into the passenger seat as the cop walked up to the car. I was shocked at what he said: "I've been following you for about twenty miles and she wouldn't stop."

I apologized to him and explained that I'd been sleeping in the rear of the car. Maybe, it was my attitude, but after I showed him my license and papers, he looked at me with the look that men sometimes share and let us go. I made a point of taking over the driving from Jane before he drove away. I was pissed off. My time with her had run out.

Our first night together, Elena and I set a relationship in place unlike any I had ever been in before. Before we had sex, she insisted on directing me on how to lick her "little man in the boat." She made sure she was completely satisfied before she took care of my needs. After a couple of weeks, she insisted on redecorating my apartment, which I went along with. Sometimes, she came over and cooked for me. I was surprised when she told me that her older brother was part of a large group of people caught in a big drug conspiracy indictment reported in the *Boston Globe*. At that time, the case hadn't been called up, so everyone was out on bail, sweating it.

The boyfriend of Elena's oldest sister was a student at the University of Massachusetts, at the Boston campus, who was in a master's program dealing with Chaucer. Sometimes, he would review my papers as a favor before I turned them in. He and Elena's sister were always welcome at my place. Elena also turned me on to more business in the Watertown-Cambridge areas through several of her girlfriends. I was dealing with an overflow of business at this time. Sometimes, I'd end up doing deliveries at a three hour stretch. Other times I'd get a call for a two hundred dollar purchase at two in the morning. It was a stressful undertaking, but I thrived in it.

One night, Elena talked me into traveling to Montreal for the day. It was a dumb idea, but I went for it. I drove most of that evening till dawn and reached Montreal in mid- morning. We spent the day there. But on the way back through customs, I had to put up with an inspector who checked our luggage and asked me trick questions such as: "Did they tell you to come this way?" People don't usually visit Montreal for only a day from Boston.

Sometimes, when her sister wasn't around, Janey would sneak over for a little rock and roll. She also introduced me to one of her girlfriends, Joan, who stopped by occasionally. Oh, my, my, my, I had, as it were, a full plate of women on my table, and, in fact, there were too many for one man like me trying to make a living.

I went to a lot of parties, but I was seldom out on the floor dancing. More often than not, I would find myself in a room isolated from most of the people, doing my business. Once in a while, a woman would come in to meet me. Sometimes, I'd end up at someone's place in the suburbs and not get home until the next day. I had so many women around me without having sex with them that I'd often end up passing some of them on to my friends who wanted to have sex with them. Anyway, there wasn't enough free time in a day to handle them all. Talk about a ball of confusion. There were times when I forgot the names of my bedtime companions before we went to bed.

☙ ❧

Chapter 13:

Always Keep your Eye on the Ball

I was constantly working to keep my sanity under control. I found myself dealing with people almost around the clock. There were times when I had a need to disappear. I was determined not to have a beeper. Cell phones weren't available in those days, although I had an answering machine in the apartment.

One day I ran into an old friend of mine whom I'll name Terry. I knew him when he lived in the Lennox Street projects in Roxbury, growing up. He now owned a house in Newton. He was, I quickly discovered, also, a fellow dealer. Although he was a competitor, we began to buy drugs from one another.

At other times, we'd go in on something together; we'd pool our money for a large drug purchase. He was always telling me that he didn't want to meet anyone, not customers, dealers nor anyone I knew. Nevertheless, I managed to introduce him to a few of our best customers, in case I wasn't around.

Terry worked as a technician at the Polaroid Corporation in Waltham, where a major scandal occurred. A group of workers were caught making crystal meth in a laboratory on the premises. The rotten egg smell of the stuff was so strong that it had given them away.

There was also an old high school classmate of mine, a lawyer, who "hipped" me how to cut coke and make more of a profit on the drug. Lenny grew up in the South End, but he attended college, where he majored in college chemistry. He also taught me a lot about testing cocaine for purity. Lenny, Terry and I spent a lot of time together in those days. It was Lenny who brought me a lot of high income clientele.

The Democratic Party rose up with a vengeance in the fall election of l976. It was payback time. Whenever the Democrats rally together, nothing can stand against them. Ford was paid back for his pardon of Nixon, along with a lot of Republicans across the country who were turned out of office. It was like a tidal wave sweeping across the land.

I voted for Jimmy Carter, but I wasn't all that excited about him. There are a lot of 'born again' Christians in the South. They can still have the same feelings about black people as the KKK. Sunday is one of the most segregated days in America. Politically, the decade will be remembered for two one-term presidencies, an impeachment and a hostage crisis with the Iranians. One thing Carter taught us was that it was all right for men to embrace one another. I'll never forget the sight of Carter embracing Anwar Sadat, while his wife shook hands with the leader.

In l977, I was dealing with a major basketball player on the San Antonio Spurs, who had a girlfriend in Winthrop. Every time the team came into town for a Celtics game, I would be treated to a V.I.P. suite at an expensive Logan Airport hotel. Sometimes, I'd go to a barbershop near the Christian Science Center on Mass Ave to meet the player. I never did business with any of the Celtics, Patriots or Red Sox. But I knew of others who claimed they did. One day, during the summer, Lenny brought the brother of one of the star hitters of the New York Yankees by my place for some business. But I never met the player, himself so, I don't know if the purchase was for him.

One night my mind was blown when Lenny showed up at my door with a world famous jazz musician whose album I'd just been playing. I wish I'd thought to get the album autographed.

Another time, I went with Lenny to a prison farm in Plymouth to visit a man convicted of fraud in a housing scandal in New Bedford. It was a facility for white collar criminals and mafia gangsters who were doing short time. It was a cool place, everyone was laid back. There were large cells that held four inmates in the section we visited. Each cell had four bunk beds and cooking facilities. At the time we were there, the cell was empty except for Lenny's friend.

Of course, I was there for business, working under the guise of a legal assistant. We had passed through a metal detector but I didn’t have any metal on me only a little powder. This was a minimum security facility with minimal security.

The day I realized that I was on the top of my game was when I and a friend sniffed a couple of coke "lines." We were in the Records Room, the top floor of the old downtown Boston Courthouse, Pemberton Square, the Scollay Square neighborhood once populated by speakeasies, bordellos, and strip joints.

The 1950s-1970s were the decades after the Blue Hill Avenue-Grove Hall Jewish Mafia had moved out of the drug business, illegal gambling, and the black market in money laundering, bootleg liquor, loan sharking, gun trafficking, smuggling tobacco, wholesale garments, jewels, and just about anything else that could be traded. Many of the Jewish criminals and their families in the 1970s became involved in legitimate small businesses, casinos in Las Vegas, Nevada, and elsewhere, the stock market, and start-up venture capital corporations. New England's Italian American Mafiosi, operating out of Providence, Rhode Island, and Boston's predominantly Italian neighborhoods of Revere, East Boston, and the North End-Haymarket Square area, were still handling most of the largest drug shipments into the city. Of course, at the street level distribution end of the city's illegal drug trade, the market in the college student, the black and the growing Hispanic community was full of opportunity for anyone to make money. No matter one's ethnic or racial background, there were plenty of customers for everyone "to score" in those days.

Bennie had moved away a few months earlier, after one of our friends from Beacon Hill had gotten busted with a trailer load of reefer in Arizona. He had squealed on someone named "Mister Bond," a major street-level distributor. My last visit with Bennie to Bond's place in Waltham was to buy the last of the reefer in the apartment, before the "Staties" arrived. How my fortunes had changed!

Carlos was still my exclusive cocaine supplier. Whenever he ran out, I'd contact Terry or go through another contact until he had re-upped his store. One day Terry and I almost got busted after making a pickup. It was a close call, the kind you don't see coming, because the statistical odd chance of it happening, as I reckon the odds, are about 50 million to 1. This is what happened.

We had just bought a package from one of my customers on Beacon Street in the Back Bay. It was a fact of life in those days, that some of our customers had access to other distributors for the illegal drugs. Boston was a wide open city with plenty of buyers and sellers, middlemen and labs for manufacturing some of the exotic products traded on the street. Anyway, we had just made a purchase and the customer had opened the front door at the top of the stairs for us to pass through, when we looked down the stairs behind us into the eyes of two white middle-aged detectives rifling through the briefcase of a black guy handcuffed and prone on the landing. The guy behind us read the situation and shut the door. He had no choice. If we'd gone back inside the cops would have probably waited for us to come out or would have contacted the landlord. We continued down the stairs to the sidewalk, where the black guy was arguing about being stopped. We tried to appear unconcerned and continued walking away, feeling their eyes on our backs. It was all we could do, feeling the cold sweat of fear while our hearts raced madly, to keep from breaking into a run until we turned the corner. As soon as we turned the corner, we broke into a run, knowing they were going to come after us.

My car was parked behind the building which faced the Charles River. Clearly, with the possibility that the fuzz were on our heels, it didn't make sense to either of us to be together if we were pursued; so almost instinctively, we turned in separate directions. As soon as I started my car's engine, I slammed the accelerator down with my foot, burning rubber. In a flash, I was out of the alley without looking whether I was running over someone or about to collide with another vehicle. In my rearview mirror, blocks away, I glimpsed Terry as he disappeared over a foot bridge that led to the banks of the river.

I don’t know if the "Dicks" tried to catch up with us but if they had followed us, we must have lost them. I called Terry a little later, to share a laugh about our close call. I also called the customer who told me there was nothing else he could have done, but not let us back into his apartment with potentially incriminating evidence. I had to agree with his decision, much as he was throwing us, so to speak, to the wolves. But had I been in his shoes, I surely would have done the same thing.

I had also started doing business with one of the old tough guys from Vernon Street, during the Fifties. He was an Irishman who owned a bar on Mission Hill. His girlfriend worked with one of my other friends from the old neighborhood at the Brigham Hospital. They bought a lot of Quaaludes from me. I had customers everywhere I turned, even among the toll collectors on the Mass Turnpike. Once I even walked through a secret police tunnel that crossed the highway underground.

The summer of l977 was the highlight of a remarkably pleasant year. I worked in the Vet Program under my good friend Norman. He and I worked at the "Mass Media," a student newspaper, in my freshman year. Now my Vet Program position was a five-day a week job that paid a living wage. My assignment was to co-write a Veterans handbook for the incoming class in the fall.

Actually, we worked half a day and usually ended at Norman's house in time to see the mid-day television soap opera, "All My Children." We rarely missed a day. I'd usually enjoy having some powder; and my companion for the day might smoke reefer for our "afternoon delight."

Norman had confided in me a long time earlier that he was gay, a secret that didn't bother me because we got along as well as twin brothers. Most amusing to me about him was the general view his co-workers had of him. The administrators in the program viewed him as straight, the office rumor being that he was in a clandestine affair with a blonde director of student activities. I knew the truth about both of them, that she was actually the girlfriend of one of his friends.

One weekend, I went to New York City with Janey and, of all people, Gina. I don't know how I ended up with the two of them. Both of them swore that neither of them was going to let me fuck either one on the sly this trip. For once in my life, I didn't have anyone to contact who might put us up in the city. We shared lodging at a cheap hotel near the Port Authority. After a nice meal, cocktails, a few joints and a snort of a line of coke among us, I managed to get a 'quicky' with Janey, while Gina pretended to be sleeping. But the real absurdity of this New York adventure happened at a famous Italian restaurant named Mama Leone's. The moment the three of us walked in, I knew it was going to be an unpleasant evening. I picked up on the New York Italian chill. Of course, the chill isn't restricted to the Italian brothers alone. It was just my night to deal with them. If we'd gone to an Irish joint, it might have been the same. The whole affair could have passed for a bad comedy.

First of all, the attention given me by the wait staff was extraordinary. They must have assumed that I was a pimp selling off two Italian girls, even though I wasn't dressed like a pimp and the women weren't dressed like streetwalkers. Right away, some of the customers stared at us in an unfriendly way. The girls didn't mind. We all knew who we were. But when I caught some assholes looking at us through the kitchen doors, I lost my appetite. I've come to realize that the closer you are placed to the kitchen in a grease joint, the greater the chance that the Maitre'D doesn't like you. It was the same up-in-your-face brash hostility, racially charged, from the wait staff that I'd experienced years before at Wildwood, New Jersey, when I was with Marilyn.

As we decided whether to stay or leave, I recalled something an old Boston Police friend had once told me years earlier about restaurant workers in places like this one. He said that he would never order food in his police uniform at a restaurant. He said a large percentage of kitchen staff had criminal records so they could not find better paying jobs; this embittered them against the police and the felons couldn't wait to piss in a cop's soup, or put some foul thing in his or her food. The girls shared none of my misgivings, nor were they sensitive to the racial dimensions of the unpleasant stares from the staff and customers. Most black Americans, particularly in that period, almost had to have a sixth sense just to survive into middle-age.

When it came to white racial hostility, we could almost smell it. Women who grow up aware of male sexual interest, most of it unwelcome, probably have the same kind of sixth sense. But rarely is a male stranger's sexual attraction to a woman hostile, confrontational, demeaning, menacing, or at times, even violent; as it usually is to some degree when racial animosity is involved. So when the girls asked me what I wanted to order, I told them I wasn't hungry.

The overly solicitous waiter hovering over us seemed to take delight in my response. The girls were irritated at me. This was a locally famous Italian restaurant in their eyes, and they expected me to appreciate their choice of the place.

I was uncomfortable, all the while tense, while we sat there; and I didn't want to get into a relaxed conversation with the waiter listening, looking over my shoulder, to overhear something provocative. During the meal, a surly black kitchen worker came out of the kitchen to check me out. His appearance, not to mention his ill-behaved scrutiny, was no surprise. I was accustomed to that kind of black conformity to white attitudes that insulted the servile black support for it as much as it did the black target humiliated by the whites.

The women were oblivious to all of the white racist dimensions and our unusual attention from the people in the restaurant. But the antenna of a black person is usually right on point. It has enabled us to survive in the wilderness of America.

Finally, in order to get them off my back, I said I'd share some of their food. When I was asked about ordering a drink, I opted for a glass of water. The waiter ordered another member of the wait staff to fill my water glass and this guy must have been an expert because he filled the glass so full without spilling a drop, I couldn't have drunk from it without spilling water on the table or myself. They smiled about that one.

This pissed me off and I pulled rank, catching them by surprise, demanding that the waiter have some of the water poured off. I smiled to myself as they were forced to pour off some of the water. They left me alone after that.

I shared some of the food on the girls' plates and when they went into the ladies room before leaving, one of the oily waiters came over to me acting like an old friend and said in a low voice: "Some of these women like brown sausage, my friend." I didn't dare respond as though I heard him. I knew if I'd been white he wouldn't have dared approach me like that. I was glad when we were back on the street. I haven't been to New York City on a visit since that time.

Still, there was good with the bad. The three of us were sitting in Central Park, when we had a conversation with a white passerby who it turned out was on the production staff at the ABC Network building nearby. He ended up taking us onto the deserted set of "All My Children."

That was something to write home about.

☙ ❧

Chapter 14:

Roots

In late summer, I went with my mother, sister, and two of my father's friends to an uncle's funeral in South Carolina. It was my first time going down South since I was a little boy. My father stayed behind with my younger brother. My mother came from a large family. Odd though it now strikes me, I'd only met my Uncle Butler (Bee) once when he came to Boston.

My mother had eight brothers and four sisters, of whom she was now the sole survivor. I also had an aunt in her nineties, on my father's side, who lived in Atlanta. She had an excellent memory, visited every state in the union, and was still active.

The trip South was an epiphany that I'll never forget. Once we passed the Mason- Dixon Line after Washington, D.C., we drove through lush green countryside of Virginia. We were heading into the deep

South, and I felt a rare tranquility. I was thirty-four years old, wary if not wiser, street smart if not cautious. Driving along the dark highways of North Carolina in the middle of the night, while everyone in the car was asleep was a time for reflection that I hadn't experienced in years.

Coincidentally, songs on the radio by Fleetwood Mac played every hour for hundreds of miles. Often the lyrics seemed directed toward me. The wailing voice of Stevie Nicks captured my experience: "But listen carefully to the sound of your loneliness… Like a heartbeat... drives you mad… In the stillness of remembering what you had… And what you lost… And what you had…. And what you lost…"

And more to the point: "Say, Women… They will come and they will go… When the rain washes you clean… you'll know".

The Fleetwood Mac songs would always be my songs; my secret thoughts exposed in times of late night solitude. Energy pulsated within me and I was glad to be alive, to be in this place where I was in touch with myself. My senses were keen and alert. I felt no discomfort or apprehension being down South. I felt completely at home.

I could see the lights of an oncoming trailer truck from a quarter mile away, on the dark moonlit highway. Lulled into a false sense of security, I was surprised when I realized I was about to become the victim of a speed trap. I whipped by the cop car hidden in the crease of a gully beside the highway, but the driver was probably napping, for he didn't give chase even though I must have been traveling about 70 miles an hour in a 55-mile an hour speed limit.

I didn't hit the brakes as I rounded the curve, knowing that he would know I'd seen him and put on the red lights. Instead, I kept moving, racing the car into a rest area. I quickly turned off my headlights. Sure enough, the squad car I had passed in the gully whizzed past us moments later without flashing lights. Obviously, he had planned to sneak up on me. Everyone woke up and my sister asked me what was going on. I told her and we waited a while in the rest area. I wonder if the cop ever figured out what happened.

We reached Frogmoor Island in South Carolina in the early morning and after resting for a while I walked over to the National Seashore. It was afternoon. Porpoises were leaping out of the water as I walked along the beach. I could see Hilton Head Island in the distance and started walking toward it, thinking I could reach the island from Frogmoor but after an hour of hiking, I was no closer to it than when I'd started. Hilton Head, the scene of national golf tournaments, was an island, too. I gave up my quest at the water's edge, and returned to the entrance of the park, where my mother's friend was waiting for me. She said that she had become very worried two hours after I didn't return to the house or call anyone to let the family know I was safe.

That night, after I went to sleep I woke just long enough to find myself struggling to move against some force which bound me invisibly to the bed. Try as I did, I could not find the strength to raise myself or break free.

Whatever held me had never happened to me before. And I wasn't sure whether I was awake or dreaming. Often now, I still wonder, whether the experience was just an hallucination? A nightmare? Whatever, it seemed then very real.

On the following night after the wake, I visited one of my relative's home when I saw a freight train stopping behind the house. I've always had a fascination with trains and walked over to it. It turned out that the engineer knew my late uncle and, after identifying myself, I asked him for a ride. It turned out that he was pulling a line of freight cars to a main line to be hooked up with another train heading north. I sat in the fireman's seat and we pulled out. I guess my relatives must have thought I was just a stranger catching a ride.

We passed through several small towns and reached the main line where the freight cars were left on a spur. I got to pull the whistle a couple of times as we passed through several crossings. I reflected on the irony of seeing the tracks heading North that could have led me back to Boston. A couple of hours later, we returned to my uncle's place.

I knew there would be more occasions to travel down there in the future. And I knew I would always be open to doing it again. My sense of spirituality came out down there.

I really believe that for every gain, there's a loss. I was forced to ask myself why I had such shitty luck when I got back to town rejuvenated and discovered that my younger brother had taken my car without permission and had gotten in an accident. I had parked the car at my parent's house and left the keys with my father, who remained a thorn in my side. It's like having someone borrow your good clothes. You might not like it and that's understandable. But when you find your clothes torn and dirty every time they use them, then you must conclude that "they're fucking you over" intentionally! Ain't no other way to put it.

Years earlier, in grade school, whenever we'd have a fight in the house, my mother would tell us to go outside and finish it. This time, as adults, my parents were unable to control us. As I started down the front stairs, he picked up a football shaped rock, threw it, and hit me in the forehead, just above my eye. Rushing back into the house, bleeding and dazed, I took my father's rifle to shoot him. I was held back by a friend of my mother's. Meanwhile, my brother ran about a block away. To confront him, I concluded, meant that I would have had to chase him down in the street. By then my anger had cooled enough that I no longer cared to hurt him.

The doctor at the hospital who stitched up my head wound told me I could have died from the blow to my temple. I never forgot that. Ironically, "what goes around does come around" and I got to pay him back a few years later, breaking a beer mug over his dome. I did it when he tried to bully me by slapping my hand when I was holding a drink. I never realized how easy it is to break a mug on a hard head.

When the cops came to my parent's house, however, to investigate this latest confrontation, they decided not to get involved in what appeared to all concerned just a domestic fight. They admonished us for disturbing my father by fighting. Then, "Mister Bad," broken and bloody turned rat, broke the cardinal rule about snitching on a family member. In his defense for hitting me, he told the cops that I was selling drugs. I challenged him on the spot saying that he was lying, and in any case, his accusation wasn't the issue: It had nothing to do with our altercation. To add insult to his injury the cops ignored his attempt to get me arrested.

This time, I threatened to take him to court for slander and false accusation. But it wasn't necessary. He bribed me with his salary check when I threatened him. But my wheel of fortune was still spinning. I considered that as I took further risks in the drug trade, the wheel's needle could stop on the space of my misfortune, my disaster or bad luck. I suspected the cops were keeping tabs on me, waiting for an opportunity to bust me. I just didn't know who it was snitching on me or how long before my number was up. I tried to console myself that I ought not to worry, to cross the bridge when I got to it, in the event I was arrested. I determined to enjoy my last week of summer vacation.

☙ ❧

Photos

Kelly's Key Shop, Roxbury, Mass. as it remains since the 1950s to 2014 Same key shop near where Clark family lived, and still in operation. Credit: James Raynor, c. 2014

Marvin, his great nephew and great niece, 2009

Marvin Clark's elementary school on Roxbury Street. It was one of the schools considered de facto racially segregated by Federal Judge W. Arthur Garrity in his 1974 order to the city council to comply with the state's 1965 Racial Imbalance Law.

Graduation photo 1981 - credit: Eva Clark, 1981

Marvin, brother Walter in T-Shirt, and sister Eva, Boston, 2008 credit: J. Clark, 2008

Former Roxbury Memorial High School Building (Boston Latin Academy) Warren Street, Roxbury, 2014 -credit: James Raynor, 2014

The Big M, a nightclub in the largely black South End of Boston, Massachusetts 1969 Photo Credit: James Raynor

Pleasant Street, Roxbury, one of the first residences of the Clark Family. Credit: Eva Clark

The family of Marvin Clark, his father and mother, and baby sister Eva, 1946 Credit: Eva Clark

Marvin Clark, Ruggles Street Housing Projects, Roxbury, Mass. 2009

Marvin on his Motor Bike, Boston, 1962

Marvin and wife Marilyn, Brookline, c. 1970

Images of Roxbury 1955-1980

Madison Park, Lower Roxbury, circa 1950.
Credit: James Raynor

I Have Often Walked . . .

. . . Down The Street Before

1940s Roxbury near Shopping areas and Ruggles Street at Shawmut Ave. Credit James Raynor Date Unknown

☙ ❧

Chapter 15:

Right Things

A week later, I was back in the swing of a good life. I started the fall semester enrolled in journalism courses at the University of Massachusetts in Boston. This was the prelude to my final year at school. All of the old familiar faces who had begun the courses there in the past year returned to campus. In the spring semester, my student board elected me to the position of news editor for the *Mass Media*.

This time I found out about another position in the news department of a local radio/TV outlet and I applied for it right away. I got the job.

One night I invited John, the owner of the Limbo Restaurant, to join me in a visit to Carlos at his house in East Boston. I was there to drop off some money and pick some drugs up.

When we arrived at the apartment, Carlos led us to a bedroom closet and he opened the closet door. There was a duffle bag on one of the shelves; in it were a number of clear plastic freezer bags full of white nuggets of cocaine. I'd never seen that kind of quantity before. He opened one of the bags and measured out a quantity on a scale for me.

In a flash, I looked into John's eyes and saw greed reflected there. His eyes had narrowed like those of a wolf around a flock of sheep. If he could have gotten away with ripping off a stash like that without getting caught, I could imagine him doing it. Although I had never seen a look like that before, I recognized it. Greed and drugs can be a lethal combination.

There are some things you never do if you have any integrity or self- respect. People who knew me were aware that I had standards of behavior. If something was missing, I was the last person to be suspected. Sure, there were times when I fucked up, giving away too much drugs because of partying and my weakness for loose women. But the amount of loss was a forgivable amount. Someone else's greater loss could put them deep into some scary shit with their sources. My sister told me that most people trusted me and were willing to give me the benefit of the doubt. So, if there was a fuck up, I couldn't have done it on purpose. I just tended to get caught up in the moment.

How the powder Carlos showed us got into Boston, I never knew and Carlos never talked about it. He had a job at the airport on a catering truck. Actually, it wasn't necessary for me to know anything other than it had arrived.

There was a black man from Texas who worked in the airport administration building. I met him through Norman. He had two brothers who came up to Boston every few weeks with large pharmaceutical bottles of Seconal, Valium, Percodan, and Quaaludes. They also had Thai sticks and reefer. I used to have first shot at their shipments. There were always people looking for Quaaludes.

At my level of dealing, I had to be constantly aware of what was going on around me. Word had gotten around the building that I was a dealer. But I was so low key and kept traffic so minimal that I hadn't been confronted by the management. Luckily, there were people watching my back.

One day a little girl who Jackie had once babysat in my apartment came up to my apartment telling me that her mother had called the cops and told them I'd given drugs to her twelve-year-old brother. I knew the motherfucker was a lush and I rushed down from my apartment to the front hall where I confronted the woman in front of the cop. She had just given him my apartment number and he was writing it down.

I denied everything and backed her into a corner about her son. Luckily, he was there and backed me up with the truth. She was forced to retract and threw out the information that I was selling drugs. I saw the cop was becoming a little skeptical. I pushed harder and asked her who had told her that I sold drugs. I had to show indignation.

When she told me who had "dropped the dime" on me, I was surprised. It was none other than the woman who had introduced me to Gina. This being serious shit to me, and the cop, she and I went to the woman's apartment to confront her with her accusation about me. When the accuser, supposedly a friend of mine, was confronted by the other woman, she denied having said anything but I knew she was lying. As the exchange between the two women became more and more heated, the accuser physically attacked the other woman, forcing the cop to break them apart.

I went back to my apartment knowing I had to put the stopper in the bottle. I called the police station house and spoke to the sergeant in charge. I told him that I smoked marijuana and was being called a drug dealer by a drunk in my building. I also implied that the issue might have racial overtones, since my accuser was white. From the way he responded, I knew that he had heard about me but I knew he had no proof other than the woman's allegations about what I was doing. There was no way they could set me up for a buy. I also mentioned that I was a student.

The sergeant ended up warning me that I'd better not be selling anything in that building. I told him I wouldn't and hung up. I never heard from the cops again. But I'd been forewarned.

A month later, the same little girl came up to my apartment and told me that there'd been an accident with my car. When I went downstairs this time and went outside, I was shocked to see a full sized sedan sitting on top of the Z. Apparently, an elderly woman had lost control of her automobile, which jumped the curb and landed on top of my car in the parking lot. My car was totaled.

I was now in the market for another car. The body of the Datsun had already begun to rot out with age so the timing of the accident was fortunate. Terry told me about a foreign car dealer in Allston who had reasonable prices. He used a contact in the business to set up an appointment for me to look at an l974 BMW 2002. It was a beautiful car. I made arrangements and bought it. The woman's insurance paid for the car.

I met my roommate, Ginny, in my screenwriting class at U/Mass. We'd hit it off. She came from a wealthy family in the Lowell area. She had also been married with no children. The song "Rich Girl" by Hall & Oates messed with her psyche.

For the first time in a long time I began to think about starting over with someone else. Ginny had been good for me. She pushed me to apply for an internship at the news station. She also started me into eating healthy foods and getting the proper rest. I began seeing fewer pcople at my apartment and made more deliveries. I began to pay more attention to my grades. My place became more like a home than a clubhouse.

The last woman I slept with from the building was a young neighbor from across the hall that had been referred to me by the building manager. I didn't even like the manager. She came knocking on my door one night and asked me to stop by her place and talk but I learned from her that he told her after he'd fucked her that I was a dealer who might have something for her. He'd been right. We "got down" the same night we talked.

My next door neighbors were a lesbian salon owner and her niece. We got along well at first. The bitch even took me to her salon in Newton Center and cut my hair. But soon I had a few unpleasant verbal exchanges over my music volume with the nosy black woman; and in a few days the lesbian became frosty to me. She had a little poodle, which was against the rules of the management, but I never complained.

Ginny and I began to get serious and spent time around a couple who moved into the girl's apartment after she'd moved out. Michael and Lucy were an unusual couple. He was Jewish and she was Hawaiian. His family had a small franchise of joke shops. Michael became one of my best friends. He also sold a few things on the side and brought me new customers. He bought a new Honda car, the first year it came out. It was through him that I got new customers from the South Shore.

One night, Michael and I did so much "blow" that we were "fried" out of our minds. Ginny claimed that she lost respect for me when that happened and thought that I should go into counseling. She asked me a question that was meant to put me on the defensive: "Do you plan on being a fifty-year old drug dealer?" I hadn't planned on being anything. Long ago, I had considered becoming a teacher or a news reporter. I once planned to stop doing business after I got to college, but that plan never worked out. My drug contacts expanded even more after I entered U/Mass. By doing the seemingly smart thing rather than the right thing, I developed a profitable drug business in spite of my plans.

Sometimes, I thought that God must be looking out for me because my luck had been so extraordinary. My luck with Ginny changed unexpectedly, though, when she had to get an abortion through our unprotected sex; it was our fault for not using protection. I didn't go through a crisis over it. I knew I wasn't ready to start a family. I was supposed to be there when she was finished at the clinic, but I was late arriving and missed her. I didn't hear from her until hours later. She was pissed off at me.

Around this time, I knew she had begun seeing an old boyfriend, Paul. He had been in the background in secret contact with her, trying to get her back. His efforts didn't worry me, because I didn't think he was serious or ready to make a serious commitment.

I allowed Ginny to borrow my car when she visited her mother's place in New Hampshire, even though I knew that Paul was a passenger. I couldn't turn her down when she asked me. She had really helped me to think about my lifestyle in critical ways. I felt that I owed her much. She had helped me realize my limitations. I was aware that my life couldn't continue safely in the drug trade.

Her parents were divorced. I always suspected that the old man beat Ginny and her two brothers when they were growing up. Knowing her bouts of depression, I concluded that her family was a stressful one for a child. When I met her mother, in a house full of cats, it blew my mind. Almost every space in the house seemed to have a cat or kitten in it.

I didn't make a great impression on her mother. I slipped up during a dinner conversation and said the word "shit," a mistake. But I wasn't about to sweat it. One day Ginny had to go to the hospital with a serious infection in the area of her ovaries. I never did get the full story, but I hadn't given her anything. It could have had something to do with the abortion.

I always had the feeling that her family might have suspected that her medical problems had something to do with the fact she was seeing two men and probably sleeping with both of them. She spent several weeks in the hospital. She could barely walk without pain.

Ginny's grades never suffered. She was on the Dean's List with a column of A's on her grade sheet. I felt fortunate to have her there to review my class papers. She even helped me draft an application letter for graduate school.

☙ ❧

Chapter 16:

The Blizzard of '78

"But baby, it's cold outside"

—Ray Charles

When the Blizzard of l978 arrived in Boston, on Monday, February 6, Ginny had me drop her off in the South End, so we wouldn't be stuck in my apartment together. I didn't mind it all that much because I had a date arranged with Janey's friend, Joanie. Ginny always came down on me about my taste in women. She always had something negative to say about them. I had to admit that she was usually right.

The serious snow started falling at rush hour. I can remember leaving U/Mass and arriving at the Allston toll booths on my way to Newton Corner. I'd never seen snowflakes like the ones I saw that night. They looked like round cotton balls.

I got home and made ready for Joanie's arrival. I was completely prepared. I had plenty of food, drink, and drugs. I had become used to living the good life. It was going to be more fun than Disneyland. When she arrived, we frolicked around the apartment like two kids. Finally, reaching the stairs, we slid down the steps, thumping and laughing hysterically, as the Quaaludes kicked in. An old crone in a next door apartment banged on her wall between my place and hers a few times that evening. But if she wanted us to stop our loud noise, she was disappointed. Her pounding on the wall broke us into laughter. Later we simply ignored her each time she banged on the wall.

In a short while, we fell down exhausted on my bed, slipping out of our clothes. The "ludes" had us buzzing, our skins highly sensitive to the touch from our high. Soon enough, we began making out, performing oral sex on each other. After pausing for air, I dipped into my sandwich bag of cocaine and put it onto our private parts. We proceeded to lick it off each other. Finally, I slipped a towel beneath her behind and took a swig from a glass of cold water, spraying it into her vagina. Joanie shook in ecstasy. During a threesome, with two call girls, one of them had 'fizzed' my 'jizz' like I was doing with Joanie. It was a real ice breaker. Next, I entered her and she let out a loud moan. The bitch next door must have had her ear to the wall for she banged on her wall, again. And again, we ignored her. I was having a deliciously sweet time. I'd become a hedonist. Anything that made me feel good was all right. Later, I looked out the window of my bedroom at the tall trees in the park next door. The air was so white with snow that I could hardly see them.

The next morning, Joanie left for home. She was dressed in a snow suit. I gave her a little package. Driving was just about impossible by this time. Visibility was down to zero and the snow kept coming down. Traffic on the highways was crawling and most businesses had closed down. Even the MBTA busses and trains were affected. The airport was also closed.

The snow began to stack up by the foot. Governor Dukakis called a state of emergency and recommended that people who could stay home remain there. Around the clock television reports carried a stream of images of stranded motorists, traffic stalled on Route 128, and snow plows clearing roads that quickly were covered over again by the "white out." It was a blindingly relentless snow fall, almost shutting down emergency responses on the streets. The storm was to cause several deaths in the state due to auto accidents and heart attacks.

It must have been a horror to be stranded in a vehicle slowly running out of gas, being forced to leave the window partly open to avoid being asphyxiated by exhaust fumes. Thousands of vehicles were abandoned on Massachusetts roadways the following day.

The snowplows went to work on the third day, but it was a frustrating endeavor. There were few places to put the snow. Some of the drifts were as high as eight feet in places where the main thoroughfares were plowed.

Many people were stranded at their jobs in hospitals, broadcast stations, campuses and emergency response units.

Snow plow operators and emergency personnel were logging up hours and hours of overtime. One of my friends plowing the Mass Turnpike got in touch with me for a pack of coke powder. Apparently, a number of people out there were using it to keep going. I did as much business with my friend over those two days as I did during one week.

Although driving was restricted to emergency personnel or those in critical services, every dealer I knew had a driving permit. I was able to drive because I had journalist I.D.s from the newspaper and the radio station. When I reached the Mass Turnpike four days later, I was surprised to find that it had been plowed all the way down to its asphalt surface. I drove on the nearly empty highway at no charge. It made me feel like one of the elite to be able to drive past lines of people walking in the street. But once I saw someone I knew, I felt a moral obligation to give the person a ride.

Whenever cops challenged me for driving on banned streets, I simply showed them my press credentials. I was legit. A cute policewoman seemed particularly impressed by my papers as though I were some kind of celebrity television broadcaster, not a "drug dealer" on a duly appointed "coke run."

I drove out to the campus and picked up a photographer at the newspaper. We went to the coastal towns of Hull, Nantasket and Weymouth, where I saw the damage done by the ocean. Many homes on the shore were caved in like matchboxes from boulders washed far inland by powerful tidal waves. The beaches looked like a Tsunami had come ashore. Many of the streets were impassable with fallen trees and downed power lines blocking the way

Yet the beauty of the massive white carpet reminded me of white frosting in a fairytale land. It was more pronounced in the suburbs, where more attention was spent on the main roads. I made deliveries to many of my customers during that week when traffic was shut down. I never got stuck in the snow. I never suffered "cabin fever," forcing me to get outside. No, I was a man on the run and I had company every night of the week.

People were incredibly friendly to one another during blizzard week. It had been the storm of the century. I hoped to have that experience one more time, but it wasn't to be. Nothing of that magnitude ever came along to match The Blizzard of '78, during the twentieth century.

☙ ❧

Chapter 17:

No One Does It Like Me

In June l978, I graduated from U/Mass Boston with a Bachelor of Arts degree in English Literature, with a concentration in journalism. Having applied to graduate school in April, I was still waiting for a response. Everything I had published, every position paper, every piece of journalism and news writing: I cited them all in my resume. My grade point average, an honors B-plus, made me very optimistic of receiving an offer of employment. I received a response in July that I'd been accepted at the Boston University Graduate School of Journalism.

In August, I attended my first and last orgy in Provincetown. Early one morning, I received the invitation from a friend named Skeeta. We had met at a bank party four years earlier in New Bedford, the city that begins the highway to Cape Cod. Since that meeting, we had communicated several times although I hadn't seen her since the party; that is, our one night stand. I recall bringing her back to Boston for our first encounter and to spend the next day together.

A pretty "Port'egee" with long dark hair and large brown eyes, she was about 5 feet, 2 inches tall, with a fine figure. The last time I'd seen her, she asked me for a reference to a Madam she could work for. She seemed a little desperate to sell her body for cash. As she was reticent about the matter, I didn't push her for details. I just put her in touch with one of my Madam customers whom I knew wouldn't take advantage of her. Over a year now had passed since I'd heard anything from Skeeta. But my intuition all along was that she would be back in my life.

On the phone, she told me that she'd been living in California with a rich guy and was staying at the exclusive Ritz Carlton hotel on Arlington Street. She had also called her Madam to meet with us at the hotel. I had never been to the Ritz before. I knew that a lot of famous people stayed there when they came to Boston. My friend Lana, her boyfriend and I arrived there at the time Skeeta gave me. We drove together in my car.

The interior lobby of the hotel immediately felt to me like entering a time warp. The furniture in the lobby was retro 1940s. Persian carpets covered the floors. The elevator was old fashioned with polished brass fittings and a uniformed operator.

Skeeta's suite was set up like an apartment, furnished expensively. I believe we had drinks sent up. I was comfortable with her friend, Howie, a jeweler from San Francisco. I don’t remember bringing anything with me, but I must have brought something to sniff.

When the visit came to an end, Skeeta said that she’d call me the next day. She kept her word. The next evening she invited me to dinner with her and Howie at the Maison Robert (Maysohn Robayr) restaurant on School Street in the basement of the Old Boston City Hall. It was a classy looking joint, unpretentious, definitely a four star out of five-star rated restaurant. The food was excellent.

I recalled the eating etiquette that I learned from Ginny, who had schooled me on which spoons to use and how to carry oneself in formal settings. At the table, I didn't skip a beat when we sat down. I immediately and properly placed the linen napkin in my lap, sipped my water, placed a roll on my bread saucer to the left of me, and enjoyed myself all through the salad, and entree of lobster Rockefeller that I ordered.

It turned out that Howie was going to return to California the next day and Skeeta wanted me to go down to Provincetown with her. I don’t remember where Ginny was at this time. I hired a young woman to stay in my new apartment at 101 Tremont Street in the South End of Boston and keep an eye on things. She was once married to a medical student whom I met in a summer course at U/Mass. I trusted her, so I gave her the keys to use my BMW. And "No," reader, if you should be wondering, we never “got down.” She was simply someone I trusted and a friend.

One thing I have to note here is that the people close to me in those days were, for the most part, dependable and trustworthy. I tried to treat them the way I would like to be treated.

Having visited Provincetown the weekend before, Howie gave me the feeling that he wanted to return to California rather urgently for reasons he didn't explain. I got the feeling by reading between the lines of our conversation that he was almost burnt out by his stay in Provincetown.

The following afternoon, I met Skeeta in Somerville and we took off for P-town. At her suggestion, I was to bring at least a quarter ounce of powder with me for sale. I brought that, of course, and a little more.

When we arrived, we had dinner at a restaurant. We intended to stay at a rented summer house with a friend of hers from Boston. I guess that we might have taken a few sniffs and looked around the town. I'd visited there over the years many times and had once fucked someone (who shall remain anonymous here) under a blanket on the National Seashore. It was a fun place.

I'd gone there with Norman the summer before and we had stayed at an inn owned by his sister and her husband. The husband was white and had been the best friend of her deceased husband. When the husband died of cancer, her new husband looked out for the family, marrying the sister after about a year and assuming the role of father to her two adolescent sons. Norman's mother, who also made the trip with us, warned us about the danger of smoking marijuana.

Norman and I visited a gay bar for a little while, but there was nothing there for me. While I sipped a drink there, he cruised the bar for a partner. All the while, I wanted to go to a straight club, but there didn't seem to be any time to find a straight bar on that street of gay hangouts.

Later that afternoon I went with Skeeta to a lesbian club. She seemed a little concerned that I'd be uncomfortable, but I took it in stride. I was the only man around. I ordered a drink and moved around the place. Although a few "butch" bitches gave me "the evil eye" of hostility, as a watchdog might first greet an intruder. I smiled and ignored them.

The music was slamming and danceable. I don't know when it happened but I found myself dancing with a woman around my age who'd come with a small group of friends. We began dancing with others as the night went on. I was having a good time until I heard one of the "butches" mention the movie "Looking For Mister Goodbar" in an ominous way. It was a pointed remark meant to be overheard, and to me it appeared a reference to me. Just as in the film, I, too, might be a serial killer like the villain of the fictional film. The jibe at me was a real stretch. I laughed with my partner, a 2l-year-old woman from New York named Fran, an acquaintance of Skeeta's. At the end of the evening, "Last Dance" by Donna Summer came on and everybody got out on the floor.

A number of women joined us back to our rented house. I didn't plan on anything out of the ordinary happening. I figured I might end up in the sack with either Skeeta or Fran. Altogether, there must have been at least sixteen women in the house, even a beautiful Chinese girl. Everyone seemed friendly. Maybe I don't project a threat to women as some men do, but all the women were relaxed and quite warm to me. I've always found that what works best for me with strange women is being honest.

I produced my package of coke to sell. As I distributed it, Skeeta collected money from the customers there, and dropped it on a plate. Soon most of the women started coupling and grabbing one another, stripping and otherwise dropping their pants. I'd never seen anything like it. I joined the crowd. All of the women were fine, the types who could blurt out after one drink, as the Tina Turner song goes, "Hello, hello! Can we give it a go?"

The room, at first, was full of naked women coupling, and I went from couple to couple, muff diving here and penetrating there. I made out with whomever I pleased which was just about everyone. The coke kept me from ejaculating.

Once, I did a threesome with two girls. I laid on my back, as one of them sat on my face and the other sat on my dick, moving back and forth. Another time, I formed a triangle, with two women. It proved the truth of the saying: "What the mind can conceive, it can achieve." It was like sampling twenty flavors of ice cream over three long delicious hours.

Everyone was open. I'd been hoping to try out the Chinese girl, but she was on her period, the napkin in place. We didn't have sex, but we still made out. I was in a situation that many men dream about and never get to experience. Some even make up stories about their conquests to impress people.

These women came from all along the East Coast. I even met a long legged blonde from a horse racing family in Kentucky. Now, I understood why Skeeta's friend Howie was burned out. I made the complete circle and ended up with Skeeta. We came together in the bedroom and ended up breaking the bed. It was a wild ride. Of course, the woman who was renting the house was pissed off.

But I fixed the bed and fell asleep, snoring. Three of us shared the large bed and I can remember the woman punching my shoulder to make me stop the noise. But I was beyond waking up. As they say, " If the boy could have saved up 'fuck tickets' he woulda had enough to last for two months."

I lazed around on the "topless" beach the following day with two women from Miami. It had been a hell of a time. You might say that I've done and experienced just about everything a man could want to do. But I've never bragged about my encounters. I don't have anything to prove.

Was I "a little whore just like your uncle?" It was a question I recalled from many years ago. Two barflies asked me the question when I tried to hit on them in my Uncle Adam's bar on a visit to my relatives in New Jersey. I was new to the scene, having just turned drinking age, and I was still "wet behind the ears" as they say. The women, some with sons my age, were amused by my hitting on them. And they were familiar with my uncle Adam, a hipster, my mother's younger brother, and a hard drinker. He was also one of my favorite uncles, with a voice that sounded like Alan Ladd's baritone. When the women compared me to him, I took the comparison as a compliment, rather than a complaint. My mother, who enjoyed stories about Adam with a kind of bemusement, called him a "tough customer," a hard drinking man, who led a hard life.

Perhaps, the barflies even then saw a similarity between us. But Uncle Adam was to die young, ravaged by the consequences of living a promiscuous, hard life on the edge of the law, and the father of children born out of wedlock with different women.

When I returned to Boston, a Madam named Martha, whom I knew from the South End told me that she'd heard about a black guy named "M" or some other letter who had partied with a group of women in P-Town. She concluded that "M" was me, because no one else could have pulled off something so crazy. She explained that the woman who had rented the house was an old friend of hers. When I fessed up, she shook her head in mock dismay.

That summer, I traveled back and forth to Provincetown a few times. I even took a trip down by commuter plane from Logan Airport. An old friend of mine named Mark told me that he remembers once driving down there with me to return a dress to Fran, who had left it at my place in Boston. Mark remembered the dress.

In fact, he said he bought a BMW like the one I was driving at the time, because I let him do most of the driving, which he enjoyed immensely. I don't remember ever taking anyone with me on a trip there. My memory well may fail me about the trip because at the time, I was doing some heavy duty coke on a daily basis.

When I arrived on campus for Grad school that fall, I was heading to the bookstore with a fellow student, when surprise, surprise, who should I run into but Fran! I had no idea she was taking courses at the school. Boston is such a small town city.

One afternoon, I traveled out to Walden Pond with my dog Epic. Walden Pond's a historical site in Concord, Massachusetts, where 19th century New England pacifist, journal writer, philosopher and essayist Henry David Thoreau lived. Today it is a public park, a historical preservation wildlife reserve. This is where he wrote most of his essays. The summer day was a sunny, pleasant one. A hiker asked me if I had any reefer. He was out of touch with his dealer. I told him I only had some powder and he said he understood where I was coming from. In the 1960s-70s, people were only too happy to share a joint.

As I walked beside the railroad tracks, I came upon two guys in the woods. One was about ten years older than the other. It turned out that they were brothers. I started talking with the oldest one. Surprisingly, we had a friendly conversation. They were sitting in a small area with a dog. The younger brother wanted to leave. But Jason, the older one, and I smoked a joint and let the dogs play together. After a while, two "Staties" on horseback came along and told us that dogs weren't allowed on the pond. Jason and I exchanged telephone numbers and left one another.

Later, I called Jason in Cambridge and we started hanging out together. He was a natural comedian who became the center of attention in any room of people. His girlfriend, Debbie, was also a grad student at B.U. and was friends with the roommate of one of my classmates in the Journalism program. My life was indeed a mix of unusual coincidence and circumstance.

As we got to know one another it also came to light that one of his friends, Roger, supplied one of my suppliers, in Lexington. He was also the supplier of a group of guys in the Roxbury neighborhood where my parents had bought another house. The Boston Redevelopment Authority (BRA) had demolished the old neighborhood in order to build a large housing development and a high school complex named Madison Park. It was a misguided attempt to end Roxbury's slum housing, under its then director Edward Logue, rather than an attempt to improve the neighborhood in consultation with its residents.

We had many parties with plenty of weed and coke at a large apartment in Brighton rented by a friend named Debbie. We partied with her that year and the following year. Lenny, my sister, and Jason were always welcome to come over and join the party, although they did not indulge in our vices. There'd be a plate of powder on the table and people could help themselves.

I'll never forget that Thanksgiving Day when we all partied at Debbie's place with marijuana dressing in the turkey. Later that evening, my dealer Roger came to the party riding a motorcycle with a quarter pound of coke in his backpack.

About fifteen of us sniffed all night, until the sun came up the next day. Like a kid with a stomach ache, Lenny said he had never done so much cocaine at one sitting. He complained that he felt nauseous from the encounter. At higher income levels of the consumption chain, people seemed exceptionally generous with expensive powder.

One afternoon, as I made to deliver a drop to one customer named Martha in the South End, I encountered a problem. I knew she was feuding with one of her gay neighbors at the time. I double-parked in front of the building and then waited inside her front entry for about ten minutes, thinking she would answer her door bell, when she called to me from her front room window: "That little queen called the cops," she said. "The cop gave you a ticket."

I made my way to the front steps that led to the street and looked down to see the little "queen" standing there with his arms crossed. There was a ticket on the windshield and the cop was standing by his car. Seeing me, he called out: "M!"

It was Jackie's brother, Jack, who had left U/Mass to become a cop. He walked back to the car and took the ticket off, tearing it up. The Madam and the "queen" were speechless. Legends are made like this.

Around the first of the year, Carlos left the country, having divorced his wife and, according to what I'd heard, abandoning his tenement in East Boston. There were tenants there, according to rumors, who didn't know where to send their rent. Before Carlos left town, he forgave me about two thousand dollars that I owed him; and he forgave a debt close to my amount of another friend in the same boat. Few people get rich in the cocaine business because of the seductive quality of the drug once you start consuming it. Once you started sniffing, it was easy to rack up a balance with your supplier.

Another dealer named John, in the meantime, had already left town with his family. He gambled away a large piece of money belonging to his suppliers. It was his greed that undid him. I often warned him about gambling, but he hadn't listened. I think I remember Carlos complaining that John owed him money as well.

By the spring of l979, I was on the way to completing my first year at the Boston University School of Journalism. That year, the university's instructors and professors went on strike to protest the conservative administration of the tyrant of the hour, B.U. President John Silber. For me, the strike was a lesson in politics. It seemed to some faculty members, that Silber had spies in every academic department. Other faculty, however, thought that a strong leader was needed at the helm of a great university and they excused his excesses.

My professor was also the dean of the department and he refused to participate in the strike. Always a company man from his days as a news director in New

York City, he fought against the strike although his position came under union guidelines and he was not exempt from the work action.

As students, we had to decide for ourselves whether to honor the picket line. Most were in favor of the strike, an easy position to take when you didn't have to give something up in support of it. But to give up your classes that you were paying for? That was a horse of a different color. Even some of the students from union families were put in the middle, between their self-interest and their principles. I was in favor of the strike and stayed away for a few days.

One of my professors who taught us FCC rules and regulations was a white-haired Jewish man who took the strike seriously and ranted at those who crossed the picket line. When the strike ended, there were still some hard feelings in the department.

In the real world outside the universities, the 70s' decade was one of one-term presidencies: President Gerald R. Ford, a bungler; President Jimmy Carter, a good man, but one too politically pragmatic rather than principled, especially about advancing civil rights for racial minorities and women. Carter gave the impression that he would not push from in front of politically contentious policies, but from behind. That is, he would offer to lead a winning constituency promoting an agenda that he supported, but not until the constituency was winning its fight would he enter it to lead them. I can't put my finger on anything specific to document my concerns about Carter, but it bothered me that the blacks within his inner circle of advisors were "good ole boys" like Rev. Andrew Young. I even had questions about the meaning of his religious faith. After all, so many of those "born again" Southern Christians like Carter were as prideful and hateful in their heart of hearts toward black people as the regular whites, that I was unable to fathom the difference.

I began to view President Carter with dismay after he forced Andrew Young, his "ace boon coon," from office after the Israelis complained about his off-the-record meetings with officials of the Palestinian LIberation Organization (P.L.O.). Yet informal "off-the-record" meetings for non-attribution of our diplomats with an adversarial group was a practice long part of our diplomacy. Even the Israelis, who led the protest against Young's P.L.O. meeting, themselves, secretly engaged in lately publicized meetings with Palestinian leaders.

Carter also wasn't interested in reforming the drug laws and gave the same lip service to the problem of illegal drugs as his predecessors. There was a mini-scandal about coke sniffing in the inner circle during his presidency.

The hostage taking of our Teheran Embassy staff following the fall of the Shah doomed Carter's re-election as President. I will always suspect that the Reagan campaign encouraged the Ayatollah to draw out the release of our hostages in negotiations with the Carter administration to win the election. Refusing to release the American embassy staff until after the election, the Iranians gave Reagan a weapon to keep the Carter rescue failure on the minds of the electorate when they entered the voting booth.

But back to my situation, I concluded now that the bitch next door was eavesdropping on me, listening through the walls to my conversations and running to her peephole to see who was coming to my apartment. I knew she had an intense dislike of me and was dangerous. People like her, when they fucked over or snitched on the wrong person in the neighborhood at the time, wound up in the garbage dump. And while I would not have gone so far as to violently retaliate, I could easily have named her as a dangerous snitch to my dealers, who might well have silenced her for good. I was on to her, so I never let down my guard when I suspected she could observe or hear me. Besides, she didn't have any evidence of my dealing, neither did she have witnesses against me; and she did not have more credibility than me with the police.

She once publicly challenged me in the building parking lot, accusing me of selling heroin. I felt miserable, unable to physically throttle her, because she didn’t know what she was talking about. She even mentioned part of a general conversation about sports I’d had with a friend; it was to let me know she could listen to my conversations through the wall between our apartments.

One afternoon in the spring, I had a Sunday afternoon function with a number of classmates and good friends. It wasn’t a noisy gathering; and for the most part my guests were having quiet conversations. But the shrew called the cops and tried to get them to come out claiming I was making a lot of noise. One of my friends who was a Boston cop was also at the party. There was hardly any drug activity going on. The cops on patrol that day refused to take her complaints seriously and didn't come out to the building. A neighbor told me that the woman was going around to other apartments trying to get them to complain about me, too, but there were no takers.

As a precaution, I then all but closed my apartment to any business except for two or three people. Someone took the nameplates off the bells for the four apartments in my section, forcing me to test out each bell so I could fix things. The woman then tried to accuse me of the nameplate mischief.

It was a new customer, then, someone I'll here call Rex, a student from U/Mass, who brought matters with her to a head. He worked with me at the student newspaper, wore glasses and semi-long hair like a hippie. By provoking an incident I'll describe below, he enabled me to confound my enemies living with me as neighbors.

Rex and I had problems early on in our relationship. Soon after we met, I had it out with Rex about his practice of going into the bathroom as soon as I sold him a package of coke. One night I soon discovered a drop of blood on the floor near the toilet, just after I sold him some coke and he had returned, yet again from my bathroom, his face flushed bright red. He seemed quite high; and clearly he was shooting up in my bathroom. Not only was he ignoring my demand that he not shoot up in my place, so as to expose me to the law, but he showed maximum disrespect for me. He was jeopardizing my safety and his by carrying needles and syringes. I threatened to cut him off after that. Lucky for him, the AIDS virus among drug users was still years away from the states. But from then on, I insisted that

Rex use the emergency stairs whenever he came to my place to buy a "hit." The stairs were three steps away from my door and the building exit door; and I could hear my neighbor running to her front door every time my bell rang. I knew that the broad was trying to set me up for a bust. One day I decided to fuck with her, blocking her peephole with my hand as I passed by her apartment door to let someone buzzing my doorbell come inside.

A few days later, I was summoned to a meeting with the management and the cops; and she was there, accusing a tenant downstairs of buying drugs from me and using the stairs to reach my apartment. She was adamant in her identification of the tenant as my customer. But the only thing this tenant had in common with Rex was his white skin color. Otherwise, although the same height, the two white men looked nothing alike. The bitch was so far off the mark that the tenant, who had never stepped inside my apartment, nearly slapped her. The police didn't believe her. All of this was happening under my nose and I didn't have a clue. This goes to show you how people can get ambushed out of nowhere. God must have been on my side.

Two weeks later, the bitch was evicted by the management and the reason given was for having a pet poodle, which was a crock. A week before that the tenant came up to my apartment and told me what had happened.

Everything settled down and another couple moved into the apartment next to me. It was a black guy and a white girl, Lenny and Terry. From the sound coming through my walls between our two apartments, Terry's screams, the loud curses from Lenny, the sounds of someone being slapped, the shaking of the floor and loud bumps against our common walls, I gather that he beat her on the sly, that is, behind closed doors. One night, soon after one particular beating, when, as they say, her morale had not improved with his pummeling her, she came to my apartment and asked for refuge, which I gave her. Lenny kicked her out because he had rented the apartment in his name.

We slept in the same bed that night, but I didn't try to seduce her or take advantage of her situation. The next day, when we heard her boyfriend leave the apartment, she said that she wanted to retrieve her clothes and belongings before he returned. She decided to then re-enter his apartment, climbing over the railing of my balcony to his adjoining balcony and sliding open his patio door.

Lenny knew that she was staying with me, since he could probably hear her sobs and our conversation as I tried to calm and reassure her that she was safe with me. When he returned to his place to find her things gone, he knocked on my door and wanted to know whether I had been in his place while he was gone. Before I could deny it, he began to get testy and "bad ass" with me. He had a body like the hulk only he was shorter. But he knew I wasn't prepared to let him intimidate me. He knew that I was well connected, but he didn't know what I had to defend myself. So I shut my door in his face without bothering to answer him. And he walked away. The next few days passed, and he seemed to cool down. We passed each other without incident. By the end of the week, he was calling and apologizing, promising and begging her to forgive him; incredibly to me, she gave in to him. Although I had my reservations, she decided to move back into his place. To my surprise, a pleasant one for sure, I had no more problems with my neighbors.

At the end of May, I came home one afternoon and saw a couple of fire engines in the parking lot of my building. I was curious enough to park up the street in front of the building, and observe. As I stood on the sidewalk, a little girl, the daughter of a neighbor who knew me, came over and said there'd been a fire in my apartment. I walked into the building with a feeling of dread. Taking the elevator to the sixth floor, I could smell the smoke damage. I reached my duplex apartment where the door was still open and walked into my place. I was in a state of shock. The smell was noxious. Much of the upstairs hallway rug leading to my place and my bedroom had black smudges left by the firemen's rubber boots. But the rest of the building suffered little damage other than smoke stains on the hallway ceiling and walls. Inside my place, I found my living room to be nearly impassable. The floor was covered with uneven stacks of burnt wet furniture, and what had once been a twenty-five year collection of record albums and books.

My album collection of 33 r.p.m. vinyl records, once a source of immense listening pleasure, was melted together and stacked unevenly in a pile a foot high across the floor; the record jacket covers were burnt to a crisp; all that remained of them were ashes. My precious memories! Now, just a pile of ashes! As I swept them into a trash bag, I realized that even though I had enjoyed the fruits of my illegal labors, an accident had now made it all for naught. Sure, I'll admit that with my ill-gotten profits from dealing drugs, I enjoyed new cars, fast women, foreign vacations, even traveling to Peru, land of the Incas—things I could never had done without drug money. But fate was starting to play cat and mouse with me. My sudden misfortune told me that my gods were abandoning me.

In my life as a street hustler, I never believed that I was all that special. What I tried to do was to make the best of a tricky life situation, the dice life had thrown me to play. I lived by the adage: "If you're gonna do wrong, you'd better do right."

Several of the maintenance men came up to my burnt-out apartment. I knew they didn’t like me and were secretly pleased with what had happened. But I also knew that since I hadn’t left any cigarettes burning in my place, the fire was not my fault. Although I could have screamed in frustration at finding a lifetime of memories destroyed, they never saw me sweat. Putting my mind to work, I figured that someone had probably reached the roof, crossed to my patio, and forced open the sliding door. Someone like the Lenny next door who beat up his girlfriend? Who knows? I was resigned to never finding out for sure; I didn't have the time to investigate, nor the funds to hire an investigator to find the reason for the fire.

The Fire Marshall report found no arson, however, which rejected my suspicions. The source of the fire on the report remained unknown. And as I didn’t have the apartment insured, I knew that I wouldn’t be getting any money from insurance, either. It was bad luck all around.

Tina, a girl who lived in another apartment, came up to my place, hugged me, and simply put five hundred dollars in my hand that I didn't have to pay back. Neither Lenny nor Terry offered to help me. One of my new suppliers gave me a used sofa and table for an apartment in another building next door.

My new apartment was above ground about two stories, but was bordered by a hillside next to the living room window, between the two buildings. The only way I could feel safe would be for me to have bars inside the window. Otherwise, I was sure that I'd suffer a break-in before I could settle into it. All the while I moved, I was hoping to get my old apartment back after it was fixed up; it being the best apartment in the building. I suspected that the management was determined not to give it back, which turned out to be correct. So I was living in limbo, unhappy with my new place and wanting to move again. But where?

I had been keeping my stash at my parent's house on Mount Pleasant Ave; but I discovered that some was missing when I ran out of product sooner than I should have from my accounts. I suspected that my brother was hitting my stash with a vengeance to the point that I was in debt for four thousand bucks and would have to sell my car to cover the loss. I found out later, too, that my creditor, who, deeply in debt, had to be bailed out by my mechanic in Cambridge. For a long time, unbeknownst to me, he had been one of his bankers. The mechanic now needed cash from my BM, to cover the money he'd put up to help my creditor for the drugs my brother had consumed without paying me for them. I was so angry that I told the creditor that my brother was responsible and told him to have his people contact him for their money. He believed me and someone contacted my brother. But my brother was so defiant that they couldn't reason with him and I was forced to let the car go. No one, least of all my brother, was going to be killed over four grand.

It was like being hit by three strikes. The wheel had come full circle with a vengeance. I lost my scholarship to Grad school and was forced to look for work. The grant papers had arrived to be signed, but the mail went to my mail box for the old apartment and I'd missed the application deadline. I wanted to reapply to the school but I was told all the money for the first year was due in full. I didn't have three thousand bucks. I left Brighton and the friends I'd made and returned to Roxbury to regroup. I let Ginny stay in the new apartment and got a call about two months later. She said, "You're not going to believe this …." What happened was that the entire building at 101 Tremont Street had burned to the ground! Isn't life strange?

So it was that I faced the 80s and the Reagan years, busted and broke. The good news was that I had escaped the initial scourge of AIDs hitting the streets among drug users and others. Just in time, I also managed to keep myself away from the crack epidemic and violent street madness. I still had my health and freedom.

A number of people who were friendly to me, I suspected, were happy to see me down and busted. But I knew my luck would change. It always did. I remember calling Marilyn one night to tell her I'd changed and a man answered. I wanted to let her know that I had finally accomplished something. I'd graduated from U/Mass and was going to go to Grad school. "There's a man in my life," she told me. We hung up without further words. There was no going back.

All I had were my memories of the two decades that changed America. For the life of me, I can't figure out why things ended up the way they had. All I knew for sure was that there were better days to come. I meditated on regular readings from Psalms in the Bible as much as possible. I believed that if things were to come to a head and I was going to fall, I'd rather not think about it until it was over.

☙ ❧

Chapter 18:

Everybody Had a Hand Out

The 80s were the decade of the "Just Me Generation," as some pundits would label it, when greed everywhere seemed to be virtue. At least that's what Michael Douglas said in the persona of his character Gordon Gekko in the block buster movie "Wall Street." Corporate raiders were on a buying frenzy, taking over and selling companies in a wild west atmosphere endemic to the early days of the "Gold Rush." It was a decade when the rich got richer and "voodoo economics" became a part of the popular lexicon.

On March, 28, 1979, an accident in Dauphin County, Pennsylvania, at the Three Mile Island nuclear reactor seemed to threaten major urban communities north of the reactor such as New York City. Media photos of poisonous radioactive steam rising into the atmosphere from the reactor caused national panic in many communities. The accident made real the fear of a nuclear meltdown from a reactor, seemingly just as opponents of such reactors had predicted. The accident occurred just as a film thriller, "China Syndrome," hit national theater chains with a plot centering on a fictional meltdown. The story involved a reporter teaming up with a nuclear activist (played by Jane Fonda and Jack Lemmon) to expose to the public the mismanagement and cover-up of a radioactive leak. The film's release on March 16, less than two weeks before the Three Mile Island breakdown, was a hell of a coincidence. The Hollywood film studio producing the film had struck it rich with a blockbuster. Suddenly politicians were demanding a halt to new nuclear plants as a source of electric power for domestic consumption. It would be years before many politicians returned to defending nuclear power for civilian use.

In November, Republican candidate Ronald Reagan won the election for President. Although I didn't care much for Reagan, I had long ago soured on Democratic President Jimmy Carter who Reagan defeated for a second term. As previously mentioned, I didn't respect Carter after he'd given Civil Rights leader Andrew Young the boot as our United Nations Ambassador. The reported reason was political, of course. Not long after taking office at the U.N., Young met informally with the Palestinian U.N. observer mission. As soon as the Israeli lobby found out about it, they leaked accounts of Young's secret meetings to the media. Israeli supporters in Congress and editorials protested across the country even though it was widely known in the media that the Israelis had been holding talks with the Palestinians.

Clearly, what Israelis could do in their national interest was forbidden to Americans acting in their country's interests. At least, that appeared to be the case to many leftist critics of Israel. The Israeli lobbyists were politically better organized on Capitol Hill than the leftist supporters of the Palestinians were. They complained to Carter about Young's secret talks. A public firestorm in the American press was mostly supportive of Israel's criticism of Young. It was also critical of the White House for not distancing itself from Young's apparent acting undiplomatically or unilaterally without instructions from the White House. To limit the political damage to Carter's re-election prospects, the White House issued a statement saying that Young's meetings were unauthorized. President Carter accepted Young's resignation, which most people believed Carter had demanded. Many African American supporters of Carter began to share my view that Carter was weak and unreliable as an advocate of Civil Rights for us. We clearly had to look elsewhere for a leader on the national stage.

When Ted Kennedy challenged Carter for the presidency in the Democratic primary, Ted gave Kennedy lovers like me dreams of Camelot's return; but a disastrous interview where Ted was unable to articulate the reasons he deserved to be president had taken him out of the race, at least for most Democratic delegates at the convention where he won the re-nomination.

Carter's publicized collapse while jogging, however, was another sign of weakness to me, as was his claims of being attacked by a rabbit in his fishing boat, and his botched attempt to rescue American hostages in Iran.

His failed Iranian rescue did the most to destroy American public confidence in his leadership during the 1979 campaign. And he didn't stand a chance against Reagan.

While I had expected changes in the drug laws during the Carter Administration, nothing happened. There'd been rumors about coke sniffing in the West Wing, but the President made it perfectly clear time after time following such press rumors that the rumors were false.

Closer to home, I was pleased about the house my parents had bought on Mount Pleasant Ave, in Roxbury. The neighborhood on our end of the street was quiet in the evening and bustling during the day. A Catholic school was located across from our house. However, the other end of the street was known as a haven for drug addicts and other miscreants who gave the street a bad name.

The highlight of the previous year had been the visit of Pope John II to our area, when he came to Boston. I had only to walk down the street to the corner of Mount Pleasant and Dudley to see Pope Paul II, helicopters flying overhead as he rode through Roxbury to demonstrate that we were "somebodies," too.

Soon I paid off my creditors and was working at a new job delivering lunches to senior citizens. Although I'd been hired at the social service agency as a staff photographer, I was shifted to my waiting position after the photography position wasn't funded. Lenny had warned me that I was going to lose many of my customers with my change of address but I wasn't worried. I had more than enough clients. Besides, working allowed me to be less dependent on drug money.

There was a store near Dudley Station where nickel bags were sold. It was the only store I'd ever seen which was completely boarded up. If you didn't know it was open, you would have thought it was an abandoned building. Just about everyone in Roxbury knew about the place. I had once sold a couple of pounds to the owner, who was an old man. But he got a better price from his regular supplier and no longer did a lot of business with me. I never gave him my phone number or my real name during our deals.

On this particular day, the place made the news headline. Local newspapers reported that the old man shot and wounded a detective visiting the place with several other cops. The report I read described how a cop, who had returned inside after looking through the front window, observed the old man passing a bag of reefer to someone. But the "skinny" to the story I heard through my sources was that a detective had gone inside to threaten the old guy for more payoff protection money; and when the man refused, the "Dick" leaped over the counter and the old man shot him. Word around the Roxbury Court labeled the detective a corrupt asshole.

The incident was blown up in the press, because the old man claimed he shot the cop in self-defense when the cop threatened to beat him up. It was a big story. As I thought about the news account, I concluded a different scenario. Unless the cop had x-ray vision, he couldn't have peered through the wood panels nailed over windows into the store. There was something fishy about the shooting. I had to say something to someone.

I contacted a friend in the press and asked him if he had seen the storefront. He said he had. All I had to do was ask how anyone could look through a boarded up window? And that was all it took. The case heated up, with community leaders calling for an investigation into the shootings, and the feds got involved. When the investigation made public revelations of the crooked protection payoffs to the police, the shooting incident was responsible for a shakeup in the command staff of the Boston Police in Roxbury.

The old man went to prison for shooting the detective, but I learned from my sources that he snitched out the cops as part of a plea deal reducing his sentence for attempted murder to a lesser charge. The "Dick" retired under a cloud on a disability pension. He tried to file a suit sometime later, but I don’t think the law suit went anywhere.

I had just made the acquaintance of several new contacts from the Dominican Republic. The Dominicans were taking over the distribution of cocaine in Boston. My friend Jason moved to California, but I still had access to a mutual friend, Lena. I had gone to school with her and her first husband during the years when U/Mass was located at Park Square in Boston. A friend of Jason's who had livened up my Thanksgiving party the year before was her supplier. One thing about the Boston drug scene was that everyone sooner or later ended up knowing the same people.

I was on a roll. I'd been given the formula on how to make rocks by a South American student, after having spent years trying to figure out the formula in the labs of several colleges. Rocks were a method used to determine the quality of "pure" cocaine. The more rocks in a package the more you could charge for the product.

Of course, knowing how to make rocks gave me an edge in the coke business: access to the major suppliers. You might call me a chemist of sorts. I must have been smoking too much of my product. Sometimes, I compared myself to the chemist in "The French Connection" who tested out the purity of the heroin. I usually charged an amount of product for my services.

I hardly thought about the dangerous consequences of my actions anymore, telling myself that if I were caught in a major bust I had only to keep my mouth shut. But it was never a well-thought out plan, for I had no idea what I'd do when and if I were busted. Anyone facing ten years in prison, even in the act of protecting a relative could be expected to have second thoughts about taking the risk of arrest. I knew many people who talked a good game about "taking the weight," until they got busted.

I remember once visiting a house off Quincy Street in Roxbury where a family of Dominicans lived. I'd gone there to buy a large package, but they were new to me, and really strangers. I'd run out of product that day and had customers getting in touch with me for a "hit." Once at the house, I found a black guy making a buy from the dealer. I'd never seen the black guy before, but as I walked into the room where my contact was talking with him, he immediately refused to make his transaction. The contact called me to come back to meet the person, but I ignored him. Something caused me to back away. I followed my instincts.

The following night when I went to see the contact, the street was blocked by state police cars. The cops were packed inside the house. The other guy had been an undercover "Statie." Nobody knows how many snitches are potentially out on the streets. The former convicts turned police informants are the most dangerous to dealers, but the ones undercover are almost impossible to spot until it is too late.

A few Colombians had recently arrived in Boston but those in the know warned me to beware of the Columbian dealers. Although the Colombians were some of the nicest people you could want to meet and would give you whatever you wanted on credit, if you fucked up on paying them back, they would not only kill you, but if they couldn't find you, they would kill your family.

By this time, I had gone over to the wild side with a vengeance, even as I was determined to keep a regular job. It was the smart thing to do. I was thirty-seven years old and divorced. The times were changing. Smoking a pot pipe was becoming the "in" thing for users to do but there was always a new fashion in dealing and consuming.

In 1979, I recall meeting a black man with a cane at the Piano Factory Building on Tremont Street in the South End. He had paraphernalia that looked like a small chemistry set with vials of liquid in a back pack. Lenny was our go-between, arranging for the man to show me what freebasing was about.

Taking a portion of powder, the man mixed it with ammonia and rinsed the solution with ether. He then poured the solution through a cloth until there was a small pile of crystals remaining on the surface. This he scraped together into a pile and put a portion onto the edge of a knife blade.

Opening up a small carrying bag, he took out a long stemmed glass pipe and put the crystals into its bowl. I watched in fascination as he took out a small repair torch from the bag, ignited it and pointed its blue flame at the bowl. The substance sizzled and disappeared into a stream of smoke which he inhaled through the stem.

After everyone had taken a hit, I wanted to go again. I got my wish. My powder, which I had donated for the demonstration, was again my tuition for his lesson. When freebase smoking came on the street scene, the dealing game changed. And I was one of the first dealers to experience the future, just before the madness began.

The end of 1980 turned on a low note, December 8, when the former Beatles John Lennon, then only 40 years old, was shot and killed in New York by a crazed fan. Lennon's murder cast a pall over Christmas and set up a spike for companies offering personal bodyguards for anyone able to afford one. For someone to shoot John Lennon made no sense. From this day forward, celebrities realized, it had become dangerous to be famous.

☙ ❧

Chapter 19:

Do You Believe in Magic?

New Year's Eve of l981 started out to be rather depressing. I had little money and nowhere to go. Often, there was a drought of drugs around the new year. Everyone I contacted that month was either out on the town or sold out. So, I stretched out on my bed and watched the festivities from Times Square on the TV. But like a magic moment, a call came out of the blue, as it were, to relieve my boredom. The call was from a Brighton Madam here named Merrilyn who supervised a house with a group of girl clients of mine. She came from South America, a very attractive woman in her mid-thirties, with long black hair and sparkling blue eyes that lit up her face when she smiled. She had a kind of Spanish accent reminding me of Ricky Ricardo, the husband of Lucille Ball on the television comedy.

Merrilyn and her married boyfriend, Jorge, owned a restaurant on Commonwealth Avenue near Kenmore Square, a fancy place that wasn't making a lot of money. I planned one day soon to get down with her girlfriend, a pretty blonde girl. Presently, however, the girl was the last thing on my mind. I needed revenue. And when Merrilyn called me about a deal, it was just what I needed. I don't know how I managed to have so much luck in such a cut-throat business as the drug business, but I did. Merrilyn asked me to come out to her place. Since she hadn't mentioned wanting anything I presumed that she had something. She'd also asked me to bring my scale. I borrowed my sister's car, without telling her of my mission, and went to Allston where Merrilyn lived.

When I arrived she sat me down and told me that she believed I was the only person she could trust and she needed my help. After a few moments of small talk, she went to a closet and brought out a quarter pound of cocaine. I hadn't seen that much powder since the time I visited Carlos' apartment in East Boston. I assured her that she was absolutely correct in choosing me. I was one of the few nice guys in the business, someone she could trust.

She explained that she had met a “trick” who liked her a lot. He had returned to New York and had given her this powder to help her get out of the sex business. That was all right with me. I let her know that I’d help her move the powder.

As I proceeded to measure packages of powder for sale, she told me she'd had a falling out with her girlfriend over this stroke of good luck. I knew that jealousy was a deadly sin in this business and that women in the life had a tendency to get jealous over stupid things. It came with the territory. Sometimes, men got into pissing contests as well.

After I'd finished making her the packages, she gave me a little package with three grams inside. I thanked her and left. She was the persona of the hooker with a heart of gold. There was no way I wouldn't do all in my power to keep her safe. A longtime wish of mine had come true; I had control of all the cocaine I could ever want.

Before long word went around the call girl circles that Merrilyn and I were in business together. It was impossible to keep something like that a secret for long. All I could hope for was to move the powder as quickly and as safely as possible. The best method for moving this kind of "weight" is to move it within a certain time frame. Not too fast or too slow. Keeping in mind that an urgent time factor must never govern your actions by causing you to do something stupid is the best way to survive. One fatal example would be to deal with someone you didn’t know very well because they had a fistful of dollars. The man from nowhere with big pockets would always set off alarm bells for me as a possible police informant.

After moving a large load, the ideal move is to lay off doing anything for about a month before starting up again. This allows you to see the forest and the trees, while enabling you to keep up with what is happening with your customers. I had ears in law enforcement that kept me abreast of who got busted or was being watched.

Once, a prison guard tried to set me up for a police grab at a small package drop in a borrowed car. We were in a large housing complex on Huntington Avenue, near Brigham Circle. He and a young boy who had gotten in the car suddenly tried to grapple with me from the back seat. I managed to smash an elbow into his face and break free. When I threatened to go over to a police car parked a short distance away, advising them that I was working undercover and, if they didn't back off, I'd signal my partners, the "guard" flashed his badge at me and they left me alone in the car.

I went to police headquarters, where a friend was running the night shift. He made a call to the Commissioners' Office of Prisons and after talking to someone there gave me the news that the guard had been suspended for a drug violation and hadn't turned in his badge. I concluded that the guard was trying to have me busted to win his position back.

My friend told the party on the other end what had happened, and after hanging up the phone turned to me, saying that the guard's badge was going to be picked up. If I'd been so inclined, this gave me an opening to set up a target for reprisal. But I decided to wait for another opportunity to expose him to the police, a time when I needed to save myself. If anyone was expendable, it was going to be the guard, not me.

Merrilyn and I had become very close. I liked her boyfriend, Jorge, who was married and lived in Lowell.

We moved the quarter pound in two weeks. I'd done most of the work through my contacts, selling packages of a half ounce or less. I knew she wanted to take advantage of this opportunity to change direction in her life and I told her I'd try to find someone to take over her call girl business.

It was a satisfying feeling the first time we stacked all of the money on a table. The stacks amounted to over eight thousand dollars. I had no car at this time but with the powder and the money I controlled, it was easy for me to rent a person's car or get a ride whenever I needed it.

Just as I had enemies, however, Merrilyn also had people who were jealous of her for reasons I couldn't understand. There was another madam named Marcel who was jealous of Merrilyn, despite being the success story of a woman in "the life." Marcel lived in an apartment building she owned in the last block of Marlborough Street across from the Boston Public Gardens. The property was priceless, worth close to a million bucks. She was extremely tight fisted with her money. Yet, Marcel was a trip. She had demons that caused her to get drunk at times and pull her hair out. Once she'd made a bet with one of her girls that the girl couldn't sniff up all of my powder without fucking me. The girl who was black had succeeded and won the bet after staying in my room for almost two days. The bet might have gone the other way, except I tired of the girl's relentless chatter, losing any interest in sex with her. I never forgave Marcel for setting me up. But, as in many human endeavors, one's enemy today might turn out to be a friend tomorrow.

☙ ❧

Chapter 20:

Everybody Needs Somebody Sometime

I'd come in contact with an old friend from my days in Holiday Magic named Arturo. He had done well on the retail side of the cosmetics business and had a large group of customers. Even after the company was shut down, he'd continued to sell the products to his customers. Arturo had put me in touch with his brother-in-law, Elroy, who owned a 280 Z. I ended up using the car whenever I needed it.

Arturo knew what I was doing in the drug business. He was only interested in marijuana. He was a self-taught fix it genius, who owned several apartment buildings. He had also worked in his father's printing shop for years. He could repair any of the machines in the shop, which was located near the other end of Mount Pleasant Ave.

Before long I found myself spending time around Arturo, who came from a prominent family. One of his uncles was a doctor who had an office near Grove Hall. One of his brothers was also a physician. Another brother, who was my age, lived at the family home on Dudley Street and had shocked me one day when he showed me a photo of myself as a teenager, taken at a junior high track meet. Sometimes, it seemed that I was always getting surprised.

One thing I noticed about Arturo was his business acumen. He was always busy making money at his different pursuits, which also involved furnace and water heater repair work as well as home renovations. He seemed to be getting work orders whenever he had any spare time.

Arturo was still a square in many ways, but he wasn't anybody's fool. On weekends, he could usually be found in his private den, which was off limits to his three sons. He had a VCR set up inside so that he could watch porno movies undisturbed. Still he wasn't a wanderer outside his marriage.

Being a landlord enabled Arturo to have a licensed pistol. One day I had him buy a blackjack for me with his permit. Although I had a firearms I.D., a blackjack was off limits for purchase because it was considered to be a dangerous weapon, on par with a handgun.

My mother liked Arturo and his work ethic. I remember her telling him that she hoped he could influence my behavior in a positive way. To my chagrin, anyone who worked hard automatically scored high with my mother.

She always seemed to be more critical of me than my siblings. I realize now that what I was doing didn't make parents feel very proud of me. After all, why had I spent all those years in college to end up risking my freedom on the other side of the law?

The predatory nature that comes with being a dealer gave me the mindset of always trying to bring someone with money over to my side. Hence, Arturo had a special place in my universe. My feeling was that unless someone had some real use to me, there was no benefit in having them around. I had no use for deadbeats or lackeys. This feeling was also extended to anyone who didn't get high. That was the nature of the business.

Although Arturo couldn't seem to get high from smoking freebase, I had to give him credit for trying to get a buzz. Some people couldn't get high when they tried smoking "base" for the first time. It would take Arturo months to finally reach "Cloud Nine." In the meantime, I had other things to be concerned about.

I had kept Merrilyn out of the limelight until one evening when I brought her to my parents' house to meet my sister. They got along very well. This led to us being invited to a party in Newton at the home of a lawyer friend of my sisters. Merrilyn enjoyed it so much that she told some of the other madams about it. She'd never been around professional people in a social situation. A woman selling drugs is more acceptable to most women than a woman selling pussy. So she was able to gain easy acceptance as the owner of a restaurant who had access to a lot of cocaine.

My Madam friend, Martha, had needled me about the party and I was a little uncomfortable when she asked me why I hadn't taken her out to meet my friends. This was the same woman who had seen the cop tear up my parking ticket years before. I gave her the silent treatment, until she stopped bringing it up.

Merrilyn was my number one. I had tried to get into her pants, but she told me that we should keep things on a business level. I respected her wishes because I could get just about any woman I wanted.

I also had access to more cocaine than I would ever need and all the TVs, cassette recorders, cameras and clothes I could ever use. I was living life at the top again. But this time I was more aware that things could change at any time. It wasn't like a game, anymore. The stakes were higher.

A second package arrived. This time it was a pound. Merrilyn moved some of it through one of her friends who worked at a rare coin brokerage in downtown Boston. He and a younger man were regulars at Merrilyn's apartment. There was also a black couple who lived next door who were always welcome. They were students at Boston University. They were the only other people besides me who came over to socialize on a regular basis.

What I'd discovered was that if you acted around cocaine like a monkey in a banana factory, you were going to end up like a dead monkey. A "Scarface" character couldn't exist in real life, making coke lines with the edge of his hand. Nor would he be allowed to exist, not on the mean streets of the drug dealing life I knew.

Among my main concerns about the large amount of coke were the Madams and their whores who knew about Merrilyn's good fortune. Sometimes, Marcel would call up just to be nosy. I knew she could change like the weather and was capable of almost anything. I always delivered the product to my customers rather than use her as a distributor. None of my regular distributors or clients knew about Merrilyn. Even Elroy had to wait outside when I went to her place.

One night, Merrilyn and I ended up leaving the apartment in a snowstorm. We had one hundred grams in a plastic bag because Marcel started calling us constantly, making inquiries for bullshit reasons, such as wanting to buy in to our operation with referrals to customers. But I wasn't letting her into our thing, although I knew that she had all kinds of connections and could be vindictive.

I didn't fool myself that if someone held us up, they would probably kill us because of the possible ramifications that we might recognize them. At the time, I would have shown no mercy to a thief or anyone else who robbed us at gunpoint, in the event that I survived a robbery. It was the law of the jungle. What else could I do? I couldn't use the law for justice.

Merrilyn and I, however, had nothing to fear that night. We met her friend from the rare coin brokerage who took the package off our hands for the night. Having a large quantity of drugs or cash on hand would have been a stressful undertaking, even without traveling about with it on the street. Every phone call could be a tip-off that someone was clocking your movements, waiting for you to leave the apartment or planning to come in on you. Babysitting a package is usually done with a loaded weapon at your side, just in case. Sometimes, I'd take the package home if I became uncomfortable in the apartment.

Keeping my section of Mount Pleasant Ave "hot" was a strategy I used for safety. Any time I saw a strange car with people inside near the house, especially at night, I'd call the cops to check it out. There were only two white families on the street and they were on my end. I knew the cops were tired of my calls, but I preferred to be safe rather than sorry. I don't think they realized I was black.

I was also aware that a stakeout would be revealed if the car stayed where it was or the cops didn't show up. A couple of times, cops responding to my calls discovered a surprise in a car parked suspiciously around my building: a local whore's "trick" got caught with his pants down, the whore, too.

One night I stopped by to see a former co-worker at a weekly card game. He also had access to large amounts of powder through some Dominicans with whom he did business. I had a package with two ounces and let him see it. He bought a small amount from me. But he did it as a favor to me, to help me profit because I didn't compete with the kind of large quantities he handled. He was a major distributor in the city. There was no way I could match his Dominican connections.

Among the problems I was forced to deal with was my younger brother who had a drug problem, as did some of his friends. I wasn't very impressed with this younger crowd and didn't really need their business. But they were the source of a steady supply of hot stuff like cameras, stereos, tape recorders and cassette players.

Two days after I saw my friend at the card game, I had an ominous visit. My sister arrived home and noticed an unfamiliar car parked a few parking spaces down the street. The car had two people inside. As she tried to make out the car's license plate, the driver backed it away out of her view to keep her from taking down the license plate number. I knew that kind of feeble attempt to conceal one's car plate number from a person in a window wasn't a cop move. Suddenly backing one's car out of identifiable range when someone observed a stranger in a strange car was suspicious behavior in my neighborhood. In my experience, real cops would have come out of the car or stayed parked where they were, unlike a thief canvassing buildings for a house robbery, or unlike a hit man!

Now I knew no one would make a move on my parents' house in the daytime. There were too many residents on the street, and too many windows in the school up the street within view of our house. In the daytime, there were a considerable number of people on the street, coming and going, and we often had visitors. Also, I lived with a Doberman and two shotguns in my apartment above my parents downstairs. That day, two new tenants were moving into the next door building.

At this time, there was a set of scaffolding placed against the front of my parents' house because of outdoor gutter work. I didn't like the setup but I couldn't complain to my father. I had every reason to be concerned because the scaffolding was placed next to my window on the top floor. During that time, I clashed with my brother over some missing powder only to discover that I had misplaced it. I later acknowledged my mistaken accusation and apologized to my brother; instead of shrugging the incident off and accepting it, he went off on me, threateningly, and he went looking for one of my shotguns. But that day he couldn't find them. I would never have shot him over something so petty, but I would have defended myself against him. I was in possession of a two-shot derringer as a defensive measure against personal assaults. On the streets and in my business dealing dope, one never knew when one needed protection from assault or robbery. Dealing was a high risk business. A Madam of a local brothel who had befriended me gave me the derringer to hold for another Madam; it was my security for a package of powder.

My brother and I both cooled down in a few days. By then, so I heard, he was shooting up heroin. I believe to this day that my parents blamed me for his heroin addiction. Soon he stopped bothering me, but one of the wise guys whom he had referred to me for deliveries, came to my place looking for him. The man was so angry about a botched deal with my brother that he threatened to hurt my dog if I didn't give him a package, or deliver the whereabouts of my brother to him.

Although he became aggressive in his tone, he didn't show a weapon, perhaps assuming that his loud voice intimidated me. I didn't let him inside my front door, so he didn't see me grab my shotgun in the hall corner. I left the door open with him in the hall. If I had felt he was about to move on my dog, I believed then that I would have shot him.

But years later, as I write this, I ask myself: What would shooting him, perhaps fatally, have done to my parents? To have someone shot in their home? It would be like déjà vu for them because there had been an accidental shooting involving my brother at the other house on Oakburn Ave about ten years before.

I could picture my mother demanding that I explain cleaning up the blood and pieces of skull on her dining room floor. Knowing now what my killing someone would have done to hurt her, I thank my lucky stars that I didn't ever kill anyone. And though the guy at my door looking for my brother annoyed me no end, I gave him a small package to cool him down, and he left. When I saw my brother, I let him have it about sending his friends to me. He said he'd take care of it and have a talk with his buddy.

Incredibly, a few days later the guy came back and paid me for the package. And he let me know that he'd been so strung out that he'd wanted me to shoot him. I didn't want to shoot anyone over some leaves or powder. It wasn't worth it. But I had the minority opinion. Most dealers that I knew wouldn't have thought twice about blowing someone away. I could see that cocaine was causing people to lose their minds, especially the ones called "baseheads," that is, people who were ingesting, smoking, and otherwise addicted to cheap rock cocaine.

Base or "crack" was causing problems on a major scale across the country. There had even been a scandal at the MBTA, in Boston, when a train operator getting high on the job nearly derailed a train entering Dudley Station on a sharp curve. This was followed by a rash of firings at the Transit Authority and the introduction of drug tests on the job that brought the problem under control.

One night when I pulled up to my parents' house, there was a young black man about my brother's age standing next to a large tree in front. At first I thought he was waiting for my brother, until I noticed he was carrying a knapsack and was checking out the scaffolding still in front of the house. I knew in a flash what was going through his mind. I could have played dumb and waited inside for him to climb up to my window and come inside. I believed then that I would have been justified in shooting him. My firearms permit card allowed me to keep a rifle or shotgun in the house. Or I could have waited and when he reached the top of the scaffold, I could have forced him to jump off the scaffolding at gunpoint. The crazy part of all this was that there wasn't much of anything of value, drugs or otherwise, in our house. Walking over to him and memorizing his face, I gave him a warning about the consequences of fucking with me that had a chilling effect on him. I let him know that if anything happened at my house, I'd be waiting outside his house. I let him know that his life meant nothing to me, and I was deadly serious.

I never had any more problems after that incident. I first suspected my brother might have been behind what had nearly happened but I found out later that it was one of my old " buddies," a customer. Having once seen me in a 2-bit coke deal, he decided that I stored quantities of the drug in my house. What a stupid snake! If one of my packages had been ripped off, I would have gone to the Colombians to deal with the slime bag and I wouldn't have let anyone other than Merrilyn know of my plans.

About six months later, my "buddy" proved the truth of the saying "What goes around comes around" when he was tossed off a building by his Dominican suppliers whom he'd fucked over. The rumor on the street was that he got so strung out that he'd tried to commit suicide by leaping off the roof, which never made sense to me based on what I knew about him as someone who loved life. Sooner or later, I always got the truth. Although he was lucky to survive the fall and to walk around another day, he got out of the business.

☙ ❧

Chapter 21:

Coming Out of the Closet Could Be Dangerous

One evening I had someone give me a ride to a psychiatrist's apartment in a building undergoing renovation at the intersection of Brighton and Commonwealth Avenues in the Allston neighborhood of Boston. It was a two hundred dollar delivery. While "my ride," a female friend, waited downstairs for me, I entered the large luxury apartment complex. There were only a few people living there at the time.

The doctor opened the door to let me inside. We made small talk and he prepared to pay me when the bell rang. He answered the intercom, acknowledged his visitor, turned to me and rather bizarrely, so I thought at the time, smiled nervously: He informed me that he had to take a few moments alone with the man downstairs who was about to knock on his door. He said the visitor was a "hit man" needing to meet with him on urgent business, so he couldn't reveal that I was with him. Without letting me know more details, he asked me to hide in one of his closets. I couldn't believe my ears. But who was I to doubt this doctor? He had a deadly serious tone. Besides, the customer in such times was always right. Better to be safe than sorry. I had no need to meet a "hit man."

Leading me to a bedroom near the entrance, he directed me into a closet. He said that he wouldn't take more than a few minutes with his visitor, apologized for the inconvenience to me, and shut the door to his closet. Sitting in a corner of the closet on a pile of his dirty clothes, I waited, steaming mad. I didn't dare take a chance on being seen though. I was also unarmed.

In a few moments, I heard the apartment door open, and in the hall the murmur of voices. The scene for me was totally crazy! Who would have expected something like this to happen at a doctor's apartment no less? I badly wanted a cigarette but I knew better than to light up. I was even worried whether I was breathing too loud. What a predicament if the guy found out I was hiding in the doctor's closet. Then we'd both be in trouble. I was very tense and worried. What if I had to pee? Why was it always one thing or another fucking up my plans?

Having been in a number of bad luck situations running the streets of Roxbury, I knew just enough about bad luck to consider a troubling possibility: What if the "hit man" and the doctor got into a fight? What if the "hit man" shot or killed the doctor? And what if, after the shooting, before I could get away from the apartment, the police found me there? ...Yi-Yi-Yi, I shuddered silently to myself: I could then be involved in a whole lot of shit. I knew "the ride" was probably wondering what the hell was keeping me? Thank God, she didn't know which bell to ring. All I needed was for someone to ring up and ask how much longer I was going to be there, while "the hit man" and the doctor were meeting.

After spending about forty minutes in the dark, I heard the front door close. I stayed where I was until the doctor returned to his bedroom and opened the closet to let me out. There was nothing much for him or me to say. I took the $200 bucks he handed me, said nothing other than thanks, and rushed out of the apartment.

"My ride" was upset at my delay, even after I told her what happened. She didn't really believe me. To thank her for her trouble, I gave her a little extra powder for the wait and that seemed to calm her down. The experience was just another lesson for me of what could happen when you least expected it. Sometimes you just don't see it coming. It's a truism in any trade: "Anything can happen." And again it did.

On the 29th of January, weeks later, I got a call from Jorge, his voice cracking as he told me that Merrilyn was dead. The news stunned me, so I hardly heard him describing how she died. It happened, he said, as she left the apartment with two black students from Boston University, a man and a woman who were good customers of mine. The three of them were on their way to a café for an evening meal, about to leave Merrilyn's building. As she stepped outside, she collapsed on the sidewalk. As she lay there, she lost consciousness. Unfortunately, neither of the couple could revive her. Jorge later said that they told him that they tried to do so for a few minutes, but no matter what they did, Merrilyn was unresponsive. As their efforts failed to revive her, the girl became hysterical. Only the man kept calm enough to realize their other predicament, that if they called the city rescue ambulance, the police would soon arrive, and they would have to answer police questions that might raise suspicions. The man was savvy enough to know that the police usually called into the dispatcher the names of witnesses in an investigation, even for non-criminal ones, for a background record check. There was no telling what the police would find about Merrilyn. The man convinced his partner that the two had to abandon Merrilyn on the sidewalk in hopes that someone would find her. The girl agreed with his assessment of the situation, except to insist that he call Jorge to tell him what had happened. When Jorge finished his description of Merrilyn's death, I suddenly felt my blood run cold. The worst thing about it all was the image in my head of my good friend Merrilyn abandoned on a dark street.

Giving Jorge my condolences, I promised to call him back later when I had time to absorb the news. I hung up the phone. As I recovered from my shock, I recalled that in the past few weeks, whenever I saw Merrilyn, she seemed distracted, agitated, or exhausted. I wondered now whether she was showing some minor signs of a psychosis. I recalled vividly how in our last few meetings she often attempted to get a laugh out of me about washing her crack, or something that didn't strike me as a good laugh. Worse, when I didn't get her joke, or laugh with her, she kept repeating it long after I wanted to change the subject and get down to business. The last time we met, her coin collector joined us and she kept repeating herself again and again. When she repeated herself a few more times, the coin collector gave me a bewildered but amused glance. I thought at the time that she might be turning into her best customer for much of her product. But I didn't have any evidence for concluding that about her. Besides, I trusted her. She was a good friend to me.

But the truth, I had to admit, was what it was. Jorge revealed to me that she had been getting high, more and more frequently, in the weeks leading up to her death. Getting high and then some, every day, he said. Had I known about her binges, I would not only have been deeply worried for her, but I might have called her out on it. I would have pointed out to her that she was consuming product at about ninety percent pure, a dangerous level of purity, which no one I knew could live to consume for very long. At that level of purity, I would always cut the stuff with lactose before selling or consuming it. I would turn an ounce into another ounce and a half, without diluting its potency for the average user. But she apparently blasted off with the harmfully pure stuff around the clock. Every time I came over to make up some packages, she'd take a little and urge me to join her getting stoned. And I usually joined her, although now I felt guilty for encouraging her. In the end, it probably had killed her. But my diagnosis was not the only one that could have been true. When I spoke to Martha, Merrilyn's Madam from Tremont

Street, she told me that Merrilyn had suffered brain damage from a beating she received from a trick. I never knew of that injury from Merrilyn, and do not know whether it had anything to do with her death. Only the Madam revealed then that Merrilyn was scheduled for an operation to repair damage to her head from that beating. The prospect of going under the knife, I supposed, may have so frightened and so upset her that she started binging on product. Maybe I should have spent more time around her, looking out for her. Maybe, maybe, but now it was all too late to save her.

Sadder still, no one, it seemed, knew how to contact her family in Argentina. Jorge said he knew that her family were prominent people in the country there, but he was otherwise vague. Another story I heard was that she had been married and had left her family in South America to live in Boston. All that I knew for sure was that we had to make funeral arrangements ourselves. My sister, Jorge and I went down to the city morgue, but we were unable to see the body. It was all as depressing as hell.

Still, we managed to contact a local funeral home near the hospital. And we managed as well to arrange for her cremation. It was a shame that for all the money we had handled in our dealings, none of it was available to help us pay for her service back in her own country, even had we known where to send her remains for burial.

Later, during a discussion I had with her pathologist about the circumstances of Merrilyn's death, he informed me that her brain had a large amount of cocaine covering it. I had never known up until that time that using large amounts of cocaine causes some of it to settle on the brain. Perhaps the reason some drug tests can be taken from hair samples relates to the concentration of the drug in the head. We also discovered that the EMTs hadn't entered her apartment. Lucky for all concerned that they hadn't entered it, because had they done so, they might have alerted the police with what was probably in plain view: her stashes of coke, pot and other illegal drugs.

We knew that certain people on the outside knew about the product being kept there. But none of our little group knew how much product she had left in her place. At a later meeting of her friends and me, we discussed the need to find out what of her product remained. And when none of the others present volunteered to enter her apartment, I offered to do it.

The Madam on Tremont Street Martha was at the meeting. And she told me to expect to feel lingering signs of Merrilyn in the apartment. The next day, Jorge gave me the key and waited outside. I entered and could feel Merrilyn's presence, plus the faint smell of her. I wasn't afraid. She was a good friend.

I had just entered the closet and was going through coat pockets, when the phone rang. It was Marcel snooping around. The phone had a long cord so I went back to the closet with her on the line. I suspected that the coin man was with her, because he intended to score at Merrilyn's for his regular package delivery. It seemed like everybody knew what was going on. Marcel, however, kept me on the phone, talking about nothing. A moment later, I found an ounce of product and involuntarily said something like "Uh." Marcel picked up on it right away and I knew that she knew I'd found something. I told her to tell her friend that I'd found his package. I also found a couple of hundred bucks which I gave to Jorge. I didn't find anything else in the apartment except a book with amounts of money that had been collected. The young man from Hyde Park owed a couple of hundred bucks. But the big money had been sent off as fast as we made it. I had a couple of grams at my parents' house.

When I was back in the car with Jorge, he told me that Merrilyn had been planning to surprise me by buying the 280Z for me. That caused me to sink a little more into a depression. A couple of days later, Jorge, the coin man, and I were in the crematorium at the Forest Hills Cemetery looking at Merrilyn for the last time. She was in what looked like a large wooden match box. There was a large black furnace, nearby. Her eyes were partly open, blank and glassy. The three of us said a prayer. Then, it was all over. We left before the box was placed inside the furnace.

Jorge and I got together a couple of days later. We went out to Hyde Park to collect customer money. A young guy there told me he had been arrested and the cops had taken the product. I recognized his story as an old trick to get out of paying. But I had a trick, too. I asked a customer who worked in the court system to check out the arrest reports from the South End district, where the guy lived, and my source found the man's name in the records of arrests. According to the record, he had indeed been arrested on a minor drug charge. When I explained my problem to my courthouse source, the source advised me to tell him that his probation officer wanted to hear from him.

I returned to meet with the guy the next day, gave him the message about his probation officer and told him that the Colombians still wanted their money. But he had the sense to consult his father, who contacted me, and advised me that he would tell the cops that I was using someone in the court system for extortion and black mail of his son over illegal drug money. I had no clout over the father, and I had much to lose by his threat. As I considered the father as an obstacle to my business, and as the money owed to me was a relatively small sum, I decided to chuck up the debt as a cost of doing business. I dropped the matter and never heard any more from either of them.

When I informed Jorge of our loss, he tipped me that our Colombian dealers had been curious about me, whether he thought I might have taken anything from Merrilyn without permission. He assured them that he didn't believe so. I realized from their concerns that Merrilyn might have been the source of their suspicion: Both Jorge and I knew that she had consumed more than a couple of ounces on her own from time to time. I posed the question: how much of the product meant for her to distribute to her customers did she herself consume? Clearly, the answer was something only she knew. Jorge agreed with my assessment, and I never heard anything else about the suspicions of our Columbian partners.

A few days later Jorge gave me the okay to reach out to Merrilyn's contact in New York for new business. I got a print-out of all of her long distance calls from and to New York. The Colombian connections were good ones. Every number turned out to belong to a different restaurant. I called the connections from a secret phone office at New England Telephone, one of the kind used by law enforcement. Promising as my efforts seemed, the whole development soon came to an abrupt end before we could realize any returns on them. It started when Martha called me to relay a message for me. It was from Marcel who wanted to pay me a reward if I would let her have Merrilyn's client book. Now Marcel knew better than to call me herself. But when I asked Jorge about it, he told me that he'd found the book and had thrown it away. Whether he was telling the truth or not, I didn't care. I passed the message along.

A couple of months later, there was a new program on TV similar to '60 minutes' called "Day One" with Forrest Sawyer. It featured a segment on a Colombian with the same name as Merrilyn's man, who was setting up a cocaine network across the country. A nationwide alert had been issued for his arrest. But he was never caught, so far as I know.

A month later, I met a new supplier who had recently arrived from the Dominican Republic. The man and his wife had a group of illegal aliens crowded into his apartment in South Boston, sleeping on the living room floor. They were simple farm boys for the most part who barely spoke English. They were for all practical purposes his slaves forced to sell drugs as part of the price for being smuggled into America.

The players were changing in the drug business. A lot of the people who had started out with me were no longer on the scene. I would discover later that the normal turnover rate is each season in a business where there's no guarantee you'll survive more than a year. I was a lucky son of a bitch.

I'd been planning to buy the 280Z from Elroy; but he asked that instead of my putting money down as a deposit toward buying his car, I would give him powder. Later, I would find myself on a collision course with him when I was unable to buy the car.

While Elroy was in the service he had gotten himself locked into a long term financial arrangement with GMAC that bordered on robbery. He'd wanted to buy the car so badly that he'd signed the papers without checking out the interest rate which was so high it could be called legalized usury, which means the terms were close to those of a loan shark. The figure at the end of the contract was over $3,000 more than the car was worth. I'd even called GMAC trying to make a deal by offering to make a payoff two years ahead of time at a reasonable price. They refused to entertain my offer, saying they wanted the full amount regardless of an early payoff. Then, for reasons entirely his own, Elroy began a hostile attitude towards me.

One day, he told me he wasn't going to pay me back for the powder I'd given him to secure the purchase of his car. Now the deal was dead. In other words we would both have to take our losses, which really meant tough shit on me. What angered me most was that I had been generous to a fault with Elroy since he had helped me out over time. His greed now canceled out my obligations to him for his past help to me. When he realized that the gravy train with Merrilyn had come to an end, his true feelings about me appeared. It suddenly became clear that he had no interest in helping me any longer. He only was interested in helping himself.

I decided to consult with my sister who had just passed the bar. I looked at powder as a form of currency that was as good as money. You could use it to get automobiles, goods, services, and sex. I'd even used drugs to get auto repairs and in another case some dental work done.

We decided to take him to small claims court for the cash value of the powder. Even though illegal transactions are off limits in the court system, we were confident that Elroy would never admit that our dispute involved drug money. By doing so, he'd be labeling himself a snitch, as well as incriminating himself with drug possession. Because Elroy worked part time for Arturo at a small ice cream stand, I let him know of my plans to sue Elroy. If I won the case, I wanted Arturo to pay me back the money I had lost on the powder down payments for Elroy's car, by deducting it from Elroy's salary.

Arturo made it clear that because Elroy was being paid under the table he didn't want to get involved. He had a talk with his brother-in- law and told him to work out a payment plan with me. Soon I was receiving payments every week. As a result of our deal, Arturo and I became close friends.

If Merrilyn had lived, I believe firmly that she would have bought the car for me regardless of the cost. Given all my expenses for school and what not, I couldn't afford to buy Elroy's car with cash at that time. For my business deals, I either borrowed my sister's car, or a Volkswagen owned by a female law student living at my parent's house. I also had a list of clients eager to taxi me around for a deal on drugs that they purchased from me. Having a large customer base, a good distributor list, and a growing contact base built up over twenty years, I had access to product and customers when nobody else knew where to look for them. I even had channels for Peyote and magic mushrooms.

Before very long the Dominicans became the principal players in the coke business. As I had learned enough Spanish to communicate with them, I was even able to get a package from them on credit. When my customers were often strangers, dealing on credit for a large quantity of drugs proved to be a lot safer than my coming in and out of someone's home five times a day to pick up small quantities. One could not be too careful to avoid suspicious behavior in the city neighborhoods, given the increasingly dangerous world of the trade in Boston.

The first time, in fact, that I had a gun pointed at me came when I least expected it. It involved a low-life character named 'Little John," a kid from a large family in Roxbury. I knew him from years earlier when we attended the same junior high school. But he was younger than me. One of his older brothers and I were in the same class, the two of us belonging to the same R&B singing group in the school. Because of our age difference, I didn't know "Little John" very well, other than that he was a classmate of my younger brother.

But out of the blue one day, "Little John" showed up at the front door of my apartment at the top of my parent's house. Right away, I told him that I knew what he wanted, but he said it wasn't for him. He asked that I meet a stranger on the street in his car. At first, I refused, telling him that if he wanted to deal with me, I would accommodate him. But if he wanted me to meet the stranger outside, he'd have to go somewhere else. He decided to leave me. There was nothing else to talk about.

That evening, he showed up again with one of his younger brothers. They were looking for a score, which I was happy to oblige them. My dog Epic stood next to me as I opened the door and let them inside my foyer. Before I retrieved what they wanted, a $30 package, I put Epic inside my living room and closed the door.

As I handed the package to "Little John," he turned and made a bum's rush to the street, without handing me the $30 bucks. I turned to grab the arm of his likable brother, who started pulling away from my grip. Suddenly he flashed a small pistol at me, aiming the gun at my chest. I let his arm go and backed away. It was bizarre in many ways, not the least because I'd been working with his older brother, my classmate from junior high school. He not only had invested a lot of money with me, but he was making up rock packages with product I sold him. And he was a middleman dealer for rock distributors.

Now I knew that the older brother had little to do with "Little John" and the brother with the pistol. I suspected that the brothers were competitors, even that there could be a jealousy factor at play, a sibling rivalry. The way I analyzed them, "Little John" seemed to be banking on the fact that his associate's reputation as a gunman would protect him. To me, of course, his calculation was very naive in a business where stupid people didn't survive very long. The harder they came, the quicker they fell, usually to a bullet. But in some families that I knew, blood ties tolerated behavior that would be dangerous in a business like mine. I also knew that the drug trade didn't reward family ties that hurt the business.

All the same, I knew I couldn't make a serious retaliatory move on "Little John" or his armed brother without fighting my friend, their older brother. I had good reason not to start a fight with him. For one thing, he had a violent reputation, the stuff of legend on the street. For another thing, I wanted to keep him as a friend. Later, I heard about other incidents with his two younger brothers. Yet because of the fear inspired by the older brother, the victims informed me that they, too, had not retaliated. They had let "Little John" rip them off the same way he robbed me.

For me, it was just another punk play over a little package. I decided to get back at them in a punishment proportionate to the crime. I called up his mother and told her what had happened, saying I'd been held up by her two sons for thirty bucks. In that way, I put the problem to the family in such a way that the older brother would have to get involved. I also passed the word through the grapevine that "Little John" was playing stick-up man.

Needless to say, the mother was very concerned and said she'd take care of the money. The older brother called and wanted to know why I hadn't called him. I said that he was out of town when it happened. I knew that he had always tried to build up his family as being high class, a fiction he attempted to engender by driving an antique car as a status symbol. I knew he'd be more concerned with his family's reputation than the fact that his brothers had brought a gun into my family's home.

From him, I then learned that the guy his brother had tried to get me to meet was a violent maniac known to be dangerous. He said I had done well to refuse to meet him. Things might have turned out a lot worse if I had gone against my rules and had gotten into that car.

My call to his mother very clearly dealt his ego a significant blow. He said that he didn't want the news out on the street that his younger brother was a street thug. And yet over time, although he assured me then that he'd repay me for the stolen package, he never did.

About a year later, the younger brother confronted me at a funeral ceremony. It was for a friend who had burned to death in a fire that had also killed his small son. The word among the mourners was that the fire had occurred while the father was smoking coke and knocked something over. A street rumor was that the apartment had been littered with so much junk, it had blocked the possibility of any escape by the son. His father's attempt to rescue the boy in his state of mind left little chance.

At the funeral, "Little John" brazenly came over after the ceremony and offered to have it out with me, mano a mano. I turned him down saying it would be disrespectful to our deceased friend and his surviving friends and relatives. When I caught him involved in a conversation with others in the lobby, I went outside to the parking lot and slashed one of his tires. For me, at least, that brought our contact and business to a satisfactory ending. I wouldn't see him again for years, and only then in passing.

A few weeks later, I began going to Chelsea to do business with several Dominicans. I always came back with the money for them from my dealing the product I got from them on credit, and I paid up just when I said I would be there to do so. I was determined not to do anything to anyone that I wouldn't want done to me. My dependable payments got me big respect from the Dominicans. Even a Bolivian woman who had gone to U/Mass with me had turned me on to a contact.

All throughout this period in my life, I still made efforts to get a number of well-paying legitimate jobs through my contacts, including a news position with Lenny's brother at a TV station out of state. I didn't want to stay in the drug business forever. But none of my efforts came to anything.

Perhaps my friends in legitimate work were reluctant to take a chance on recommending someone like me, fearing that I might embarrass them or scandalize their reputations were I to be arrested for drug dealing. On the other hand, some of my best customers were reputable people—lawyers, M.D.'s, policemen, court officials, teachers, nurses, business owners, insurance agents, airline pilots, managers and others with something to lose. And they were the ones I would expect to watch my back, while they were watching out for their own safety.

At this time, I also began going to Montreal for a little business and relaxation. One day while on a week's vacation there I decided to apply for a job at a Canadian Broadcasting Corporation (CBC) radio station. I dropped off my resume and an audition tape to their office. A CBC administrator told me to call the station in a couple of days and when I contacted them, they told me to come in for an interview.

I was happily surprised to find out I was in the running for a news broadcast position on the national program. My elation came to an end however when the interviewer asked if I could speak French. I didn't study French in school, wasn't raised in a French-speaking community, and so I couldn't speak it. I wasn't qualified for the job in Canada's two main official bilingual languages. According to the interviewer, I couldn't qualify even by taking French language classes; the station expected its broadcasters to be able to discern the nuances of the language. And that was something that only someone familiar with the language on a social discourse level over many years would be able to do.

I was unsuccessful in finding a journalism job in Montreal probably due to timing as well. I happened to be there as an ongoing political dispute was brewing in the province of Quebec. It was long-standing, and it pitted the English-speaking residents against the French-speaking ones over the use of the English language in business and in the schools. Quebec was largely French speaking, so I probably didn't stand a chance of getting a bilingual job even if I were fluent in French. In the western part of the country, where English-speaking residents were in the majority, bilingual French didn't seem to be a requirement then. I might have stood a good chance of getting a position in broadcast media. The interview, although it turned out badly, still lifted my spirits. It showed me that I had skills for a "real world" job. I figured that my problem in finding a decent media job as a career was networking or the lack thereof on my part. I didn't associate with professionals from the "news business," and I had no idea of where the job openings were. Having isolated myself from straight people, I was spending more time with women who got high and had little incentive to do better for themselves. Most of my male customers were working or middle class with homes and families. And I didn't socialize with most of them. The most important thing to the women I socialized with seemed to be seeking out guys like me to satisfy their habits. Of course, they were also willing to satisfy our wants in return. But partners like them couldn't be depended upon for anything except sex which in turn made them undependable for anything else.

Almost six months to the day of Merrilyn's death, Arturo made the decision to enter the drug business. I suspected that it wasn't only about the money. Cocaine is a very seductive drug and I suspected that the move had something to do with his wanting power and control.

Everyone usually starts out with the intention of making a lot of money in the cocaine business. But if you looked as closely as I did at the revenue streams and the risks of dealing cocaine, you found that more people were successful at selling marijuana than cocaine.

Contrary to the myths propagated by the drug police, the drug kingpins are few and far between, most of them living in South America and Mexico. There are thousands of black people in the Nation's prisons doing "Kingpin" time for petty drug offenses. In fact, there were over 600,000 drug arrests in one year for the simple possession of marijuana.

Arturo once explained to me that he thought he could make money and do it on his own terms. As he had saved money from his legitimate businesses, he believed that he could start at the top with the purchase of a lot of cocaine—a "big package," as we called it. I persuaded him to start off with four ounces.

I knew that he could make money easily. Nobody I knew had ever put a gun to anyone's head to force them to buy cocaine. Still, I couldn't shake the feeling that he wanted to spice up his life by dabbling on the other side. When he asked me where he could buy a package for the cheapest money, I told him that the cheapest dope was in Florida. And it just so happened that I knew someone in Florida who could put together a deal for Arturo, my old mentor Bennie.

☙ ❧

Chapter 22:

"You Talkin' to Me?"

One week later, I contacted Benny in his adopted paradise. I was on my way to Florida on a silver bird. At the time, the price of cocaine in Boston was $1,600 per ounce. We settled on a price of $1,200. Coincidentally, my seatmate on the plane was an ex-boyfriend of the girl I earlier named Carol, who had nearly caused me to crack up my car while she was on Quaaludes. Her boyfriend happened to be on his way to New York to pick up a package.

When I arrived at Miami International Airport, I picked up a rental car which had been reserved from Boston. Calling Bennie from the airport, I got directions from him to a motel in Key West. Our plan was not to meet my contact there, as Bennie would do all the work to "cop" the stuff and bring the package to me at the motel.

Until the 1960s and 1970s, Civil Rights laws forbade racial discrimination in public; it was not easy for me to adjust to the social life of the South. But most black men accustomed to the North's lack of openly hostile racial laws and customs would find life in the South a challenge. I found in the 1970s and 1980s that going down South was like going back ten years in time. Bennie and I didn't even have to discuss how to conduct ourselves while I was there. We made sure to keep a low profile around the "crackers." Southern cops had a notorious image around the world for vicious racist attitudes and behavior to black people, whether blacks were innocent or guilty of possessing and trading illegal drugs. Few can disagree with the observation that southern jails are filled with black petty drug offenders sentenced to long hard time, largely because of racism and unequal justice in the courts. To this day, a good majority of white southerners still have anti-black feelings left over from the Civil War era.

At the motel, I settled down to wait for Bennie to pick up the money. Late in the afternoon, there was a knock at the door and I opened it to see Bennie in the flesh. He hadn't changed all that much physically since I had last seen him except that he no longer had a crew cut, and he sported a moustache. Although he was still as stocky as I remembered him, he hadn't gone to fat. We settled back and reminisced about old times. It was good to see him. After we counted out the money I had with me for the purchase, he left to make the deal. I was told it would take a few hours.

I can't stress it enough that at certain levels of the drug trade, personal trust is all you have. I didn't know if

Bennie was going to use the time to cut the package. Nor did I know whether the time of the exchange was going to happen in two hours. I had only his word that the deal would go down the way he said it would. If I'd known someone in New York, I might have done the deal there, but I didn't have a contact I trusted in the city. If Bennie came back to our room to tell me he'd been robbed, there would be nothing I could have done about it.

Three hours later, Bennie returned with the package. I checked it out. It appeared to be all right. Satisfied with the transaction, I had some time on my hands. Bennie invited me to visit his home in the Keys. I accepted the invitation and hid the package in the room. I wasn't about to leave it in my luggage or anywhere a thief might look should he break in.

The Keys could be described as flatlands based at sea level, a principal reason that hurricanes are so devastating when they hit the Florida coast. I didn't see any hills. There was little to keep the water from sweeping across the coastline.

On the way to his house, we stopped at a tavern where the boat from John Huston's 1951 film "African Queen," starring Humphrey Bogart and Katharine Hepburn, was dry- docked. The boat seemed much smaller than it looked in the film.

The houses in Bennie's neighborhood were constructed on stilts. I'd never seen anything like it. He explained that it was necessary to keep their homes from being swept away during a hurricane. Having seen films of hurricanes hitting the Florida coast, I could only imagine what it would have been like to sit out a raging storm in a house on stilts. Later that evening, I sat with Bennie and his wife on his balcony of his house listening to the sound of the cigarette boats ferrying drugs from ships offshore to the mainland. The engines had a sound similar to revved up hot rods. O, Florida!

The next morning I checked out of the motel and headed for the airport. I decided to carry the package in my underwear. I wasn't going to chance carrying it in the luggage. This was before the terrorist scares of today. At that time, there had been a series of airline high- jackings.

By now, I'd become a professional trafficker. I wasn't affected by the stress of passing through checkpoints. Even customs inspectors didn't rattle me. I played the game as an average type of guy by becoming the average type of guy. It wasn't a game for the faint hearted. I was aware that there were profiles designed by the experts to flush out people like me but my background had prepared me well. I thought the same way that the inspectors thought and I knew what kinds of things set off their curiosity. I was good to go.

The question at the reservation counter came out of the blue. I didn't know at the time that the Florida cops had a special patrol at the airport to toss drug suspects who fit their profile. It was pretty simple when you got down to it. They'd walk up to you and ask you courteously, if you'd mind if they checked your luggage. If you refused, you were automatically under suspicion and they'd toss you anyway under probable cause. I didn't think the procedure was legal, but neither is being stopped for "driving while black."

It was posed innocently by the woman at the reservations counter: "You've only been here for a day. Why are you leaving so early?"

This was said with the undertone of: "You haven't stayed long enough to enjoy this beautiful place!" I hadn't expected the question. Maybe she wouldn't have asked it if I'd been white. None of this mattered. I thought quickly and knocked the ball out of the park.

"I went to a wedding and have to get back to my job." I responded.

That ended the small talk and I was soon on my way to Boston. If you were to ask me at that time why I was doing what I was doing I might have responded that I didn't believe the drug laws were fair. Another response of mine might have been that people had a right to do as they pleased if they weren't hurting anyone else.

But the truth of the matter was that I was in denial, trying to fool myself and doing a lousy job. After losing Marilyn, I'd lost interest in remarrying again. My parents were always reminding me of that blunder. I saw myself becoming arrogant and self-centered; much as I enjoyed dealing drugs, in quiet moments as I reflected on my life, I seemed to be squandering it away. Once I went into a one-week treatment program. My therapist informed me during my exit interview that I was so embedded in "the life" that I'd need extensive therapy to get out of it. He said that I might have to move out of town in order to escape its power over me and to fully recover a healthy life. According to him, I needed to "hit bottom" in a catastrophic event such as being busted to force me to change my behavior. The way things had turned out, I had such a large group of customers that I didn't have to pay for my habit. I could either dip into a package and take something out or I'd be given a piece of product for my trouble, a thank you tip to me from a gratified customer. Sometimes, I would even get free packages for the business I brought to suppliers.

I was living with my parents after giving up my own apartment. I worked at jobs for which I was overqualified. I felt uncomfortable when I ran into old friends who asked me what I was doing with my life. All the time I tried not to face the reality that I wasn't building up a nest egg for the future. I was only living in a "here and now."

I returned to Boston and went to my sister's house to cut the package up for resale. Lenny was present along with my sister, when I had to leave the apartment for something. I put the package to the side and left for about twenty minutes.

When I returned with the liquid chemicals to make rocks and added them to the powder, the stuff turned gooey. I was shocked. After I tasted the dry powder, I detected a sweetness that I hadn't noticed before. I commented on it to Lenny. Half of the package was destroyed and I called Arturo to come over. I knew I hadn't overdone anything.

When Arturo checked out the gooey substance that wouldn't dry, I could tell he was disappointed. I had done this exercise many times without a problem. Yet, I couldn't help but feel defensive. The product hadn't tasted like this when I'd checked it out in Florida. Now, we had two ounces of product left that couldn't be cut and had to be sold "as is." It was Arturo's first loss in the business. He never had any others of this magnitude.

Months later, after Lenny and I had begun spending less time together and he had stopped seeing my sister, the incident with the gooey powder came up. We were in the company of several friends and he dropped enough hints to make me wonder whether he or my sister had done some tampering with the package. He paraphrased my comments about the powder tasting sweet and cracked up laughing.

Although I never found out for sure who might have done what, I never again left a package in the hands of anyone other than myself or the buyer. Cocaine brought out the larceny in people. From then on, it was no longer the fun drug that you could sniff and use for good sex with a partner. It became fake fun when people started smoking it. In smokable form, it caused some people to hide in closets when they got too high and certain women to begin removing their clothes. Others transformed under the influence and exhibited scandalous behavior. For example, some women hid pieces under their fingernails, when people weren't looking.

Unlike marijuana, cocaine didn't bring people together to have a good time. It caused strains in relationships, pulling people apart. Often creating a sense of unease around strangers, the drug caused some people who smoked to withdraw into familiar settings and to socialize with people of like minds.

Others did it alone, exhibiting the secretive behavior that the drug seemed to bring out on occasion. Becoming an observer from the sidelines, I watched in fascination as people I thought I knew transformed into strangers. I tightened up on credit for anyone who smoked. As well, suppliers became wary of anyone who smoked the pipe. They couldn’t be trusted.

I had begun hearing rumblings about something called AIDs in 1981. At first it was called a sexual disease that affected homosexuals. The rumors about the disease spread quickly throughout the play-for-pay business but it wasn't known to affect straight people.

In the late summer of 1982, AIDs began to spread all over the country. By this time, there had been cases of people who had gotten blood transfusions coming down with the disease from infected blood. As a result, homosexuals were discouraged from giving blood. Lenny and I had speculated on the possibility that a mosquito could pass on the disease, if it bit an innocent victim after biting an AIDs carrier.

At this time, I had begun to fuck around with a neighborhood coke whore who gave out "head" for hits. Bettylyn was also a thief who didn't know that everyone knew about her. Even her mother didn't trust her. I'd been given the heads up before I let her come into my room to mess around. Sometimes, I'd leave her alone in my room with the plate of powder, expecting her to fuck with it. I got a kick out of seeing how careful she was not to take too much.

Once I experimented with dangerous behavior through a gay couple, allowing one of them—a nurse—to inject coke into me with a syringe to see what the high was like. If he hadn't been a nurse I wouldn't have done it. This happened before it came out that intravenous drug users were susceptible to the virus. My luck held out and I never did it again. But I can't deny that drug use has caused people to do stupid things.

Letting Bettylyn into my parents' house came back on me, after the house was mentioned at a neighborhood "watch" meeting as a drug house by one of her loud-mouthed male friends. The man was old enough to be her grandfather, but the girl didn't let age stand in the way when it came to getting high. One of my mother's friends who was at the meeting called up in shock to tell her what had happened and from that moment, my ass was in a sling.

The family meeting with my parents was short and to the point: I was not to sell drugs out of the house or I'd be kicked out. The nuns in a rectory down our street, so they said, would be keeping an eye on their house. And the nuns agreed to notify my parents of any suspicious activities. My parents promised my neighbors that they would call the cops on me if I was found to be dealing drugs. My parents were well respected members of the community, so the weight wouldn't be falling on them.

The next day when Bettylyn came by I let her know that her mouth had gotten her ass and me in trouble. I told her to pass the word to her friend that I was ready to let his cat out of the bag, if he didn't shut up. I knew he had to be getting high with the bitch for her to have talked about me.

I stopped all traffic to the house and started meeting certain customers on Blue Hill Ave. Often I had a ride pick me up to make deliveries. After things quieted down, I let Bettylyn visit my house again. But my mother didn't like her; and I had to slip her inside without any fanfare.

There was an uneasy truce between me and my parents. Drugs had become such a part of my life that I found it very difficult to let go. I had inverted the old dictum that said : "Even if you're a street sweeper be the best street sweeper you can be." I'd reached the upper levels in an illegal enterprise by becoming one of the best.”

It had been hard, dangerous work. There's a certain truth that if I had put as much time into a career or planning for the future, I would probably have reached legitimate professional heights as well. My weakness caused me to delude myself that I was still making progress in my life; but when I began to consider that was true, while I continued my same behavior, even the admission seemed to feel like just another form of denial.

By l983, I'd begun to hang around with Marcel of all people. I'd begun to see one of her girls, whom I'd taken with me to Canada. By this time, I'd made several friends up North. Back then, whenever I went to Montreal, I had a place to stay. I also had a choice of playmates to play with. I introduced Marcel to one of my friends who didn't mind playing the "pimp" game with her. Although the two of them were attracted to each other, my friend had another woman in his corner that was legit and had more money than Marcel. For a while, he played them off against each other, until Marcel managed to contact the other woman. All too soon, it was only a matter of time before he left the scene.

I did good business with Marcel, her girls, and their clients. It was enough to enable me to take time-outs without feeling a financial pinch. I still had old customers from the '70s. Sometimes, it amazed me that I had survived for so long.

☙ ❧

Chapter 23:

"I Coulda' Been a Contender!"

When a Boston television station owned by Boston Broadcasters was sold to new management, I made an effort to join the news staff. One of the owners was the mother of one of my classmates at Roxbury Memorial High. What made me an attractive candidate, some of my professors said to me, was my relationship with the camera which enabled me to project my persona from the small screen. It was an ability you either have or you don't. And I had it, as I discovered during my mock newscasts in Grad school. I strongly admired NBC news anchor Jessica Savitch, (Feb. 1, 1947-Oct. 23, 1983), a television broadcaster and news reporter, briefly host of Public Broadcasting Station's Frontline, and a dynamic news presence elsewhere on NBC news. I wanted to have the same ability with the camera as she did. She was my role model and inspiration. Her life and career came to a sudden end at the age of 36 in a car accident.

Coincidentally, she'd once had a cocaine problem and had beaten the demon only to die in the accident. Given my own profile with drugs, I felt that we shared some experiences. And I wanted to meet her. Back then, I read an on-air editorial at the television station before the new owners assumed managing it. My editorial ran on the evening after a popular movie, which gave the station a large audience share and my on-air editorial broadcast a larger than average exposure from the audience spillover still tuned to the station.

A number of my mother's friends called her to let her know they'd seen me. I even received my first fan letter from a viewer in New Hampshire who agreed with my position on a topic which I no longer recall. I subsequently had an interview with one of the new owners. He had seen my audition tape and was favorably impressed with our informal interview. When he informed me that he was scheduling a second interview, I felt that I stood a chance of doing either editorial commentaries or street reporting to start. It was another chance to turn things around in my life without having to leave Boston as so many people born in the town have had to do in order to make it.

The next evening I got a call from Sherry, one of the black girls in Marcel's stable. She lived at the opposite end of Marlborough Street in a basement apartment. Sherry wanted to buy an ounce of reefer from me, but I was reluctant to deal with her. She was a pain in the ass because she was always trying to get me to give her credit, when I didn't even know her real name. Her favorite and apparently sole bit of wisdom that she often repeated was: "You can either do the smart thing or the right thing."

She told me that a friend of hers wanted to buy the package. She had talked about him before to me, and had offered to introduce him to me, a man she called "Bertie." I was sitting on a lot of pot, so it wasn't a big deal to sell a paying customer; besides, I knew Marcel well enough to know that Sherry was on the up-and-up about her friend, and I was going to get paid.

When I arrived at her place, she invited me into her living room to meet her friend. I walked through the door and came face-to-face with the man who had interviewed me for the TV job. We were both stunned to see one another. I became extremely uncomfortable; but I was in no state of mind to observe whether he was as nervous as I was.

Sherry picked up on the vibes. Although she didn't know what was going on, she knew the atmosphere had changed in the room. Greeting the man, I excused myself immediately and left the place. When I told Lenny about what had happened, he told me to forget the job. And he was right. When I called the office to speak to him and to confirm my second interview, the receptionist told me that he wasn't available. I never called back. Later in the month, I received a letter from the other owner who had been backing me, which suggested puzzlement that there was no interest in me. She suggested I contact a documentary filmmaker she knew. But I'd already given up on a media job in Boston.

In hindsight, I see clearly that the professional media circles in Boston, much more so than working class employers, limit access to gigs for regular people. In that professional environment, sooner or later you'll run into people you know or people who've heard about you, and much of your chances of getting hired will depend on the personal chemistry established between you and one of the media in-crowd.

For example, it would have been likely that had I met "Bertie" in Sherry's place after he'd hired me, our chance encounter would have been a different story. We would have been on a level playing field with both of us having something to lose from an indiscrete tongue. But for him to be consorting with someone he didn't know very well was a deal buster for me. The risk of distributing product to him wasn't worth it. Nor was it worth hiring me for him, given what I now knew about his tastes in women and his habit. Nobody wants to risk his business coming out on the street.

The station manager's dirty little secret was no secret anymore, at least to me. But my friend Lenny, who worked with several of the station owners and their attorneys, already knew about the man's secrets.

For years, I'd heard scuttlebutt about judges, cops, famous and infamous people who fooled around with the call girls. The women were always gossiping about someone important they knew as a client. It was something that came with the territory. This was another reason that consorting with "low-lifes" could be hazardous.

I most certainly didn't want my business known to everyone and his brother. That my secret had been kept for as long as it had been was very fortunate for me. I still had hopes of walking away from the drug trade and doing something else. I saw too much human depravity associated with it. Long ago, I realized that when you see people at their worst, in vulnerable positions, as when they're strung out on drugs so much that they would sell their souls to the devil, usually a dealer like me, it causes them to resent the dealer. It's human nature. Once, a woman I considered a friend told me that there was a ritual she followed whenever I was expected at her home. She said she had to go to the bathroom and take a dump because that was how the thought of ingesting cocaine affected her.

So whenever she saw me, she couldn't help but think of going to the crapper. It didn't make me feel attractive to the woman after hearing that true confession. Truth was, it made me feel like shit.

☙ ❧

Chapter 24:

The Blizzard

Things really began to tighten up for me economically in the 80s. The signal that Reagan was going to play hard ball with his adversaries came when the air traffic controllers went on strike and Reagan fired them all. There would be more right-wing attacks on organized labor under Reagan and his Congressional allies.

Life also became financially tighter for those down the food chain. Federal and state governments slashed social welfare programs, food stamps and unemployment benefits. Information on how to apply for benefits was restricted by government officials at social service agencies unless you knew someone who knew how to get around a myriad of red tape used to disqualify many recipients.

To my way of thinking, the early 1980s were a time of unequal opportunity. Politically, the Democrats couldn't complain about Reagan's actions because they gave him everything he wanted. I'll never forget when Reagan ended up at a local bar in Dorchester with House Speaker Tip O'Neil for a few "suds." They seemed very close friends, drinking buddies in a local bar after a day's work.

I don't remember Reagan ever doing anything of any financial consequence for poor racial minorities. I found little remarkable about him as a president or a leader. The only thing outstanding about Reagan was his ability to get Congress to do whatever he desired. And the only thing remarkable about the Democratic controlled Congress was its support of the Republican programs, while trying to give the illusion of fighting against them.

In the Reagan re-election bid in 1984, public polls showed early in his bid that there was no way he was going to lose. Most people approved his push for tougher drug laws. He had the support of the Congress just before his Iran-Contra arms deal behind the backs of Congress came to light. Meanwhile, he supported the push for the "Just Me Generation" to pay their student loans which a lot of us had been loath to do. A lot of those well-paying jobs we'd expected to get to pay for our student tuition loans just weren't there when we graduated, loaded down with debt.

When a blizzard defied weather predictions and struck the East Coast that winter, the unexpected storm caused the wholesale price of cocaine at $500 an ounce to jump to $1,300 an ounce but weeks later, the price dropped. Word on the street from reliable sources was that a massive shipment of cocaine arrived in the country through some new players in the game. The East Coast was buried in powder and the shit was very good. The best thing about the delivery to the country was that most dealers like me could make money.

Later it would come out that Oliver North had testified behind closed door hearings chaired by Senator John Kerry that the CIA was working with the Contras smuggling drugs into the country with the tacit support of the Federal Drug Enforcement Agency (DEA). Illegal drugs like cocaine were flown in by the DEA and weapons flown back in the same cargo planes to our right-wing allies in South America and Iran. Interestingly, Kerry kept his mouth closed until almost a year after the fact. For once in a lifetime, my colleagues in the trade could say that buying drugs amounted to an act of patriotism.

The bulk of the drug shipments measuring in the tonnage went to a warehouse in south central California, where a dealer named Ricky Ross parceled it out to large, well- organized street outlets run by the "Bloods" and the "Crips," two ruthless black street gangs. According to Pulitzer prize winning Journalist Gary Webb in a speech in 1999: "This CIA-connected drug ring played a very critical role in the early l980s in opening up south central (Los Angeles) to a crack epidemic that was unmatched in its severity and influence anywhere in the U.S."

Apparently, some of the cocaine from Central America also ended up in Mesa, Arkansas when Bill Clinton was governor, but I've yet to see any proof that he might have been involved. One can only imagine how easy it must have been for the drugs to be brought into the country through the CIA.

In l986, the Little Rock office of the FBI concluded a four-year investigation of a businessman named Dan Lasater (founder of Ponderosa Steak House and other businesses). He was the alleged drug kingpin from Mesa who was the chief cocaine supplier for the banking, investment and bond community in that part of the country.

Lasater's arrest brought down his operation. He and 24 other defendants received prison sentences ranging from 4 months to 10 years. The government seized an auto, an airplane, warehouses of marijuana and cocaine, and $77,000 in currency from the Lasater enterprise, a large haul at the time. As the "brains" behind the outfit, Mister Lasater ended up with the four-months sentence, spent in a half-way house! His deep pockets as well as his political connections clearly mitigated his punishment.

Sometimes, in such drug cases, truth surpasses the credibility of fiction. Was this American justice another example of "just-us" in action? Meanwhile, Nancy Reagan and Michael Jackson were at a bizarre White House gathering urging young people to support First Lady Nancy's "Just Say No!" to drugs campaign.

It was frustrating for me, as well, to watch Sam Donaldson, an ABC-television correspondent on the 6 o'clock nightly national broadcasts. Most viewers of Donaldson's reports on the Reagan administration were accustomed to his crusading media persona as a journalistic pit bull. But in his dealings with the Reagans, he began to throw softball type questions in his interviews with them. In one interview with Nancy Reagan, Donaldson never brought up the Contra scandal. It was headline news in the national press. Some in Congress voiced suspicions to the press, for non attribution, that the Reagan White House was behind one of the largest drug conspiracies in history.

Details of the Iran-Contra scandal of l985 became public when the Nicaraguans shot down a Contra supply plane and captured an American CIA contractor. Reagan began issuing denials about knowing anything about Iran Contra or the drug operation. This was but one of many lies he would utter while president.

In l986, auto maker John DeLorean was convicted of money laundering and drug trafficking from a government sting operation. His conviction seemed vindictive and so far outside the boundaries of federal sentencing for white collar, first time felons, that DeLorean was acquitted of all charges on appeal to a higher court. Both his professional and private lives were then in ruins, however, from his arrest and highly publicized trial.

It was during the Reagan years that the "maximum–minimum" drug sentencing guidelines began to impact upon the black community, with devastating consequences. The very hypocrisy of the Reagan-Bush Administration was to victimize black people by making them both the targets and the villains of the Iran-Contra scam.

It was an unequal decade with unequal treatment for all. Al Pacino captured the essence of the 80s with his performance in the legal film "And Justice for All." It seemed like justice was somewhere else and there was no help coming out of Washington.

When it came to the drug trafficking by the Contras to the tune of forty million dollars there wasn't a mumbled word from our government. It's enough to make you favor jury nullification as the main leveler in this phony drug war by the feds and their local cohorts. In some cases, it's the only way for justice to be done.

During the period when the Iran-Contra affair was happening, an anti-drug campaign against cocaine was launched. It was called "Cocaine-The Big Lie." When I spoke to a well-known disk jockey about the commercial that was running on his station, he responded to my query as he sniffed up a white line. I said no one I knew was saying that cocaine was a safe drug. He explained to me that this was called using the "Spin." The aim of the ad wasn't to question what users were saying about the drug. It was to create doubt about the drug itself. He said the technique had been used during the McCarthy era of the 50s to create the "Red Scare." He explained further that some people are more easily influenced by short propaganda lines, rather than the truth, which might require more thought.

Rush Limbaugh, the drug addled gas bag, and the others of his ilk attacked Congresswoman Maxine Waters as being a "nutcase" when she exposed the illegal drug component of Iran-Contra to the Nation on her own after it became apparent that the yellow press in this country was either unable or unwilling to do so.

The sad truth is that as of l999, little else has been reported out of the Congress on Iran-Contra. Oliver North has his own radio show and most of the others involved in the affair were pardoned by former President George H.W. Bush.

ℭ ℜ

Chapter 25:

Buddy, Can You Spare a Dime?

My personal crisis occurred in the summer of 1986. I ended up living in a number of different places after I was put out of the house on Mount Pleasant Ave. It had happened after one of my female customers ignored my warning not to come to the house and rode up to the front door in a taxi cab. I was fit to be tied. She wasn't that stupid. I had even chosen her to take over Merrilyn's call girl business because of her intelligence. Recently, I found out that I took so long to meet her down the street that the cab driver had started getting restless.

My odyssey was to become an unforgettable experience when I found myself living with other people in their apartments. Some tried to take over my movements or dictate what they thought was a fair amount of powder that they should receive for their help. Some tried to make an issue of the number of phone calls I should receive. Others got so ridiculous in their demands that I left them high and dry on the first night.

Actually, I came with my own set of baggage. The plus side of having me around if you were an addict was that you would have cocaine on hand almost every night. The down side of the situation was that unless you were disciplined, you'd get caught up in the madness, neglecting your friends and family by overindulging yourself.

Again, I managed to keep a job and was able to pay my rent. I had long ago gotten used to having a group of customers following in my wake. All I needed was a telephone on the premises and I could hook things up in very little time. I would even pay a phone bill if it was necessary. It was a novel situation for a roommate to be in. But it wasn't always a healthy one.

I'd come to the realization that I was no longer interested in living life at the top. Things had gotten too dangerous with the "crack" epidemic. I wasn't about to go out on the street and deal with those fools selling drugs on the street corners. It was a whole new game. It had become the decade of thugs and drugs in the inner city. The business was changing before my eyes; it was becoming a young man's game. I was reminded of nature's way of dealing with change. The old lion gives way to the young lion when his time is past. He has a choice of leaving gracefully or leaving after a struggle. But when his time has come, he has to give way. I decided to move to the background, keeping a low profile. I knew it was only a matter of time before a crackdown took place. It was a deliberate act on the part of the authorities to allow drug selling on the street in Roxbury and Dorchester. It wasn't happening in Quincy or Milton. It wasn't happening in Brookline, either.

In l988, a part-time pimp attempted to get some powder for himself by introducing me to two young street girls he knew. I was on to his game and didn't fall into his trap. The girls ended up coming to me anyway, like I expected. One of them, Shari, ended up living with me and almost caused me to throw her out of the third floor window of our room in the South End. It was a match made in hell. She was what I called a "base head bitch."

Nineteen when I met her, Shari had an extremely slick way about her, manipulating and dealing, playing others to her advantage as though you were merely one card in her deck of cards. She gamed you for everything, doing whatever it took to get over on you at your loss. At 19, a grafter, a liar, a backstabber—you would trust at your peril. I fell for her, trustingly, as ignorant and innocent of her plans for me as a calf about to be taken to a slaughter house. I was still working full-time, but back living at home, so when she asked about us living together, I began to look for a place that was inexpensive yet large enough for me to spend part of the week with her overnights. In a few days, I found a room we could share off Saint Botolph Street in the South End of the city. I considered our living arrangement there to be a means of getting some stability in my life and in our relationship. How little I then knew!

My mistake initially was to let her convince me how to see our relationship as a partnership without an emotional commitment. And although I agreed to that view of us, and though I considered her to be more of a roommate than a girlfriend, I cannot deny that I was smitten by her. She, of course, knew all along what she was doing to set me up, leading me to believe that our relationship, deep down inside of her, was based on an affection not at all connected to our business relationship. I fell into the trap. It was the worst kind of entanglement and it was mainly so because I let her pull the wool over my eyes to make her happy. I felt that I brought her closer emotionally to me the more I agreed with her view of our relationship. Her happiness, of course, was never really about getting closer to me. And that became clear as she began to openly run around with other guys who would pay her in money or powder for her sexual services, and she began to return with nothing to pay me for my powder. She expected me to continue giving her free powder and other drugs for her consumption. She also expected me to trust her.

She'd gotten a job in the Prudential Center at a Brigham's Ice Cream shop. But she was doomed not to keep any job involving cash transactions because she was a thief, so out of control that whenever I came in the shop she'd charge me for the food and, instead of putting it in the cash register, she'd pocket my money for herself. Those were crazy times.

We split the rent on the room but there was seldom any peace there. I knew she was constantly at work trying to play on guys in the building. In the eyes of people who didn't know our living arrangements, her flagrant prostitution made me look like a chump. I was not oblivious to the humiliation. Sometimes, she'd slap me during an argument over something stupid and I'd slap her back. This made things interesting for the neighbors who could hear her screaming. Nobody ever called the cops on us though. I suspected that the other tenants in our building didn't consider me to be the abuser in the relationship. For one thing, I knew that they had a low opinion of Shari. For another, they could hear her assaulting me until I had to return her slaps to stop her. I never initiated our physical altercations, but I always ended them.

I had a book with my customers' numbers inside. On days when I might get careless and leave my book of numbers with her, she'd tear out pages from the book. She was always playing the jealousy card as though I was none the wiser. But I was becoming wiser to her game.

At some point, she revealed to me that she'd been sexually abused by an older brother. That probably had a lot to do with her actions and the way she related to men. Still, you can only excuse so much to childhood traumas, as, for example, a person's childhood sexual abuse. After a while, everyone has to take some responsibility for their actions.

The one thing that most drove me crazy about this woman is that I wasn't hard enough on her to keep her from interfering with my business. Every time she got wind of a package I got to sell, without being able to sell it the same night, I was as good as not having it. Once she knew that I didn't have a ready buyer for it, she would hound and hound me to get stoned with her and have a good time in bed. As soon as she plied her wiles on me, I got stoned and she ended up sniffing or smoking up the whole package. Mixing business and pleasure was never a good idea. I seemed to never learn that lesson.

She'd have no money on hand to help me pay for a new package and would try to blame me when I had trouble with a supplier. I knew that things couldn't keep going on like that. The shit hit the fan when I found out that she had paid the full rent only once and had been using my share of the rent money to buy drugs for over six months while keeping it a secret.

The landlady told me what had been going on when I had approached her about taking a separate room. I liked the location of the building and the neighborhood. It was the final straw. The owner who lived in a building next door alluded to the fights we'd had since living there. She had no interest in having me for a tenant.

The first thing that came to my mind was helping Shari to take a long leap through the window. My rage was flaring out of control. Luckily, I knew how to cool down. She knew how to piss me off and tried to use that as a means to control me. It all came to an end in a few minutes. I gave her a reality shock when I put all of my things in a couple of shopping bags and walked out the same day. The good part was that I still had a job. So, I could still be independent. Years later, after we became friendly again, Shari died of cancer. She had graduated from college and left behind two small daughters.

At this time, Aids was in the crisis stage. It had reached the point where just about every family in America knew of someone who'd been infected by the Aids virus. I had begun to lose people I considered to be friends, including two young men who had lived in my parents' house on Mount Pleasant for a while. I'd been stunned by the loss of a very good friend who was married with a family and who had always been cool with me and my family. He had been active in the church and hadn't lost his edge on the street. I often wondered if he'd been bisexual.

Some people believed that Aids was God's payback for the sexual excesses of the 70s. The disease was like a plague that ate you alive from the inside, all the way down to your bones. Transforming you into a living skeleton, it punished you with unendurable pain for your transgressions with members of the same sex. It was the ultimate price to be paid for "ass whacking" and "rump wrestling" at the "Y" and other places. I was still fucking around with "basehead bitches," but I had become a lot more selective about my sex-mates. Even, sexual behavior on the street had changed. A lot of male customers no longer wanted to fuck, preferring to get "head" instead. Nobody wanted to die over a piece of ass.

Since Rock Hudson died of Aids in l985, everyone had taken notice. This stuff was serious. I still wanted to have straight sex, because "head" had always been a part of foreplay for me. There were times that I didn't use a rubber. But those times became few and far between as the crisis spread.

A few months later, I was staying at the apartment of a middle aged woman who I'd met through my sister. This was the first time I got to see the negative effects of the crack epidemic up close and how it destroyed lives. This woman who I'll call Fedora had received a settlement of about fifty thousand dollars for an accident. She lived with her daughter in a well-kept apartment with nice furniture in Mattapan. She had a younger man as a boyfriend and an older man who was in competition for her affections. She played them off against each other.

When I first met her, she had just begun to spend the money on cocaine. It was a trip to watch her and her entourage of about eight people as she went from place to place spending an hour here, two hours there. She was into a power trip, making people wait in line for her to give them a crumb or two, as if they were little children. She tried the stupidity with me only once. The first time it happened, I had gotten something for her and when she attempted to "diss" me like the others, I told her off. I made an impression that night when I left the place to get something for myself. None of the others would have dared to challenge her as I had. But I'd been around drugs for so long that I could see the game quite clearly.

Some people make the mistake of allowing drugs to define who they are. If they have a lot of drugs on hand they're important. If they're out of drugs, they're nobody. My fortunes had changed from the days when I rode around in BMWs and Corvettes. But I was still standing.

Two months later, Fedora had gone through all the money and the entourage was gone. The first thing I would have done in her position would have been to buy a decent automobile. But for some reason a lot of people who aren't used to having large sums of money often do the stupid thing. In a way, I suppose my experiences in the business gave me an outlook more in line with that of a dealer rather than a consumer.

Fedora ended up not only losing her apartment, but having to sell her furniture. It was another in the long litany of horror stories I was to hear about and occasionally see firsthand as the crack epidemic bankrupted lives on a scale almost equal to the destruction caused by Aids.

☙ ❧

Chapter 26:

Down for the Count

It all started innocently enough. First I had a cold which refused to go away. Then, I got the chills and a fever that sapped my strength. Not knowing what was happening, after taking cold medications and feeling pain in my back, I ended up becoming so weak that my survival instincts caused me to return to Mount Pleasant Ave.

Hoping my mother's care would make things right, I faced a chilly reception after I arrived there. The house had been sold to my nephew by my parents. He and I hadn't gotten along since he'd bought the place. My mother had planted the idea in his head that he could help her straighten me out when I was staying there on one of my infrequent visitations. I'd refused to let that happen and had left as soon as I found other digs.

Previously, Arturo had offered to buy the house, promising to allow my parents to remain there rent free. He wanted to rent out some of the rooms and put me in charge of the property. My mother claimed that because neither my sister, brother, nor I was capable of getting credit, my nephew was the only one suitable for keeping the house in the family.

My nephew was insufferable and seemed to relish the opportunity to throw his weight around. He even cut the line to my phone in the attic but I continued to use it by forwarding my calls to the places where I'd moved. I'd threatened to report him to the telephone company for destroying their property which increased the tension between us. Once, when I'd stopped over for a weekend visit between a change of locations, I had wound up sleeping outside in my father's truck.

My mother told me that my nephew who was at work had better not find me there. I refused to listen to the hype and fell out on the living room couch. When he arrived, I was out of it and ignored him completely. I might have told him to call the cops if he didn't like me being there.

The next morning, the pain in my back had intensified and every breath I took cut like a knife. I convinced my other nephew to drive me to the hospital where I dragged myself into the emergency ward. It wasn't long before I was stretched out with a bottle of saline dripping liquid through my arm to hydrate my body. My temperature was 105 degrees.

After I was settled in a room, I sent word through my sister that I didn't want visits from any other family members. I was pissed off at the way I'd been treated. I had other friends to visit me. Several of my suppliers paid visits to me. One of them even brought me some powder, which I shared with some of my new acquaintances on the floor.

I found myself starting to write the outlines of what was to be this story as a means of passing the time. Until I began to write this section, I'd forgotten how long ago this project was in the works.

When I arrived at Mount Pleasant Ave, after spending a week on my back, my nephew forced me to help him clean the yard. This pissed me off to the point that I threw a "nutty" with the rake which caused him to back off. After I returned inside, I began to make calls to friends about a place to stay. I really didn't want to deal with the dumb shit.

Toward the end of the 80s, drug houses which had been operating on a 24-hour a day schedule were being raided and shut down. Street violence was on the increase as young thugs sold their wares on the corners. Gangs from out of state had moved into some of the housing projects and Jamaican bosses were flexing their muscles. I knew a crackdown by the authorities was coming. I continued to operate outside the mix, minding my own affairs.

Arturo had continued to dabble in the business and had invested with other dealers. Some of the deals had worked out but he had become more aware that he had to keep an eye on things. A couple of times, he had to chase down his money from people he thought to be reliable.

We'd had a falling out of sorts because running things his way meant running things on his time, meaning an hour wait or more. I didn't have that kind of patience and would go somewhere else rather than wait for someone on my time. Arturo wasn't happy with my attitude. He'd gotten it into his head that I owed him some kind of loyalty.

I had begun doing business with a Dominican named Jose and his cousin Tony. They lived in an apartment building near Field's Corner in Dorchester. The neighborhood itself was bustling with drug activity from Geneva Avenue on one side to Dorchester Ave on the other. Undercover cops were everywhere pulling people over to toss suspicious cars. Managing to swim through the nets, I'd avoided cop trouble. Sometimes, a warning came from the least expected place. One evening Tony and I were waiting in front of the Jackson Square train station to pick up a package. There was a paddy wagon parked in front of us. I'd left the car and was walking past the paddy wagon when I heard a low whisper with an urgency to it. "Get out of here!" were the barely audible words.

The voice came from inside the paddy wagon. The cop was in shadow and I didn't want to draw attention by trying to see his face. It turned out to be Bettylyn's neighbor. He lived around the corner from me. I returned to the car and left. He had never spoken to me before and never did again.

One evening, I went to see Jose at his apartment on Mission Hill. He'd begun renting there after my female customer who owned the building went behind my back and after speaking to him in fast Spanish, started seeing him without me in the picture. A friend of Elroy's was standing in the doorway of the woman's first floor apartment as I passed on my way to the top floor. He didn't say anything and only grunted. This person had been one of my suppliers of pharmaceutical lactose which I used to cut my packages. He also used to order absolute alcohol for me through his job at a medical lab. Another of his specialties was glass pipes which he made and sold on the side.

I reached the top floor and finding the door open, I was about to enter when I heard a strange voice that caused me to freeze in my tracks. The cops were inside with Jose in the kitchen. They hadn't heard me because they were talking loudly. I backed up as quietly as possible and managed to get back downstairs. When I reached the first floor, the apartment door was closed. I never found out why I hadn't been warned about the bust. Shortly after the bust, Jose went on the lam after making bail.

About a week before this incident, my former friend who owned the building pointed a gun at me while my old buddy Lenny was visiting her. She stopped me from going up to Jose's apartment to buy a package. She said later that too many people were coming to his apartment and that the gun was empty. It didn't matter. That was my final visit to the place.

By the way, when I was in the hospital last year on what had become a seven-day stay for a respiratory infection with pneumonia, Arturo, who was picking up meds in the hospital pharmacy died of a massive heart attack. Arturo had been smoking cocaine like a chimney stack for years. If I'd been doing the drug like he had, I would have been long dead. He'd given up driving after he suffered a stroke on his motorcycle one afternoon. Later, he explained to me that he was riding around the neighborhood where he grew up and couldn't remember where he was. In addition, the stroke had affected his vision, so he could no longer drive. When my sister brought me the news of his death, I cried like a baby in my hospital bed.

☙ ❧

Chapter 27:

Happy Trails to You Until We Meet Again

If you were into the pipe, chances were you'd end up changing your circle of friends. When I ended up at what was going to be my last stop on my trail of disappointments, I never thought it would happen to me. One thing I remember about the 80s is that a lot of friendships forged over the years came apart because of the cocaine crisis.

Norman and I went back a long way from the days at U/ Mass. We had always gotten along. In fact, because we had a slight resemblance physically in height and manner as well as names that could be confused, we were sometimes mistaken for one another. I related to Norman like a brother. I could talk to him about my problems without feeling the awkwardness I might have felt with a relative. Despite his being gay, I was never uncomfortable around him. We'd spent hours at his place when I was working in the Vet program at the university. He'd become one of my closest friends.

Once, I asked him how he'd act if we came across two women who were attracted to us and he said he'd never wimp out. Although it never happened, I believed him. One thing I noticed about Norman is that he cruised the gay clubs in much the same way as Melvin used to do in the subway stations.

Norman also had a black belt in Karate which he'd achieved when he was stationed in Germany with the U.S. Army. He had my kind of luck and worked as a clerk behind the lines in Vietnam. Back in the 70s, I gave away powder to Norman who used it to soften up his male conquests, who were, primarily, young white males. The psychiatrist on Comm Ave who had forced me to hide in his closet acted in a similar fashion, but culled his prospects from troubled young patients he was supposed to help rehabilitate. The doctor ended up losing everything after becoming embroiled in a sex scandal that rocked the psychiatric institution where he'd been in charge. He liked young men.

Norman had suffered a similar fate during his two-year career as a recruiter at B.U., after he became caught up in a sexual scandal of his own making with some rich students from New York. He never admitted this to me. He only told me that he had retired from B.U. It was one of his relatives who gave me the real skinny.

When I arrived at the apartment, I came bearing gifts. It was a comfortable feeling being there after all those years. We hadn't changed all that much that I could tell. I felt just as close to him as I'd always been. I had a large couch to sleep on in the living room. The space would be shared with a Jamaican friend of Norman's who had a fold-up bed in the corner.

When I met Norman's nephew Wolfie for the first time he seemed to be quiet and subdued. He was in his late twenties, husky and tall, and lived at the apartment with his girlfriend. My assessment of him changed radically when I got to see Wolfie's temper up close when he went off on my new roommate. Whatever had happened between them caused Wolfie to begin screaming at the man and start pushing him around. It was obvious to me that the guy was going to get a beating if someone didn't do something. Norman's mother had even come upstairs to see what was going on. Finally, Norman talked to Wolfie and calmed him down. I would have hated to be drawn into a disturbance if he had turned on Norman.

After things quieted down, Norman and I had a smoke together, in his room. Not long afterward, there was a knock at the door and Norman let Wolfie come in. He shuffled around for a moment not quite knowing how to explain why he wanted to come inside. His uncle smoothed things over as he had a talent for doing and Wolfie asked me for a hit. Norman and I continued our conversation about old times, while Wolfie listened in encouraged by Norman who elaborated on some of my exploits with the women. I was flattered by the attention as Norman held his interest talking about pleasant things. Later on, when I would visit in his room to smoke I would find it necessary to make the room off limits to anyone else. Otherwise, I would find myself besieged by people for free hits.

As the weeks passed, I came to see that Norman had a steady stream of people coming to see him. Some were generous, while others would have him clear the room when they arrived. Everyone who came to visit either brought something with them or would send out for a package. There were only one or two people who didn't mind sharing with others. Norman had a couple of Dominicans who delivered by car. When they weren't available, I would often get a ride to Mattapan to the apartment of my friend who used to live in the South Boston apartment. I usually got something for my troubles. The one time that one of Norman's relatives refused to compensate me, I let them know that it was the last time I'd do anything for them. Norman had a minor disagreement with me about my refusal to jeopardize my safety for petty people.

Sometimes, he acted like he was in another world, telling me it was better to give than to receive. That was fine for him, because someone was always giving him something. Norman never had to buy anything for himself. For the life of me, I couldn't figure out how many of his guests were closet gays and how many were straight.

One of Norman's relatives who was gay told me that Norman was what was called a "queen." He told me that years before, as a teenager, Norman used to dress up in women's clothing. Still, if you met Norman, there was no way you could tell his sexual preference unless he told you. Upon being introduced to a man, Norman would always declare that he was gay.

There were times I'd become exasperated with Norman, telling him that he didn't have to give up sex if he wanted to get high. There were guys who came to see him just to get high away from home. I couldn't see him in the role of a "queen," despite knowing his lifestyle. All of his friends knew better than to fuck with me.

I had made it clear I wasn't like Norman. Sometimes, I had to keep an eye on Norman, because of his tendency to beg for my product to give to his friends. For example, there was a young friend of Norman's who lived around the corner from the house. One day when I had a package, Norman ushered him into the room where he began a dialogue about our history. He knew I didn't want to share what I had with his friend. Yet, I ended up sharing after he asked me to do it in the presence of that person.

The next time his friend came to visit, he had something. I went to Norman's bedroom and asked his friend to share with me. Not only did that little bastard refuse to share, but he shut the door in my face. That was okay, I had a trick for him. Later, as he was leaving the room I cursed him out, thoroughly and forcefully. If he had even made a little move, I would have laid him out. Norman didn't say a word, but he was put on notice that his little "friends" had better leave me alone.

Wolfie was a different kind of cat. Once I heard him say he didn't believe in buying cigarettes because he could always bum them off somebody. After hearing that, I was determined that I wouldn't be that "somebody." Another thing I didn't like about Wolfie was his laziness. Refusing to work, he slept all day living off his girlfriend, a tramp with dirty feet, who walked the street giving out blowjobs in order to keep Wolfie in drugs. I couldn't stand to see her smiling face. There was a final straw that put me on notice that things in the apartment were out of control.

One day I went shopping and had brought a fruit dish and a pasta plate to the apartment, putting them in the refrigerator. When I returned, Wolfie and his girlfriend had eaten most of the pasta, while Norman was sitting at the table with the same little friend who had dissed me sharing my fruit with him.

Then Wolfie's bitch had the nerve to ask me if she could heat up a plate of my pasta for me. I refused her offer. That was the first and last time that I bought any food to the apartment. Norman ate at his mother's apartment every day.

I began returning to Mount Pleasant to eat breakfast and dinner, before going back to Norman's place. Sometimes, I would do my business from the house before returning. Because the phone Norman used was in his mother's apartment, I had to have calls for me coming to my parents' house. Often, I had to hear complaints about my nephew's rudeness when customers called and I wasn't there.

After a while, I started staying between Norman's apartment and a second location down the street with an acquaintance who shared the place with his girlfriend of several years, someone who knew my family personally when I was growing up on Vernon Street. It was more relaxed there and I didn't mind sharing with the two of them. Plus, there was a telephone that I could use to get calls from my clients. The traffic at Norman's could be draining with people showing up at all times of the day and night. After a while, I met two brothers through Norman who became my friends and had a place where I could bring women and have a good time. One of them used to joke about Norman's breath after he'd had visitors.

When I first met Carl, he was giving up all kinds of merchandise like stereos, color TVs, jewelry and even a mink coat for product. I didn't know if all of the stuff was his or had been stolen. Suffice to say that he did a lot of business with me for several months.

When I won an unemployment settlement, I bought a package and sat with Norman, Carl and a friend of Norman's named Perry, who had always been generous with me and smoked the day away. We forced Norman to keep his door locked against Wolfie and enjoyed ourselves. Later, I sent Norman out with a crumb for Wolfie. Carl said I shouldn't have done even that.

Wolfie was extremely selfish and when he had something he would lock himself away in his room. The only time he came out was to chisel something out of Norman's friends. He was a slime bag.

One time a friend of his bought something from my connection in Mattapan and had given me a ride to pick up the package. There was no chance of his being allowed in the apartment to meet my connection. During our conversation, I mentioned that some Dominicans hid their packages outside their buildings. Wouldn't you know that one night when I went out of the building, leaving through the back door, who should I find in the parking lot with a flashlight but Wolfie and his friend.

Sometimes, I couldn't help but wonder what was going on in people's heads. I didn't think I'd transformed or lost my basic sense of integrity because of drugs. I was constantly surprised that so many others had done so. By believing I had remained true to myself and by not changing, I was in reality denying myself a myriad of opportunities to do the things that would give my life a positive direction.

Norman and his mother were extremely close, but on one occasion when we were talking about marijuana she made a statement about Norman not having his head on straight. Actually, I think that most mothers of dealers, like myself and people like Norman, knew what we were doing and in their own way did little things to enable us to continue in the direction we had chosen. Perhaps this was the reason that I'd failed to listen to my mother's criticisms, taking them as attacks rather than warnings that time was passing me by.

How was I going to improve my life? I couldn't expect to continue as someone's house guest indefinitely. Yet I'd gotten used to sleeping on a succession of sofas. There had been signs that I was living closer to the mean streets after moving to Norman's place. The quality of the people who continued to visit his place to get high with him began to get under my skin. I didn't care to associate with most of them and began to see Norman's continued association with some of those "low lifes" as being detrimental to his health and well being. Some of them were out and out con men, while others were thieves and liars. Some of them actually smelled bad. Yet Norman seemed oblivious to my warnings and after a while his door was closed so often that I hardly saw him except for brief moments.

I had another incident happen, this time involving an old friend of mine who was also a friend of Norman's. We had gone to high school together and also had gone to the prom in my father's car. I'd known him for years or so I thought.

We were walking down the street one night minding our own business when a car pulled up and these guys got out calling to us. One of them had a baseball bat. They thought I had beaten one of their friends out of some money on a drug deal. I knew it was a case of mistaken identity and I began talking to the guy. As he came closer, I could see that he was beginning to have doubts. Suddenly, my so called friend took off, running away. Knowing him for as long as I had, I would never have run away but would have stood toe to toe by his side. I guess the era of unequal opportunity had also fostered a climate of unequal friendships. If I had been beaten to death or attacked, there would have been nobody there. I would have been shit out of luck.

If this had happened during a wartime situation, I would have been justified to shoot him as a coward. He'd shown his true colors to me. Luckily, the man realized I was a lot older than he'd thought and he apologized. But

I might as well have been hit on the head for the way my friend's action impacted on me. I never looked at him as a friend again.

I was becoming sick and tired of being sick and tired. I also began to question my direction in life after I had a close call while picking up a package from Jose at an address which wasn't far from Norman's apartment. Jose hadn't yet left town and was unaware that he was being watched. Fortunately, I was driving my father's truck at the time. When I arrived at the apartment building, the hairs on my neck felt like they were standing up, causing me to become extremely watchful. There wasn't anything I could see that was out of sync but every step I took toward the building seemed to add weight to my feet. I couldn't turn around and go back to the truck, because if there was a watch on the building that would draw attention to me. I wished I'd brought along a shopping bag to make things look more innocent.

I reached the apartment and went inside. I mentioned to Jose how I felt and warned him to be careful. Then, I took the package, put it in my underwear and left. When I reached the street, it was all I could do to keep from breaking out in a run. My heart was pounding like a drum.

I got into the truck and drove away at a normal pace. Keeping my eye on the rear view mirror, I saw nothing out of the ordinary. Then, after rounding a curve on the American Legion Highway, I saw the car. No wonder the cops were able to get on top of someone as if materializing out of the air. The unmarked car was traveling with its lights out, darting in and out of the lines of parked cars on the street. They were using what was called a "loose tail" on me. This is a technique where the tail stays a distance away from the subject, not getting too close or too far behind. I decided to beat the tail. As I got near the corner of Blue Hill Ave, I pulled into a gas station and parked, turning out the lights. Glancing down the highway, the car was out of sight. They might have been planning to follow me to my destination, before pouncing on my dumb ass. Or, so they thought.

I got back in the truck and timed the traffic and the stop light. I pulled to the edge of the parking lot next to the street, lights still off and waited for a break in the traffic. When I saw the break, just before a second wave of cars reached the corner where the light was about to change, I shot into traffic, crossing Blue Hill Ave, racing up a side street, turning off my lights again. When I reached the end of the street, there was nothing behind me and I disappeared into the night.

Thinking about my actions a little later, I knew in my heart it had been a stupid thing to do. The risk was no longer worth it. I'd been dealing too close to the street since moving into Norman's place. The case of mistaken identity and the escape from the cops were signs of something disturbing. There's a saying that some things come in threes. It didn't take long for the third shoe to drop.

At this time, Norman had partially moved around the corner from his mother's house and was living in a third floor apartment in a building owned by his family. This had all come about because of the noise people made climbing the wooden stairs to Norman's, which had kept his mother awake. Wolfie was going to have a rent free apartment on the second floor. Two weeks prior, one of Norman's little friends had beat a Jamaican dealer out of a package which he'd shared with Norman. Since it had happened, the dealer had been trying to catch up with the jerk without success. On this evening, the friend was upstairs in the new apartment waiting for Norman to arrive. Unexpectedly, the Jamaican happened to show up with two of his boys carrying clubs. After they went up to the top floor, all I could hear from the steps outside was the sounds of wood whacking flesh and cries of pain. Everyone downstairs was laughing about it.

When Norman arrived after the Jamaicans had left the scene, he actually felt bad that his "boy" had gotten his ass kicked for lying. There hadn't been any effort on his part to take care of the matter. Apparently, he thought the Jamaican was going to take the loss like a little wimp.

Later, it came out that Wolfie or his girlfriend had gotten a package from the Jamaican for letting him know when Norman's friend came around. I was still spending time at the old apartment which was a lot quieter. But I was playing a game of cat and mouse with Norman's mother. Wolfie hadn't helped matters by convincing her that I was a bad influence on her son.

A couple of days later, Norman took me to the side and told me that he had the virus. I wasn't really surprised. He had been burning up his sheets with all manner of people, some of whom had no redeeming value to justify their existence.

One of my aunts had recently died and her house was vacant. My sister had moved into the place and I was making plans to go there. Norman was planning to take off for the weekend and asked me to do him a favor and keep an eye on things. It was the least I could do for someone who'd been a close friend. Wolfie and his girlfriend were supposed to be moving to the other place that weekend so I was supposed to make sure that no doors were left open. Norman's mother had put her feelings about me on hold. I didn't realize at the time that this weekend was going to be my signal to walk away from the madness.

After my near death experience in Norman's room, I finally got the message. No one had made any kind of impression on me to change my ways after all those years. Maybe, in a way, I should be thankful that Wolfie did something beneficial for once in his life. I stayed away for close to a month before I returned.

I saw Norman for the last time a month later when I had him order a package for a friend on the Boston Police force. The package which cost forty dollars had been fucked over before we got it and my friend was close to making a move on the house. I explained to him that Norman had Aids and he let it go. That was the final straw. It was the end of a friendship that had lasted close to twenty years. I didn't want to see Norman again. The hurt was too deep. He had been the closest thing to a brother that I had ever known.

A year later I ran into a mutual acquaintance who told me Norman had died of complications a month before.

He didn't ask me if I'd gone to the funeral. He hadn't gone to it.

It was the first year of the rest of my life.

☙ ❧

Chapter 28:

The Aftermath

The years following 1990 were nothing nice. After being accepted back into my parents' house, I discovered the art of check cashing which soon led to my being out on the street again.

I had perfected signing my father's signature and went on a year-long check cashing binge, which was only discovered after a new branch manager at the bank, from Haiti, became suspicious and called my mother about the withdrawals. I had managed to steam open the monthly bank envelopes, removing the cancelled checks which arrived at the house on or about the twenty-third.

Ending up on the street, I found myself back in various living rooms, sleeping on couches. A couple of times, I slept in my father's truck outside my parent's house, between changes of location. My nephew was determined to keep me under his thumb. I was determined it wasn't going to happen.

After several years, my nephew's marriage broke up and he deserted the property. The house would stand deserted for nearly a decade, even becoming fire damaged from squatters who moved in. My parents, who had expected to live the rest of their lives in the place, were forced to move into an elderly housing complex.

I was still living on the wild side making extra cash by driving members of a stolen credit card ring to stores across eastern Massachusetts. It was a risky business that I remained in for only a short while. After one of my passengers was busted inside a store and I had only a small amount of gas to make it home alone, I saw the light. However, I still hadn't reached my bottom.

While continuing to work off and on during this period as a substitute teacher, I had several windfalls from auto accident cases where I was a passenger and sustained minor injuries. I had also become a regular smoker, doing hits every day.

During the mid-90s, my father died of complications from dementia, gout and a stroke. I bought the family truck from my mother. It was a good idea at the time, even though the truck had been through hell because of its use by a group of different drivers, including family members.

In my case, I neglected to keep up the insurance on the truck or pay the excise taxes, which put me on a collision with the Registry and the court system.

Because of a partial amputation of his leg, my father had a handicap plate on the truck which guaranteed me a free parking space anywhere in town. One day the truck was towed after I'd parked it too close to a construction site. After calling in the plate number, the cop on duty found out that the insurance had been cancelled and he took the plate off the truck, which meant I had to find a space off the street to park the vehicle.

I hadn't been worried about paying the insurance. I had other things on my mind like getting high. Telling myself I didn't need a car, I'd parked the truck in Turo's driveway with a group of other abandoned vehicles.

One day I had a moving job and put another plate on the truck so I could use it. After the job was finished, I continued to use the truck until I was stopped again and cited for driving an uninsured vehicle with an attached plate. This led to my going to court and being fined. The Registry also started to fuck with me, suspending my license for the unpaid excise taxes.

Actually, having a lawyer for a sister resulted in my infractions being taken less serious. I was given a lot of juice by many judges who knew my sister but I was in such a state of stupidity that I pushed my luck to the limit.

Soon I was driving without a license, getting warnings and being summoned to court. It looked like after all my years of avoiding the police and the courts, I was determined to let it all hang out. I was stuck on stupid. After several speeding tickets, my license was revoked and I was forced to go to a safe driving class before I could get reinstated. I was also forced to do community service—hours mopping up the floors at a veterans building every Saturday for three months. The court had decided to teach me a lesson.

After I completed the community service, I was told I couldn't get my license back until all of my excise taxes were paid as well as two out-of-state tickets paid, one of them an eight-year old ticket from Vermont. I also had to pay a reinstatement fee to the Registry. Luckily, I had a settlement from an accident come in and I was able to pay everything up. I didn't have enough money to register the truck this time and I put it back in Turo's driveway.

My mother took me in for a while, but it wasn't long before I went back to my old tricks. I had run out of money at that time and I cashed a few of her checks. She gave me two days to get out.

There is no love like a mother's love. It can outlast a friendship, a marriage, even life itself. When it's gone, it leaves a hole in your life. It's an all forgiving kind of love.

Everybody in the family knew I was her favorite, even though she went out of her way to treat us all the same. It was hard for me to look into her cold eyes and try to justify what I'd done. I promised to pay her back, but that didn't make it right. The worst thing about it was that I not only knew I was wrong, but if I'd been in her place I would have kicked me out.

I went to one of my "best" friends, who had the space in his townhouse, a person I'd known since childhood and asked him to put me up temporarily until I could find a place. He responded that he wanted two hundred bucks for a week up front. My mother paid him the money. Yes, that's how much she wanted me out.

He didn't give me a key and several times I found myself waiting outside for him to come home. He didn't even like me smoking cigarettes in his house. But when his little female friend came over she'd blow smoke in his face and laugh at him.

Needless to say, he wasn't my friend. On the seventh day, he showed me by his manner that I had to leave. I moved from there to the apartment of an acquaintance, an older man in his seventies who ran a smoke house for people who had no place to smoke their stuff. It was a mad house seven days a week. But, in spite of all that I discovered a beautiful person.

It was here that I used the comments of an IG at Holiday Magic to pull in a fine young black "stallion" of a woman called "Nigeria" by making her cry. She had promised to call me after we had shared crack on my dime. Of course, she didn't call; I was one of plenty. I had been waiting for her to return the favor weeks later. This time, I had money in my pockets. After making small talk, I built her up by telling her that I didn't like seeing her have sex with the strangers who used crack to abuse her. This required a suspension of disbelief: Because, I wanted to have some of her sex, too.

Still, there was no way that anybody else was going to have her that night. I really wanted to be with her. None of the regulars had arrived and I knew I couldn't allow myself to get caught up in the madness. Otherwise, I might as well stand in line and wait to take her into the bathroom. I would have one chance to get her to leave with me.

I would discover later that Nigeria had a regular job working with computers at the operations level and no children. I'd forgotten that this drug could bring anybody down. She was genuinely attracted to older men. The man of the house where I crashed was elderly. He had bragged that she was the fuck of the century. But no one had thought to reach out to her. She was an object, as much a victim as I had been long ago in Pennsylvania.

"I like you, Nigeria. I know you're better than that." I continued. I knew she had expected me to make her an offer. But I was giving her a message before the "regulars" arrived, in a quiet voice. "When you didn't keep your word about calling me, I was hurt." I paused, looking into her eyes. She wasn't smiling. I looked away, down at the floor. "I believe in keeping my word. If I told you the wall outside was white and it was black, I'd paint it white to keep my word. Can we go somewhere else?" She took me seriously. The tears came forth.

We ended up leaving the apartment in a hurry, startling the old man. Then we took a bus to my sister's place where I borrowed her car. Of course, we bought a package. My sister knew what I was up to and refused to let me use her place. Nigeria and I had become a couple.

We went to the apartment of an old woman where a friend was watching the place while she was in the hospital. It was there that "Nigeria" and I showered together. We didn't even have a towel, just a white sheet. My friend remained in the bedroom out of respect.

There was only one bed and he wouldn't give that up. We sat naked on the couch.

"I want every little drop of you." I whispered. We made out slowly, with our tongues and our fingers. Then she said something I had never heard before and would remember for the rest of my life. She reached over and touched one of my feet.

"You have pretty feet. You don't have any corns," she said, softly.

That spoke volumes about her feelings for me. Women pick up on the little things. They will express honesty when they trust you. I didn't think she would ever hurt me, intentionally.

From there, I lost myself in her and used all the magic I knew to satisfy her. I knew she'd do the same. I'd cracked her shell. For once in my life, there might be a person to eventually love. Interestingly, Nigeria went both ways. She was also "Bi." We could hunt women together.

We used the couch. We kissed each other all over. I knelt before her and she spread her legs. She looked down on me with hooded eyes, as I lifted up her beautiful ass and caressed her with my lips and tongue. I buried my face in her sweet dewy mound. I swear the taste was sweet.

When it was my turn, she swallowed me so deeply, that she took my breath away. I wanted to do the impossible and melt into her. And after we finished, using our mouths, we took a few hits and started over, with our bodies. We did everything we wanted to do to each other. We lasted until dawn, spending a beautiful night together. I knew she would never treat me like a trick again.

Over the several months that I saw Nigeria, I never visited her apartment. She always met me on the street outside the building. One night she invited me to meet her at a private club where I was introduced to a man she called her uncle. Whenever we had a squabble, it was over drugs. The only thing that caused friction between us was knowing when to stop.

She had bridled when I criticized her for spending too much money with the street trade rather than waiting until I could find better quality through my connections. She said I had no right to tell her how to spend her money.

Another time, we clashed when she insisted on smoking crack on the street, outside a subway station at night, instead of doing it in the car. I took her home, and she turned her back on me.

She had a cell phone, so I could get in touch with her. But, it was usually so full of calls that there was no room for new messages. Still, it was up to Nigeria to contact me, when she desired. She made her own choices. Business went back to normal in the living room. It was always available for anyone who had a few crumbs. Kibbles and bits 24/7! There were many nights where I got little sleep. It wasn't long before an old nemesis reared its head and took me down. One day I was normal and the next day I had a temperature that continued to rise. But I knew what was happening. Once you've had pneumonia you never forget it.

First, the air in the apartment which was room temperature seemed to chill my skin, while every breath I took cut like a knife. I wanted to lie down and cover myself with a blanket. But since the apartment was filled with people, I found myself sitting in a chair in a corner of the kitchen, shivering my ass off under a sheet. Nobody gave a shit about me; they were too busy getting high.

I overheard the old man talking about me to someone in his room, saying that my mother was one of the nicest people he knew and if she put me out, I must have done something really bad to have caused it. I'd told him that I'd been put out for getting high in my mother's apartment. No one likes to admit that they were put out for stealing from their mother. Apparently, my lie wasn't fooling anyone.

I was forced to call my "best" friend to drive me to the hospital where I was immediately taken to the emergency room, prior to being hospitalized. One night when I was with "Nigeria" and had no place to take her, I had called him but he had refused to allow me to come to his place which had two bedrooms, saying: "We don't do that here."

It was a sorry situation. I'd hit bottom with the realization that had it not been for the help of a false friend, my plight would have been worse. When I got out of the hospital, I went to talk to Mama and laid everything out for her. I didn't want to go back to the smoke house. I told her what it had been like living there. I made her a promise that I would never cash any of her checks, again. I also reminded her that I had a settlement coming and that I would give her a thousand dollars to help make up for the things I'd done. I also promised to look out for her and do my best to keep her happy. I kept my word.

I moved into the elderly complex and never looked back for close to ten years. There were changes made in the way I dealt with my "friends." If I was willing to do something for someone, I called a friend and if they were unwilling to do the same for me, when no hardship would be suffered, we could no longer be friends. This action separated friends from opportunists. It was one of the smartest moves I ever made. By looking at everyone through the prism of truth, I saved myself a lot of aggravation. I developed a rubber skin for the arrows of the users who found me a poor target. Mama was my best friend.

Word went out that I was a mama's boy by those who speculated on what I was about. I didn't give a shit.

Mama came first. After a while, the users gave up on me as I wore my indifference like body armor.

When a "basehead" bitch made a statement to a casual acquaintance that I was selfish, he rebuked her, saying I had always treated him right. I was determined not to be used by "fake friends." I did get high in the apartment but only by myself. I also cut out any late night phone calls. Sneaking a few women into the apartment once in a while, I nevertheless managed to be a good tenant.

In her own way, Mama never made an issue of my activities as long as I showed her respect. She gave me slack when it came to my need to get high, admonishing me to stay away from "those drugs" while enabling me to borrow from her in a crunch. She never let me get too comfortable, however.

Sometimes, late at night she'd wake up in her bedroom asking: "What's that smell?" This was enough to blow my high. Yet she was one of the reasons I could still get credit, because she was so well respected that her word carried more weight than mine. Once I put her on the phone with a stubborn dealer to say she'd lend me the money the following day. I got the package.

There was a time when she'd lent one of my suppliers money when he needed it, at my behest. He'd driven her to church one Sunday when she couldn't get a cab. I guess you could say that we came to depend on one another.

Sometimes, I'd find myself at odds with friends of my siblings, who'd come to borrow money from her, leaving me short of backup. She was a true Christian in her deeds as well as her words. Needless to say if someone tried to take advantage of her kindness, they were put on notice. I became a functional addict from the time I lived with my mother. I continued working at a job, teaching English. Finally getting my certification after 9/11, I had a reason to feel good about myself. She always complained about my being lazy, however. We stayed together through my diagnosis with emphysema, which put me on a disability income and a regimen of drugs that I would be taking for the rest of my life.

One morning she woke me up, speaking in what seemed to be "tongues." I noticed her mouth was twisted and realized she was having a stroke. I was scared to death, ignoring her pleas not to call an ambulance. Thankfully, she suffered little damage and kept much of her memory.

She was surely blessed, living three years after the incident. She even retained her ability to walk and read. When her final day came in November of 2005, we were all there at her bedside. I'm grateful that she knew I'd finished this book before she died, at ninety-one years of age. Thankfully, during her final hospital stay I had gotten to snuggle up next to her and was able to inhale her sweet scent in the curve of her throat. This in turn resurrected the delightful smells of her apple pies, Thanksgiving stuffing and meatloaf in my memory; the memory I'll carry with me for the rest of my life and possibly beyond.

Clark Watson, my alter-ego, has moved on. He shows up to check in about once a year. I don't have anything for him to do.

Sometimes, when I look at my feet I think of Nigeria. It can't be helped. We saw each other a couple more times. Then I heard she had gone into rehab and stopped coming to the old man's house. The cell phone had been long disconnected. When I saw the old man, shortly before he died, he said he hadn't heard from her in a long time. It was shortly after that when I came across someone who told me that Nigeria had died of an OD about a year before. We both agreed she had been one fine girl. I had been scanning the streets of Roxbury for a long time looking for her face. When I passed the building where I thought she lived, feeling the loss, I realized that I had made the choice that was right for me. I did make a positive impact on Nigeria in spite of myself. I never suggested she go to rehab. At least she recognized her behavior had become destructive. I still feel her loss. She made an impression on me.

As for my future plans, I intend to take things as they come. As long as I'm on the right side of the dirt I can't be doing all that bad.

଄ ଌ

Chapter 29:

Finality, Infinity…

There are a lot of stories out there. Everybody has one. Chances are that few will be written. I found it difficult to write about myself, hence it took years.

As difficult as my life was, in the shadowy world of drugs, even more difficult was the writing of it. This book, my revelation of my life, felt almost like the betrayal of a secret.

It's not normal to live two or three lives. Many people who think they know me don't know about my double life. They've seen only what I've wanted them to see. I realize that my encounters with strangers portrayed me to be short-tempered and often arrogant. Too frequently, I believed I could do no wrong. At other times, I was so secretive that it caused me to miss out on a number of opportunities, employment in legitimate work or educational programs that might have taken me to places of which I could only dream. My attitudes, in retrospect, I know affected the quality of my friendships and my taste in women.

My thoughts on illegal drugs are simple and to the point. Something has to change after a hypocritical and racist "Half-Century War on Drugs." The futility of the "War" shows us our inability to overcome human nature, and what I call the reality of substance abuse, the line drawn between two kinds of drug dependents: "Jack and John," the drinker we tolerate legally and the drug customer we prosecute.

"Jack" can legally take a drink, put the bottle away and go to sleep; or he can't stop drinking until the bottle's empty. Do you call the cops to help bring his addiction under control or do you put things in the hands of a doctor? This is the crux of the drug controversy, without the finger pointing or dire warnings and lies about marijuana. Yes, reefer!

Over 600,000 "Johns," on the other hand, are in the prison system for smoking and possessing marijuana and nothing else. We're supposedly living in the freest country in the world. What's wrong with that picture? The two most dangerous drugs are alcohol and tobacco; they kill more people than all of the other illegal drugs combined. Why are they legal?

Man has been getting high since the first caveman saw a wooly mammoth, killed and consumed it until he fell down asleep. Most people are not going to stop getting high.

It's been a long learning experience, this life of mine. I managed to live it without losing my freedom. I'd like to thank God for that; despite my misguided steps, for reasons unknown at this time, He kept me free.

I've also come to believe that far too many of us attribute our good fortune to luck and little else, refusing to recognize God's hand in our lives. We too often end up unable to fill a big hole in our spiritual lives, as we spend our riches like drinking our water, without a care where the next drink of water will come.

Meanwhile, deep inside us, a part of us searches for meaning and validation of our lives, a sense of contentment and equilibrium, that we never find in the things that we buy for our pleasure.

Someday, if you're lucky, you'll find yourself looking in the mirror facing the reality that you're becoming an old timer and you will watch your circle of friends become smaller and smaller.

You might be fortunate enough to find yourself contemplating the question of the ages: "Why has He allowed me to survive all these years?"

All I can say, in eternal gratitude, is: Thank you, God, for keeping me.

--M.C.

[Note: After a brief stay at the Boston Medical Center, Marvin passed away, June 4, 2011, of respiratory and heart failure—C.S.]

☙ ❧ ☙ ❧